WAR AND ITS PREVENTION

Readers in Social Problems

DONALD R. CRESSEY, CONSULTING EDITOR
UNIVERSITY OF CALIFORNIA, SANTA BARBARA

WAR AND ITS PREVENTION

EDITED BY

AMITAI ETZIONI
COLUMBIA UNIVERSITY

AND

MARTIN WENGLINSKY
BRYN MAWR COLLEGE

HARPER & ROW
Publishers

NEW YORK, EVANSTON, AND LONDON

Library of Congress Catalog Card Number: 75-109576

Contents

PART V / THE PROBLEM OF THE PUBLIC

Preface

HAS WARFARE increased in frequency and magnitude during the last 300 years? Do its causes rest in bad instincts or in bad governments? In the decline of religion or in the decline of capitalism? Is it that some nations or some eras are more "aggressive" than others? Whatever the patterns and causes of warfare, how can it be avoided? How are aspects of war such as mass mobilization and aspects of peace such as disarmament regarded by the public? These and similar questions can be in part answered by the social sciences. Apart from their moral and philosophical implications, they are open to empirical and theoretical scientific investigation.

This volume illustrates the ways in which social scientists approach the problem of war and its prevention, using a variety of orientations drawn from disciplines that are still young but continually more productive. While we cannot provide here the full range of knowledge that has been accumulated, we hope to present some of the major themes.

The social sciences command a variety of research techniques for establishing the facts of the situation. Among the authors included in this volume, Evan, for instance, uses the methods of survey research to demonstrate the somewhat surprising fact that a significant segment of the American public is willing to report on its own government in the service of a world disarmament treaty. Milgram studies experimentally the ways in which people resolve conflicts between obedient and humane behavior.

But the social sciences provide more than "soft" or "hard" data. They also analyze these data—i.e., they attempt to draw "meaning" from them. In part, this entails the drawing of conclusions from any seemingly disparate data; in part, social science's perspectives provide new ways of approaching that which seems already understood. And in part, such analysis involves the formulation of new questions to be answered by further research and more adequate theory.

Dentler and Cutright are a good example of the first instance. They use a number of quite different empirical studies to portray a post-nuclear-war world. Hertz employs concepts of political theory to demonstrate the particular problems of nations living under the nuclear cloud. Horowitz illustrates the third method of analysis: He prompts us to look for other than economic motives for economic resistance to the abatement of war tensions.

Social scientists differ considerably in their views of the causes of war in general and of post–World War II developments in particular; for example, they differ in their explanations of the weakness of the United Nations and the stregnth of the Soviet government. But whatever positions they adopt, they are committed to the use of the social sciences in the testing of their hypotheses. This may seem especially difficult in an area so given to passionately held opinions, but the significance of the issues at stake is precisely the reason the effort is so important.

Among those who make the study of war and peace their specialty, some view the careful balancing of armed camps as the way to achieve national security and a stable peace and tend to see disarmament as unfeasible or even undesirable. Others hold that stable peace requires disarmament and a world community and that these can be brought about. The editors of this volume believe that the second group is likely to be correct in the long run; all periods of peace based on a balance of power did in fact lead to war, while war was avoided when previously autonomous states formed a community (e.g., following the unification of Germany). Most important, the possibility of nuclear war makes the reliance on a balance of power to maintain the peace unacceptable because, however infrequently the balance must break down, the costs of even one such breakdown are far too high.*

*Amitai Etzioni studied this subject in his *Political Unification* (New York: Holt, Rinehart and Winston, 1965). His views on the more general issue raised here briefly are reported in his *Winning Without*

The specific problems selected for presentation in this volume are viewed as significant by all who study war and peace, whatever positions they take in regard to them. First, the seriousness and uniqueness of the new methods of warfare and their social consequences need to be established. In contrast to such views as that of Herman Kahn, Dentler and Cutright provide data to suggest that war has aftereffects lasting many generations. Evan offers some evidence in support of the proposition that the consequences of the use of nuclear weapons are understood at least in part by the American public; American citizens are willing to inform on their own country to avoid nuclear fallout, a condition they must view as even more serious than the action they agreed to take. Thus, nuclear warfare appears to necessitate a new orientation toward world politics.

Herz provides further reasons for Evan's concern; he analyzes the ways in which nuclear war invalidates the empirical assumptions under which the modern nation-state operates and poses a new problem: What is the role of the nation in the nuclear world? Morgenthau emphasizes the limitations of the United States' power to affect world politics and the dangers inherent in overstepping these limits. Angell notes the movements of people among nations; this indicates that forces other than the nation-state help to shape the relations among the world's peoples.

Those pessimistic about the possibilities of avoiding war often raise the problem of the extent to which the nation-state, whatever its uses, is maintained by domestic economic interests. Benoit demonstrates that the nation is not economically dependent upon maintaining a military posture. Why, then, are economic leaders hesitant to support alternatives to the military posture? Horowitz, as we mentioned previously extends this question.

Perhaps the most original contributions of the social

War (Garden City, N.Y.: Doubleday Anchor Books, 1964) and his *The Hard Way to Peace* (New York: Collier Books, 1962). A more strictly sociological treatment is found in his "War and Disarmament," Robert K. Merton and Robert A. Nisbet, *Contemporary Social Problems*, 2d ed. (New York: Harcourt, Brace & World, 1966), pp. 732–773.

sciences come in the next problem area discussed in this volume. Conflict among parties, whether they be nations, corporations, or individuals, has consequences beyond the particular conflict. The attributes of confrontation must be taken into account lest the mechanisms inherent in such instances hinder the resolution of conflict as a whole. Deutsch and Krauss use ingeniously constructed experiments to specify the reasons and conditions opponents whose interests are complementary end up dealing with one another in such a way that while each tries to profit at the expense of the other, they both are hurt. Mack and Snyder survey the range of knowledge that has been accumulated concerning the behavior of parties in conflict. Etzioni uses historical data to analyze the possibilities of lessening the tensions among opposing parties and their inhibitive effect on conflict reduction.

What is the role of the public in the persistence of war? Milgram's study of the degree to which people are willing to implement inhumane policies raises the question of the extent to which warfare relies upon the compliance of the public, as well as the ways in which such compliance can be generated and forestalled. Tajfel reports the early age at which the sentiments of antagonism become instilled. Steele, on the other hand, demonstrates the considerable willingness of the American public to try out new alternatives to lessen the prospect of war, even in reference to Communist China. However, White soberingly analyzes the ways in which the same public may construe the relations between South and North Vietnam so that the resolution of conflict between them is impeded.

A.E. and M.W.

Columbia University

Part I

The Problem of Survival

WAR, AFTERMATH, AND RECOVERY

Robert A. Dentler and Phillips Cutright

SOME EFFECTS OF THERMONUCLEAR WAR ON THE POPULATION OF THE UNITED STATES

What do we really mean when we talk about a thermonuclear war? What does the term "holocaust" mean in terms of the number of dead? . . .

. . . Even a limited thermonuclear attack upon the continental United States would have a vast range of consequences. . . . We will not deal in any detail with the effects of an attack on the different sectors of the economy, on our military capability or on the housing problem. We will speak of what we can expect to happen to the *people* of this nation if we engage in thermonuclear war.

STUDIES BY THE OFFICE OF CIVIL AND DEFENSE MOBILIZATION

Two studies by OCDM on the effects of thermonuclear war upon the civilian population of the United States have been released to the public. . . . Each of the limited attacks discussed by the OCDM assumed . . . an attack directed both at military installations on the continental United States and also at certain cities whose industrial or special locations near military bases made them prime targets. . . . The

Reprinted from *Hostage America: Human Aspects of Nuclear Attack and a Program of Prevention* (Boston: Beacon Press, 1963), pp. 9–76.
 (This article is a severely edited excerpt from the book.)

Two Government Studies of the Effect upon the U.S. Population of Nuclear Attack (Based on the 1950 population: 150,699,000)

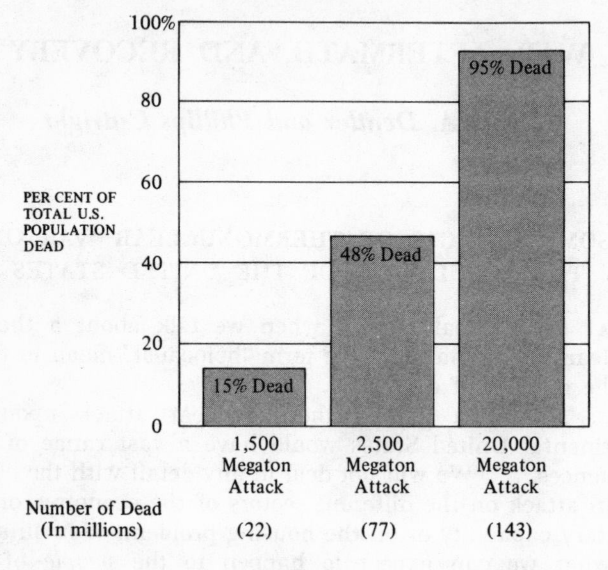

FIGURE 1.

attack reported in 1959, which involved 1,000 fewer megatons than the 1957 attack, also resulted in far fewer dead and injured. Figure 1 summarizes the results of these two studies. For reasons unexplained, . . . the Chicago urban area remains virtually unscathed in the hypothetical 1959 attack. In fact, 70 per cent of its population is completely uninjured! In Boston, 75 per cent of the population was reported dead. . . . Such variation is possible only under the conditions of a small-scale war specified by the OCDM. As you increase the number of megatons dropped, you eliminate the possibility of prime targets like Chicago going untouched. . . . As we increase the number of megatons from 1,500 to 2,500 and then to 20,000 megatons the number of dead and injured increases at a high rate. . . .

The studies of the OCDM . . . did not allocate enough

megatonnage to the targets that the Russians presumably wanted to destroy. . . . However, a May 12, 1962, Pentagon news release . . . reveals that new estimates of Russian military nuclear delivery strength envision a delivery potential of 60,000 megatons by 1970. . . . The studies that follow are limited to the situation that prevailed around 1960 and are most probably *underestimating* the devastation that is within the realm of reality [now]. . . .

. . .

WHAT POPULATION CENTERS ARE MOST LIKELY TO BE ATTACKED?

Because of their industrial and military characteristics, the Office of Civil and Defense Mobilization selected 71 metropolitan areas as the most likely targets in their 1959 exercise. . . .In our re-examination of the 1959 study we have used every Standard Metropolitan Area with a manufacturing labor force of 40,000 or more and all of the 53 largest areas (1950 census). This gave us a total of 70 urban areas, and . . . they are virtually identical with those chosen by the OCDM. . . . We . . . differ with the assumptions of the OCDM study in a few respects. We assume, first, that nuclear weapons can utterly destroy any city if the weapon is delivered and, second, that if the enemy wants to destroy the city he can and will deliver a bomb large enough to do the job. We assume that a thermonuclear war is a war with no holds barred. . . . We assume that everyone within each of these 70 areas would be killed by blast, firestorms or radiation that follow thermonuclear explosions. We do not, however, include in our estimates a single person outside of these areas; nor do we include the deaths resulting from attacks on our military installations. . . .

EFFECTS OF AN ATTACK ON 70 URBAN AREAS UPON THE RELIGIOUS COMPOSITION OF THE UNITED STATES

. . . An attack which eliminates 70 urban areas . . . results in the death of 68,755,000 persons compared to

72,000,000 dead calculated by the OCDM in its 2,500-megaton attack (1957 report). . . . One out of every three Protestants would be killed, two out of every three Roman Catholics, and nine out of ten Jews.

. . .

. . . Even a limited attack would threaten the very survival of . . . the American Jewish community and such an attack would terribly decimate the Roman Catholic Church. . . . Protestantism is not spared either; . . . the Presbyterians, Congregationalists, Unitarians, and Episcopalians would be more severely hit than would the Southern Methodists or Baptists.

THE IMPACT UPON THE LABOR FORCE

Estimates by the Rand Corporation for economic recovery discuss the prospects of economic recuperation in terms of the proportion of the capital investment or industry (for example, primary metals) destroyed and then proceed to figure how long it will take to replace the plant and get production going again. Such studies neglect the people who make the factories run and the other people in the cities who perform services that integrate the social and economic life of the nation into one complex network. . . . . . . We agree that some sort of recuperation would be likely if, after a small attack, things went on exactly as they did before the attack (it is, of course, extremely unlikely that things *will* go on as before). . . . What we want to present at this time is a view of vital sectors of the labor force that would be affected by a small attack upon the 70 urban areas. . . .

In the same attack that kills 46 per cent of the total United States population, 73 per cent of all the accountants in the United States will be killed; 73 per cent of all the architects; 62 per cent of all the physicians; 79 per cent of all salaried managers in the transportation equipment industry; 71 per cent of all foremen in the U.S. metals industry and 76 per cent of our tool and die makers. *The men and women with the very skills most in demand after such a disaster will perish in the attack. . . .*

THE IMPACT UPON THE CONGRESS

. . .

. . . Just assuming, for a moment, that elections could be held five years after an attack, what would the U.S. Congress look like? An *indirect* measure of the chaos and major shifts in regional political power potentials is reflected by applying the same procedures to the Congressional Districts as we applied to our study of the effects of a nuclear war on occupational groups. . . .

. . .

[Had an attack occurried while the] "Democratic" Congress elected in 1958 was in power, the number of Congressional Districts whose Congressmen would have a sizable proportion of voters alive "back home" is reduced from 435 to 228. A total of 207 Congressional Districts would have been eliminated. . . . Of this total of 207 destroyed Congressional Districts, the Southern Democrats lost 16, the Republicans 84 and the Northern Democrats 107. The Southern Democrats would be the dominant faction of the remaining Congressmen.

Similar effects can be seen in the results of . . . an attack on a "Republican" Congress. Of the 232 Congressmen remaining, 90 are Southern Democrats, 97 Republicans, and 45 are Northern Democrats. Although the Republicans lost the greatest number of Congressmen, they still retain a plurality in the Congress. The Northern Democratic share dwindles sharply to 19 per cent of the total, while the Southern Democrats claim 39 per cent of all the post-attack Congressional Districts. Regardless of what kind of election year we study, the proportion of all seats held in the U.S. Congress by Southern Democrats goes up from 25 per cent to about 40 per cent.

Whatever one's personal politics and preferences, it should be clear that such a shock to the political system might lead to very grave dangers for our way of life. We have come to depend upon a competitive over-all balance of the two parties to maintain the growth of legislation in Congress, and we are dependent upon a competitive two-party system to restrain the right and left wing extremists who pop up so frequently on the American political stage. . . .

. . .

PAST, PRESENT AND THE FUTURE

. . . We have summarized . . . the best available estimates of what a real nuclear war would have been like in 1959 or 1960. We have barely mentioned the obvious fact that it is no longer . . . 1960. Because the methods for delivering nuclear weapons are constantly being perfected, the number of megatons involved in an all-out attack on the United States is constantly increasing. . . . What about the wars of the not too distant future? What of the 20,000-megaton war? Would anyone be left after such an attack? How effective would civil defense measures be against large-scale thermonuclear wars? . . . Finally, even 20,000 is not the end, for, as we noted earlier, Pentagon estimates calculate that the Russian delivery system will be able to handle some 60,000 megatons by the early 1970's. . . . What does a future hold for Americans without some stable agreement between the Soviet Union and the United States?

THE FUTURE: ALL-OUT THERMONUCLEAR WAR

Far in the back of the Hearings of the Joint Committee on Atomic Energy, Congress of the United States, on "Biological and Environmental Effects of Nuclear War," is an article by Hugh Everett, III, and George E. Pugh called "The Distribution and Effects of Fallout in Large Nuclear-Weapon Campaigns." . . . Ironically, their report is immediately followed by a statement from Herman Kahn urging the Committee to embark on a national civil defense program. The irony lies in the straightforward evidence presented in the Everett and Pugh article that *civil defense preparations are effective only if the enemy does not take any counter-action. . . .*

Four types of attack are studied: (1) the anti-population attack; (2) industrial-urban attack; (3) random drop attack and (4) military air base attack. In each case the attack attempts to inflict maximum damage with a given number of megatons delivered to the target. . . .

. . .

An "unprepared" population was assumed to have had a few hours' warning that an attack was coming. It is given emergency instructions to remain under shelter during and after the attack, but it has only improvised shelters to go to. In contrast, a "prepared" population has had *six months of full-time preparation* for an attack. The effectiveness of six months of intensive activity to provide, prepare, build and stock shelters was then calculated.

. . . [Figure 2] shows the relationship between civilian deaths and the megatonnage dropped in an industrial-urban

Proportion of Total U.S. Population Dead and Total Delivered Megatons on Industrial and Other Population Centers (60 days after the attack)

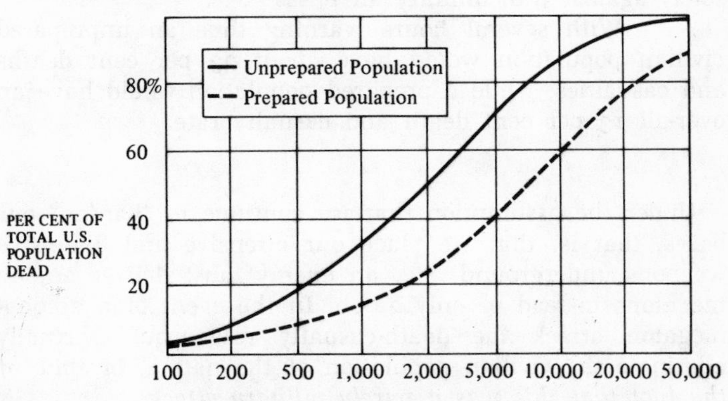

FIGURE 2.

type of attack on the United States. . . . Two things about this table are important to notice. A rather steady increase in the number of deaths occurs with each increase in the number of megatons dropped. And the difference in the death rate between a prepared and an unprepared population can be eliminated simply by dropping more megatons on the population. It takes only 5,000 megatons to kill about 75 per cent of the total "unprepared" population, but 20,000 megatons will do the same job on a "prepared" population. Remember that we are not talking here about the people in cities alone: these figures apply to the population of the nation as a whole.

. . .

An actual attack on a large scale would be directed at both military and industrial targets. . . . The calculations of Everett and Pugh did not take into account a mixed attack on both industrial and military targets. Their figures are based upon attacks that are *either* industrial or military. We can extrapolate from the results of these calculations and easily discuss what the results of a mixed attack would be.

First, . . . a limited and a full-scale attack launched solely against U.S. military air bases: . . .

. . . With several hours warning time an unprepared civilian population would have about 33 per cent deaths and casualties, while a prepared population would have an over-all 13 per cent death and casualty rate.

. . .

Under the assumption that we continue to "harden" our bases, that is, that we place our offensive and defensive weapons underground . . . an enemy must deliver 20,000 megatons instead of only 2,000. In the event of a 20,000-megaton attack the death-casualty rate would virtually eliminate the civilian population of the nation, *in spite of the fact that this was a purely military attack.*

But such a pure military attack is unlikely. Many prime military targets are not only air bases but include cities that . . . have harbors with naval yards, nuclear submarine pens, army bases, atomic energy installations, laboratories, and industrial plants. . . .

Let us assume now, along with the OCDM, that an attack will also be directed against industrial, transportation, and communication centers. The effect of even a limited 2,000-megaton attack is . . . almost identical with the OCDM results in its 1957 study. Some 47 per cent of the unprepared population is dead after 60 days and an additional 14 per cent of the population is injured. Assuming that we had taken advantage of a six-month alert period, . . . 25 per cent of the population would be dead and an additional 11 per cent injured.

But if the purpose of the attack is to destroy our industrial capacity, the aggressor must also destroy our labor force as well as the cities. . . . Twenty thousand megatons directed against our industrial, communications and transportation centers would leave only a few isolated survivors. Even a full . . . six months of digging and stocking the shelters will be of no use to 74 per cent of the population. Those people will be dead within 60 days after such an attack. An additional 11 per cent will be "casualties." *This leaves 15 per cent of the population alive and in some sort of physical condition to rebuild the nation.* One wonders how these people would survive the next few years. . . . The evidence . . . clearly indicates that any kind of civil defense is a myth and a hoax. . . . Regardless of the amount of effort we put into any shelter program, it is self-defeating, for the enemy is forced to counter our moves with further development of his weapon systems. . . .

. . .

AFTERMATH: A WARNING

This section concerns conditions among survivors in the remote areas not obliterated by nuclear blast, firestorms, fire effects or primary radiation. The partially injured, the dying and the sick, the doomed stragglers from the target areas, are neglected; . . . we are certain they would never make it to the remote areas where survival might be possible. . . .

. . .

PANIC

People in the remote areas might have as much as six hours in which to take shelter. At first glance this invites a picture of families and community groups proceeding in a fairly orderly fashion toward their shelter stations, with sufficient time at hand to collect the children and allow father to get home from work. . . . We know from the studies of natural disasters that . . . people do not necessarily collapse, go wild or flee during a crisis. . . . What looks like wild flight or panic often turns out to be an intense search for family members and efforts to get medical aid.

At second glance the picture of initial reactions to attack in remote areas becomes enormously complicated. For instance, people in remote areas are likely to behave as if they had no time to spare at all. A crisis that is defined as extremely disastrous is as conducive to terror and panic as an authentic catastrophe. After the first two poison-gas attacks in World War I, the cry "Gas!" was sufficient to stimulate the collapse of controls in the trenches. Trained soldiers fled from their posts in involuntary response to the cry, even when no authenticated signal was given. . . . A threat is as terrible as our advance definition makes it out to be.

In any severe crisis, between three and four out of every ten persons, moreover, suffer immediate reactions to danger. Among such vulnerable . . . people, severe crises . . . produce temporary blindness, stunned shock, or disabling stupor—in short, a condition of utter helplessness. Of course, many people act positively, reasonably and often heroically under extreme threats. But many others are unable to act at all. Among those who are rendered neither helpless nor heroic, finally, are the majority, who experience a sharp restriction of their consciousness to some narrow portion of their life situation. Much of what they do becomes automatic, semiconscious, a series of rituals that are appropriate or adaptive only if they are the product of long previous training in action under extreme stress.

In other words, most people will not panic, but they will not work effectively either. They will be able to get certain immediate tasks completed. They will collect their families, gather last-minute supplies, and perhaps arrange a few ways of contacting other survivors. Beyond that, those who are not incapacitated by terror and panic will not accomplish much. That people do not always panic under great danger is shown not only by the disaster studies but by experiments conducted by social scientists. . . . Panic occurs in a crisis when it appears that escape is not possible for all the people caught in it. . . . If fallout shelters in remote areas are distributed *unevenly in space,* as they would have to be, the signal of "Nuclear attack!" and the time available for action, combined with the relative scarity of shelter, would create conditions ideal for a human stampede in some locales.

In places where shelter cannot be reached, and among those who define the warning buzzer as a signal of the final catastrophe, there will be nothing to panic about. Social psychologists Snell Putney and Mervyn Cadwallader have demonstrated this in a poignant experiment. They played a tape recording through a radio at a social gathering of eleven friends, four of whom were informed observers. The tape held seven news broadcasts, interspersed with music, that reported an international crisis, an air raid alert and, finally, the outbreak of an atomic war. In their words, here is what happened:

. . .

The seventh and final announcement admitted the bombing of a nearby city, gave instructions to the civilian population, and ended with a "temporary cessation of broadcasting." This announcement stunned the entire group. One group member stated flatly, "We have been attacked." Another individual was quietly sobbing, but this reaction did not spread. Rather she was quietly told "You must think of others." All the couples were together and silently holding each other, while the unattached individuals did the few things which seemed appropriate, such as turning off lights by the windows. There was a feeling of solidarity and mutual responsibility, and nothing occurred which could be called panic behavior.

. . . The experiment . . . was originally conceived as a trial run for a series of experiments. The series was abandoned because of the intense and extended reaction of some of the subjects.[1]

. . .

So far as we know, this is the *only* experiment in which the subjects of the experiment were not playing . . . the "let's pretend we have been attacked" game that characterizes the shelter feasibility studies of the OCDM. It is noteworthy, too, that the experiment took place in a remote college town far from the nearest possible target. Further, the experiment took place in 1953, long before the general public realization of the meaning of the development of the hydrogen bomb had started to jell. . . . [And] the people in this experiment were subjected to a total of two *hours* of tension and true belief that the nation had undergone the type of nuclear attack possible in 1953.

. . . The thought of being in a small shelter and having to fight off the unsheltered . . . has gripped and appalled the imagination of many Americans. . . . The vision of panic extends far into the imaginary scene of shelter life, too, when defense officials and experts envision people from hard-hit areas, injured, weak, hungry, sick and dying from radiation, attempting to secure aid from sheltered families in remote areas. In contrast, the studies of natural disaster suggest that survivors usually help others. . . .

In natural disasters, there is, of course, the realistic anticipation of outside help. . . . There is full realization that other parts of the country are not similarly crippled. Whether cooperation and sacrifice would occur so extensively when this expectation was removed, and when the public awareness of invisible fallout becomes sharpened, is an open question.

. . .

ANXIETY IN THE SHELTER

. . . When a person is anxious, a variety of specific physical reactions occur. The heart beats faster and less evenly, breathing gets difficult, the stomach may ache and heave, and the bowels may be hard to control. In a state of high anxiety, a person's way of seeing things outside himself is changed: his perception becomes less reliable; distortions increase. Worst of all, anxiety intensifies an individual's awareness of himself; a painful self-consciousness occurs.

. . .

Psychological studies of life in submarines . . . provide significant parallels for understanding emotional reactions to life in a family fallout shelter. The important differences between the two situations are that submarine crewmen . . . are *trained* volunteers who . . . know something of what lies ahead . . . and . . . know they can count on outside support.

Even with these advantages, psychologists report that submariners exhibit severe attacks of objective and neurotic anxiety during their first dives—particularly during the first days under water. . . . Studies of people placed in situations of sensory deprivation—complete isolation—suggest the same reaction. One medical aviation study, for example, used four professional air force pilots who volunteered for the experiment. Each man was placed in a small sealed enclosure and instructed to remain there for thirty-six hours. The men were not out of contact with the outside and they had a job to do. They were to watch an instrument panel and to make a report via radio every ninety minutes. . . . Only one of the four men could stand the experiment for the full day and a half. The others insisted on being let out of confinement after less than a day. They were suffering from extreme anxiety and were hallucinating—suffering loss of contact with reality.

Individuals vary tremendously in their ability to cope with anxiety. In private shelters, this range of toughness would be maintained. There would be whole families who found they could protect themselves quite well . . . from acute anxiety.

In other families, only a few members would fall victim and they could be supported by stronger members. All forms of anxiety are somewhat *contagious*, however, and children in particular would handle this stress pretty much as they found their parents handling it. . . .

. . .

. . . The population living near target areas will have to stay in the shelters for months, not days. Roger Hagan . . . has brought us close to reality . . . with the following statement concerning life in shelters. . . . He is talking about the people on the outer fringe of the target areas who just happen to be at home and ready to jump into the ever-ready shelter. . . .

Suppose you do not live or work in a city, but twenty-five miles away from ground zero—say (using Cambridge [Massachusetts] City Hall as ground zero) near the New Hampshire border, in the town of Harvard. This is beyond the greater Boston commuting area. . . . You hear an explosion from the direction of Boston. Hopefully you do not see the flash of the ensuing fireball, although an uncontrollable reflex would have caused you to look at it! if you did look at it, . . . you would have been permanently blinded, even at distances of 40 miles from the explosion. . . . But suppose you do not see the flash, only hear the blast. You come outside to see what it was, and stay long enough to be exposed to fallout for 30 seconds. You have received 150 roentgens. If you then go inside and spend another 30 seconds looking for your portable radio or your children, you pick up another 75 roentgens. If you now go immediately to a near-perfect, self-contained deep blast shelter and stay there from this moment on, you will be in great danger of dying from radiological exposure, having received 225 roentgens in the first minute. If you remain in the shelter *constantly* for the next six months, you will receive about 22 more roentgens, provided of course that you have a six-month supply of uncontaminated air and food. Only about 2.5 roentgens of that would come after two weeks, but that does not mean that you can emerge after two weeks. The 2.5 r. is what arrives *through* the shelter, assuming a protection factor of 4000. If you go to a fair basement fallout shelter with a protection factor of 250, you will have received 600 roentgens, which, as mentioned above, is very close to fatal. (The best basement fallout shelter recommended by the OCDM has a protection factor of 1000. It is a rather expensive proposition.)

. . . All this applies only to exposure: *ingestion* of any, even the tiniest particle of fallout, even months after its original formation, will almost certainly add the fatal increment to the cumulative total of unavoidable damage, for it radiates constantly in the tissue and there is no protection factor of clothing, nor can it be gotten rid of.

If the Cambridge City Hall bomb is not the only one dropped on the U.S. in the attack, but only part of a large strike on many Eastern cities, the fallout level rises alarmingly, and the fallout patterns cover most of the Northeastern states. In such a situation one *could* get no more than a harmless dose if he stayed in an excellent shelter from the moment of detonation on for six months; but he would probably starve or die from disease, and no help would come from people similarly huddled below ground. He might be willing to leave for one hour after two weeks, then for one hour each week for six months. What sustenance could be found in the radius of a half-hour walk through a devastated area is not clear, particularly since radiation in heavy doses such as those of the first weeks also kills most vegetation, and that help would come in from any place that didn't need it itself is doubtful; but at that, he would receive about 150 roentgens in six months' time, 75 of which would come through his shelter, the rest in his trips out. This much would be devastating to a child, but an adult might be willing to risk it for his family, provided he forego future children and accept some radiation damage.[2]

. . .

But again let us return to problems of shelter life for those persons in areas remote from the threat of blast and firestorms. . . . What will these sheltered few experience as the days go slowly by and they wait for the radiation level to go down to the point where their handbook allows them to go into the unknown world for a few minutes before returning again to the shelter? . . .

Some experts on shelter life believe that this problem of initial acute anxiety is the most severe that would be faced by survivors; or rather, that unless this paralysis can be overcome, steps necessary to long term survival will never be taken. Even in remote areas, for example, the ventilation crank must be turned or the air will become fetid. Readings on the dosimeter and radiometer must be taken regularly. Communication with other shelters, or at least with some outside authority, would have to be established, casualties cared for, and rules and regulations established.

In the longer run, assuming that the first two days could be navigated by some families, the psychosomatic illness that results from severe anxiety is apt to be intensified by . . . related problems. . . . In countless shelters in remote areas, some parent or child will be missing from the group. The agony of bereavement is difficult at any time. There is not only an objective loss; . . . there is the pain of moral anxiety, the gnawing question of what could have been done to prevent the loss. . . .

. . .

. . . In circumstances of combat and military occupation, moral anxiety is often neatly displaced upon the enemy. Even among civilians, there is a prospect of fighting back. . . . In the circumstance of nuclear strike, retaliation, and counter-strike, it is impossible to imagine where . . . paralyzing feelings might be directed other than toward oneself or the inhabitants of one's own shelter.

At least three phases of moral conflict can be predicted in the event of nuclear attack. The first and earliest involves those who are absent or dying at the time the shelter must be *sealed*. This refers to family members and friends who were expected to take their place in the group. A second phase involves choices about allowing unexpected visitors to join the group. And this one implicates . . . all who seek to survive in the problem of responding to the countless stragglers, all of them inevitably casualties from radiation, who seek entry a half a day or three days after the shelter has been closed. Finally, among those who withstand psychologically and medically the confinement in their shelters for some period between two weeks and six months, there is the problem of roving bands of migrants from the more radioactive areas, in quest of better, that is, less lethal, territory. . . .

Problems of bereavement and moral anxiety are one side of the struggle against emotional collapse. Another . . . is the neurotic anxiety resulting from *inactivity*. Consultants for Civil Defense have emphasized for five years the importance of planned work and recreation for shelter inhabitants. Their experimentally verified conviction is that without the supports of meaningful activity, the majority of people cannot withstand isolation. . . .

. . .

. . . Anxiety from threat is compounded, preserved, and greatly amplified if it cannot be released or transformed into energy through work and recreation.

. . .

SOME PHYSICAL CONDITIONS

Some tough-minded Americans give little credence to the lexicon of terror, panic and anxiety. Others may admit the importance of such factors but maintain that priority must be given to the mechanics and design of shelter habitation. . . . It is in this domain that there has been the greatest investment of research and development. . . . We shall concentrate here on some features of present fallout shelter designs that could spell trouble for the inhabitants. . . . We have not introduced questions about chemical and bacteriological warfare, nor have we reflected on the problem that for each shelter design there exists an alternative nuclear attack design. . . .

. . . Human refuse and discarded waste are subjected to chemical disintegration in which gases are inevitably formed. In two separate reports of habitation experiments, . . . adults in the shelters suffered disabling dizzy spells as a result of breathing these gases. . . .

. . . An earlier West German experiment with a large

community-type shelter reported unbearably high levels of both humidity and temperature. . . .

. . . A persistent danger is that of respiratory infections, with the threat of an epidemic from contagion which would be as common to community or family fallout shelters as it is to submarine crews. . . .

Oxygen, humidity, temperature (and who has explored the implications of shelter life in northern Minnesota . . . in the dead of winter?) and chemical gases, and the medical exigencies of disease epidemics, are perhaps secondary to the graver hazards of food and water supplies. Official recommendations suggest a two-week supply of both, but the New York State medical report urged instead a six-month supply of food and a thirty-day supply of water. In a large attack, even survivors in remote areas could confront lethal radiation hazards during a two-hour reconnaissance outside the shelter. Miscalculations about supplies, and extreme distances from food reserves outside, would doubtless take an increased toll of lives among those who survived the first week or two of shelter life.

. . .

THE WORLD OUTSIDE

. . .

Major sanitation facilities would have been destroyed, making all survivors vulnerable to typhus and . . . other infectious diseases. Uncovered food and water would, of course, be contaminated, and most livestock would have died from irradiated forage or from lack of care during the period of confinement. Many arable fields, even in remote areas, would be too "hot" with radioactivity to be farmed until laborious de-contamination operations had been completed. Man's "natural" enemies are, ironically, more likely to survive high radiation levels than man himself. Viruses, insect pests and bacteria will still exist in the post-attack world. We will not have the highly developed human and technological

means to counter their effects in human and plant diseases that we now rely on for our own survival and for continued food production.

. . . Under the most expensive prevention conditions, the world outside the shelter would still resemble closely the world we have sketched in here. . . .

RECOVERY

There is a difference between staying alive somehow through a period of six weeks to six months, and surviving for a decade. One big difference for most people is that continued existence depends on renewed opportunity for economic and social cooperation among individuals and groups. . . . Some form of human or subhuman life will persist beyond even the most cataclysmic of all thermonuclear wars. . . .

But extended human survival, particularly survival at a level above that of the primitive folk community, depends for most of us on the prospects for rebuilding . . . certain life-sustaining forms of social and technical organization. . . . We know something about the minimal requirements for the survival of even the most fragmented societies. Among these, most social scientists would include health and safety standards, . . . population supply, and a complex of economic and political resources and regulations. To this list, we would add those institutions that motivate men or give them meaningful goals to strive toward. . . .

THE ECONOMY

The modern American industrial economy could not recover from a thermonuclear attack of the 10,000- to 20,000-megaton type. . . . With or without vast stockpiles of resources and equipment, and with or without the portable factory, both the United States and the Soviet Union now acknowledge there is no such thing as a "hardened site." . . . The larger bombs, triggered at ground level, have earthquaking powers that extend thousands of feet below the surface.

One careful, authoritative economic analysis, prepared for the Defense Department in the late 1950s, examined the chances for recovery from a *small scale* attack where "only" 45 per cent of the population is killed and where all military and metropolitan targets are obliterated. The economists concluded that such an attack would destroy 80 percent of the instruments, 77 per cent of the transport equipment, 77 per cent of the electrical machinery and primary metal industries; as well as three-fourths to two-thirds of these other production systems: rubber, printing and publishing, cloth and garments, general machinery, petroleum and coal. . . .

These economists concluded that recuperation of the industrial economy was possible in a period of from five to twenty years, *if* a number of vital conditions could *all* be met. First, . . . the money and credit system would have to be intact and *investment* would have to proceed as usual. Government and corporate credits would . . . make new, begin-again contracting and purchasing systems come to life. In order of importance, the other conditions they cited were these: The nation would need a favorable political environment—presumably a stable, energetic government. The surviving labor force would have to get back on the job full time as promptly as radiation conditions permitted, and the "momentum" of the pre-attack economy would have to be maintained thereby. Bottlenecks in the technical organization of production and distribution resulting from dislocation of population and material ruin . . . would have to be overcome with great speed. The surviving labor force would have to accept reduced standards of health and safety. The balance of nature . . . would not be destroyed by such effects as the wholesale decimation of mammals and subsequent multiplication of insect populations, or the death of forest cover through radiation.

The assumption about the balance of nature deserves special attention. . . . Life scientists have . . . found, for instance, that the following organisms are most vulnerable to radiation exposure—that half of all those exposed are killed within thirty days at less than 700 roentgens: guinea pigs, dogs, goats, monkeys, burros and mice. . . . Birds are less vulnerable than mammals but more sensitive than such cold-blooded vertebrates as frogs, fish of some sorts, and turtles and snails. Conversely, certain insects such as the mosquito are highly resistant to radiation: the dose of gamma rays needed to kill an insect is about 100 times greater than that needed to kill a mammal. . . .

. . . Plants are more variable in the effects they show in radiation experiments. . . . Carrots and potatoes in storage rot or fail to sprout and disintegrate at doses of ten thousand roentgens, which compares with what stored vegetables in a barn in New England or a bin in Ohio would receive within thirty days after a nuclear attack.

. . . Stunting, deformity, tumor formation, growth failure or lethal mutation are the consequences and costs of irradiation of certain plants, including fruit trees.

. . . One should relate these hard facts to the equally hard facts about the *invulnerability* of many insects and viral strains that live off plants and animals. . . . The assumption of a continued balance of nature is a most shaky one.

Finally, the economists said their estimates depended on assuming that government welfare programs would be cut back quite severely, that military spending would be kept to a minimum, that bacteriological and chemical warfare would not be used, and that no third country would follow up the initial small attack.

Economic recuperation within a decade or two, according to this analysis, requires that most or all of these conditions be met. A single failure—say, for example, that all soft wood forestation is destroyed by low-yield radiation—and the forecast cannot be maintained. The conditions also must occur at more or less one and the same time. . . . Energetic governmental regulation depends on the acceptance by the surviving labor force of lowered standards of health and safety.

. . . These economists concluded that food in sufficient quantities to feed the surviving populace for two to four years must be deposited in advance of any attack.

They reasoned that most survivors would be located in remote rural areas, hence most would be farmers. These men must be transported into the devastated cities to make reconstruction possible. On their list of critical economic problems, the "furnishing of labor forces" is cited as essential. Agriculture must be deferred for a year and a half or two. Decontamination of soil in many areas would take that long anyway.

. . . The entire tissue of the analysis is torn if we increase the megatonnage of the attack from two to ten or fifteen thousand, but in fact the argument fails when even minor premises are challenged. One small premise is, for example, that recovery within a decade or two is possible only if radioactivity in industrial areas proves low enough to permit human entry within six months to a year after a small attack. The amount of radiation that persists would, however, depend on the kind of bomb exploded and the altitude at which it was exploded, and not simply on the size of the bomb. All three considerations are open choices for the attacker, not for the agents of recuperation. The gravest flaw in the analysis is the length of the list of conditions that must be met, however. For even if each condition is given odds of nine in ten chances of occurring, the odds for all or even most of them occurring at about the same time are worse than one in a hundred.

These economists were interested in whether we could recover economically to a point of material well-being that was something like our pre-attack existence. Suppose we are less demanding and we concern ourselves with the question of economic survival at a bare subsistence level something like that of contemporary India or Iran. . . . Here, our understanding is helped by the examples of Russia and Germany and their progress in recuperating from the effects of World War II. . . . Herman Kahn presents the Russian case as partial evidence that the United States could face great destruction, yet recover.

Unfortunately, such a comparison is as meaningless as a comparison of elephants and peaches. Fairly reliable data show that the Soviet Russian economy . . . in 1945 was operating at about the same level as in 1940; and that by 1950, production had nearly doubled over 1945. . . .

How could this be? It is true that about 20 million Russians were killed during the war, or about 12 per cent of their 1940 population. But those who died were *not* strategic for the maintenance of the economy. The Soviets anticipated the routes that would be followed by a German *land* invasion (a kind of anticipation that is impossible in missile warfare), and relocated their industries and labor force before the main invasions occurred. In addition, most of the invasion routes ran through non-industrial rural terrain, and the German air offensive could not reach the inland industrial centers of the economy. . . .

. . .

. . . German civilian deaths from Allied bombings during the entire war totalled about 500,000, or less than 1 per cent of the German civilian population. . . . Such an attack would amount to the dropping of one 10-megaton bomb on New York City. . . . Considered in terms of effects on industry, the Allied forces dropped the equivalent of 20 to 30 megatons of explosives on all of Europe in the entire course of World War II.

There are other crucial differences. The German labor force was not shattered by the bombing program. The German machine tools industry was only lightly affected by direct attacks. . . . The final collapse of production was due to the destruction of transport routes and equipment and to the occupation.

If we go ahead with an imaginary comparison despite these differences, we are struck not with the recuperative power of the German economy but *with the time and wealth it took to rebuild it in spite of many favorable conditions.* Governmental stability was achieved through the machinery of the Allied occupation. . . . A substantial civilian labor force was at hand, trained and properly located, and disposed to resume work. Most sectors of the economy were intact. . . . In spite of massive outside assistance, economic recovery was not achieved even in West Germany until three years after World War II. . . . Following a nuclear World War III, what nations would be standing by with a Marshall Plan?

. . .

POLITICAL ORGANIZATION

A large-scale nuclear attack would mean the destruction of existing American democratic institutions. . . . In the period from the time of an attack until reconstruction can be attempted (from six months to two years), no one may expect any form of government short of martial rule. The interdependence between civilian defense and military defense authorities has been arranged already, and would be absolute. . . . In this period, the traditional functions of local, state and federal government would be sacrificed to the necessities of survival.

Depending on prevailing winds and the chance-like pattern of rainfall, certain states might survive a nuclear attack quite intact. . . . North Dakota, Idaho, and Montana would survive a small attack more or less completely. . . . The federal cortex of our political system and virtually all its pertinent regional extensions would be gone, as would federal communications exclusive of a fragmented civil defense radio system. National Guard units would serve under state civil defense authorities in the patches of intact society in the central northwest, and in smaller sectors of a handful of widely dispersed states. . . . In lieu of a pyramid of authorities there would exist a scatter of regional, state and municipal enclaves, only a few of which could be expected to be in contact with more than a handful of others, for a time. . . .

. . . For an intermediate period, responsibility for survival and reconstruction would rest with a uniquely authoritative few, a quasi-military elite, in each enclave.

. . .

. . . A Hobbesian choice between chaos and surrender to a central authority would eventually confront a post-attack America. Hobbes was wrong in thinking that the one thing that holds men together and makes survival possible is erection of a power able "to overawe them all." . . . But Hobbes was wrong *only for the case of a society in balance.* In the extremes of crisis, where . . . ties are shattered by terror, death, and uncertainty, law and order, to exist at all, require allegiance to a strong central authority.

. . .

. . . That the United States military and civilian defense elites would constitute dispersed, competing, and eventually conflicting cliques is simple enough to demonstrate. All the resources crucial for survival would be in unprecedentedly short supply. We might expect cooperation and coalition of authority to develop in the North Dakota–Idaho region, . . . but surviving isolated communities might depend on their quasi-military leadership for defense against inroads from towns suffering even more extreme shortages. . . .

When would quasi-military rule and democratic political reorganization begin? This would depend on reconstruction of the economic and social structure. Democratic institutions depend on political parties that . . . mediate between community and governmental authority. Party loyalties vitally depend in turn on combinations of economic and social incentives—upon *routine* expectations within family, work, ethnic and religious groups. In crisis, these routines would be broken up. The economic and social bases of interest groups would be dislocated. As we showed [above], even the pattern of two-party composition itself would be badly fragmented by a nuclear attack.

To terminate the period of martial law, individuals must have the resources, including political morale, to re-form voluntary associations, interest groups and political parties. They must have access to power and influence to affect decisions of their regime. The physical security of the individual and his family, for example, must not be threatened by economic collapse. . . .

The survivors of a substantial nuclear attack would be strung out across the most isolated rural backwaters and backlands of the country. To the interminable hazards of fallout, water and food contamination, forced relocation of families and labor assignments to individuals, therefore, must be added the obstacles of weak communication and heterogeneity. . . . Without . . . intermediate networks of attachment, the individual would have to choose indefinitely between the chaos of anarchy and surrender to the military or quasi-military state.

An extended period of marital law would further undermine the structures essential for the rebuilding of democracy. If the economy were to resume operations the new government would have to expand its powers and activities dramatically. This would challenge existing protections of individual freedom to dissent from government decrees or to test the constitutionality of governmental acts. Safety and health regulations, like schedules for decontamination and construction, would have to be so rigid as to place the regime in the position of dictating personal hygiene, diet, control over residence, material resources, professional services, and the movement of labor.

Although demoralizing despair might run deep, the prospect of a public reaction against the new leadership is slim. The scope of the crisis would be so grave that only the most stupid and inept exercise of authority would be likely to be attacked. Those charged with the administration of martial law would be seen as effective, and accepted as legitimate, by the surviving population. . . .

. . .

THE CASE OF HIROSHIMA

. . .

. . . Hiroshima, a delta city accustomed to disastrous floods and well organized to handle crises, was not rebuilt primarily by its own citizens but by migrants from the hinterlands. . . . Those who had lived through the attack suffered from extreme shock and fatigue that lingered for a year. Although American occupation authorities issued food for a year, the May Day "festivities" of 1946 took the form of hunger demonstrations. . . . Demoralization was so extreme that industrial alcohol was sold as a substitute for saki; many citizens died or went blind from drinking it. . . . As late as the 1950's, Japanese sociologists reported . . . that a fear of forming attachments and producing children was very prevalent among a majority of youthful survivors.

Hiroshima's reservoirs were filled soon after the attack, but thousands of shattered pipes had to be replaced in order . . . to start the water system. For every hole the engineers plugged by day, more were dug by citizens at night to steal a drink. Gangsters organized the sale of water as a profitable racket. They fought so effectively to prevent repairs to the system that engineers had to work at night in carefully policed shifts to put the water system in order.

. . . After the first nightmare month of locating the living and removing the dead, the struggle was resumed to keep damaged body and battered soul together. Reconstruction did not begin for five months after the attack. No gas mains operated for six months. Four months after the attack, ten buses were in operation to take more than 42,000 workers to and from points in the rubble each day. And four months after the bomb, the number of crimes reported in Hiroshima and its suburbs for one month was as high as the figure for all criminal activities throughout the entire war. . . .

Ten to twelve months after the attack, administratively undirected reconstruction efforts got under way. . . . By early 1947, amusement districts, gambling dens, brothels and theaters had resumed operations. . . . People began to erect wooden or corrugated iron huts.

. . . Catastrophic as it was, the attack on Hiroshima did not level the entire metropolitan area of the city. A few weeks after the explosion, the area numbered 130,000 inhabitants compared with the 390,000 who had lived there previously, if garrison troops are included. This, in short, was a *very limited* attack by the standard of present-day possibilities. . . . Part of the city and part of its highly skilled labor force survived. There were engineers at hand to repair the water mains. The attack on America would obliterate such urban resources. . . . *When Hiroshima began its reconstruction, there was a domestic society and an invader at hand to bring aid. . . .*

. . . The questions "How many people will die in the first attack?" and "How many people will survive the first two years?" pale before the question "How will the war come to an end?" In a major attack between 1962 and 1970, three-fourths to nine-tenths of all Americans, their European and British Allies and all Communist-bloc citizens in Europe would die. There is nothing in history to suggest that either side would cease attacking until there was nothing left with which to attack. . . . The few surviving corners of the globe . . . would themselves be struggling to survive extreme contamination of the atmosphere. In the event of a "limited attack," what remaining nations would be able, let alone disposed, to come to the rescue?

AN INTERNATIONAL PUBLIC OPINION POLL ON DISARMAMENT AND "INSPECTION BY THE PEOPLE": A STUDY OF ATTITUDES TOWARD SUPRANATIONALISM

William M. Evan

INTRODUCTION

INNOVATIONS in science are now generally valued, whereas in other social institutions they are often depreciated. And yet cultural and social innovations deemed utopian in one epoch may become part of social reality in another. The

Reprinted from Seymour Melman, ed., *Inspection for Disarmament*, (New York: Columbia University Press, 1958), pp. 231–247. (Footnotes have been deleted.)

proposal advanced by Professor Seymour Melman to include "Inspection by the People" as part of a disarmament inspection system entails a cultural and a social innovation. If methods of *physical* inspection do not afford adequate safeguards against evasion of an international disarmament agreement, then the suggestion to complement them with a *social* inspection system, namely, "Inspection by the People," assumes special significance.

According to this proposal, an international agreement would make it the legal duty of the citizens of all signatory countries to report evidence of violations in their country to an international inspection authority. Such an agreement implies that nations would relinquish a measure of sovereignty in favor of an inclusive and transcending collectivity of the nation-states of the world or of mankind for the purpose of preserving peace. The *cultural* innovation of the proposal for "Inspection by the People" lies in the acknowledgment that for the purpose of securing peace, loyalty to a supranational entity or to mankind is a higher value than loyalty to nation. The *social* innovation lies in implementing this value by devising open, two-way channels of communication between the peoples of the signatory countries and the international inspection authority. Such an international agency would necessarily create new social relationships and new rights, privileges, and immunities, as well as new duties, for the peoples of the countries which are parties to the disarmament agreement.

Present obstacles—of a political, economic, legal and cultural character—to a system of "Inspection by the People" are, of course, numerous and formidable. This paper is . . . a study of one possible obstacle: the climate of opinion regarding innovation in international law as it relates to disarmament.

In polling public opinion on disarmament and "Inspection by the People," the assumption was made that attitudes or latent views toward supranationalism were being explored. A supranational, as distinct from an international, orientation to world affairs acknowledges that individual citizens—not merely governments—have rights and duties with respect to an entity transcending the nation.

With reference to these considerations, this paper seeks to answer two questions: (1) What is the current climate of opinion regarding disarmament and "Inspection by the People" in selected countries? and (2) What are some sociological and social-psychological factors associated with opinions about disarmament and "Inspection by the People" in these selected countries?

To answer these questions, a specially designed poll was conducted in six nations: the United States, Great Britain, France, West Germany, India, and Japan. Samples of respondents were personally interviewed from March 7 to March 13, 1958, by the staffs of the American Institute of Public Opinion and its affiliates in Great Britain, France, West Germany, and India. In Japan, the Research Department of the national newspaper, *Yomiuri,* conducted the poll from March 13 to March 29, 1958.

THE FINDINGS

In order to measure attitudes toward disarmament and "Inspection by the People," the following three questions were asked:

1. Would you favor or oppose setting up a world-wide organization which would make sure—*by regular inspections*—that *no* nation, including Russia and the United States, makes atom bombs, hydrogen bombs and missiles?
2. If this inspection organization were set up, would you favor or oppose making it each person's *duty* to report any attempt to secretly make atom bombs, hydrogen bombs and missiles?
3. If you, yourself, knew that someone in (name of country) was attempting to secretly make forbidden weapons, would you report this to the office of the world-wide inspection organization in this country?

The first question refers to a somewhat abstract proposal for disarmament, which presumably evokes attitudes toward peace. Since it demands little from the respondent in the way of a sacrifice of values, it was anticipated that a relatively high proportion would express approval. In contrast, Question 2 involves a concrete proposal which imposes a unique legal duty on all citizens to participate in the enforcement of a disarmament agreement. Thus it does potentially entail the sacrifice of one or more values by requiring a citizen to report damaging evidence against a friend, a neighbor, or his own government. Hence an appreciably lower proportion of favorable responses was expected. This is even more true of Question 3, since it asks the respondent if he personally would accept the duty of reporting to a world-wide inspection organization any evidence of violations in his own country, thus raising a potential conflict of values between loyalty to nation and loyalty to a supranational or "trans-national" body. Consequently, it was anticipated that the favorable response to this question would be even smaller than that to Question 2.

. . .

National Climates of Opinion

In view of the above set of expectations, the over-all results of the poll in the six nations, as shown in Table 1, are indeed striking. The high level of affirmative responses to all three questions in all six nations underscores the widespread support for a system of disarmament inspection in general and "Inspection by the People" in particular. To the extent that favorable public opinion regarding a disarmament agreement is a necessary condition for its workability, the findings suggest that "Inspection by the People" is not considered as visionary a proposal as one might have thought.

How shall we interpret this overwhelmingly positive response to the three questions in all six countries? What meaning did respondents read into the questions, and what meaning may we read out of their answers?

One interpretation is that Question 1 presents a proposal manifestly concerned with ensuring peace, a proposal which has been debated in the United Nations for over a decade.

TABLE 1. *Opinions about Disarmament Inspection in Six Selected Nations*

Questions	*United States* (N:1,610) %	*Great Britain* (N:1,000) %	*France* (N:287) %	*India* (N:250) %	*West Germany* (N:282) %	*Japan* (N:200) %
Would you favor or oppose setting up a world-wide organization which would make sure—by *regular inspections*—that *no* nation, including Russia and the United States, makes atom bombs, hydrogen bombs, and missiles?						
Favor	70	72	85	78	92	91
Oppose	16	10	6	1	1	8
No opinion and no answer	14	18	9	21	7	1
If this inspection organization were set up, would you favor or oppose making it each person's *duty* to report any attempt to secretly make atom bombs, hydrogen bombs, and missiles?						
Favor	73	54	74	71	86	80
Oppose	11	15	13	2	4	16
No opinion and no answer	16	31	13	27	10	4
If you, yourself, knew that someone in (name of country) was attempting to secretly make forbidden weapons, would you report this to the office of the world-wide inspection organization in this country?						
Yes	80	50	63	63	73	83
No	6	17	18	6	11	5
No opinion and no answer	14	33	19	31	16	12

Questions 2 and 3 raise a novel and hypothetical proposal. The high level of approval may be taken as a measure of readiness to participate personally in implementing a disarmament agreement.

. . .

Another facet of this interpretation is that these questions are uncovering a possibly higher receptivity to supranationalism than is generally assumed to exist in a world rife with conflicting nationalisms. To ascertain whether these questions are being interpreted along the dimension of nationalism-supranationalism, it was decided to validate the meaning of the questions for the United States sample on two contrasting "known" groups for the response of establishing upper and lower limits of a supranational orientation.

It was assumed that the Federation of American Scientists, which for over ten years has publicly advocated international control of atomic weapons, would score fairly high on a national-supranational scale. At the other end of this hypothetical continuum might stand the American Legion, with its emphasis on military preparedness, national security, and patriotism. The opinions of two groups of members from New York City branches of these organizations were obtained. . . . The response patterns of these groups are indeed different. Whereas 97 percent of the group of members of the Federation of American Scientists approve of Question 1 and 84 percent approve of Question 3, 53 percent of the group of American Legion members are in favor of Question 1 and 59 percent are in favor of Question 3. The relatively high level of favorable responses of the group of American Legion members to Questions 2 and 3 would suggest that supranationalism is not necessarily a dominant meaning given by respondents to these questions. Confronted with an unfamiliar or unstructured situation, people tend to turn to familiar concepts in an effort to structure the situation. Thus, when presented with Questions 2 and 3, respondents may have had recourse to familiar concepts, such as general ideas of peace or of doing one's legal duty, since these conceptions represent widespread values in modern societies.

It is, nevertheless, reasonable to assume that respondents who answer all three questions . . . positively would have a more pronounced supranational orientation than those answering only one or two questions positively. If we construct such a disarmament inspection score, ranging from zero to three points, the distribution of scores for F.A.S. and the Legion is indeed different: 78 percent of the respondents affiliated with the F.A.S. have a score of three, i.e., are positive on all three questions, as compared with 34 percent of the group of Legionnaires. These two proportions . . . represent the upper and lower boundaries for the distribution of disarmament inspection scores in all six countries.

A second unanticipated feature of the over-all poll results in Table 1 is that [a] predicted monotonic decline in response patterns is generally borne out, with the notable exception of the United States, where the pattern of response is completely reversed: 70 percent are in favor of Question 1; 73 percent are in favor of Question 2; and 80 percent answer Question 3 in the affirmative.

. . .

A clue to the reason for the reversal is provided by the spontaneous verbatim comments of some of the respondents. A recurrent justification for opposing the proposal for the disarmament inspection system in Question 1 is that "Russians couldn't be trusted." The comments offered in support of Question 3 have as their major theme obedience to law, e.g., "If it's a law, it's a citizen's duty to report"; "Law should be obeyed"; "It would be our duty as a citizen"; "Should obey the law of the land." A strong commitment to law-abidingness as a value emerges, which is not nearly so pronounced in the spontaneous comments of respondents in the other countries. . . .

Although the verbatim comments throw some light on the anomalous pattern of responses in the United States, how may we account for the over-all national differences in attitudes toward disarmament and "Inspection by the People"? . . . Japan has the highest positive score on disarmament inspection, Germany is second, India is third, France is fourth, the United States is fifth, and Great Britain is sixth. This rank order of favorable attitudes toward disarmament is largely explainable either in terms of the military experiences of these countries in the Second World War or their present military position. As militarily vanquished countries, Japan and Germany may be particularly interested in maintaining peace. Japan's memory of Hiroshima is still fresh and radioactive fall-out from nuclear tests by both the Soviet Union and the United States has been provoking anxiety. Germany's vulnerability to invasion by the Soviet Union in the event of another war may be a contributing factor to the German interest in disarmament. At the opposite end of the rank order is Great Britain, a victorious country whose possession of nuclear weapons may afford a measure of subjective—apart from objective—security against the outbreak of another world war. France and India are in an intermediate position in the order, the former possibly because of its deteriorating military and political fortunes, the latter because of its neutralist position both politically and militarily. The United States, although a victorious country and an atomic power, occupies a position closer to France than to Great Britain. This is due to the high proportion of positive responses to Question 3. . . .

In the absence of other poll data to check the validity of these interpretations of the rank order of attitudes toward disarmament inspection, they would be at best merely plausible. However, one question was included in this poll on the assumption that it was a determinant of responses to the three disarmament inspection questions. This question measures the degree of anxiety about the likelihood of a world war in which nuclear weapons would be employed. It reads as follows: "How worried are you about the chance of a world war breaking out in which atom bombs and hydrogen bombs would be used—very worried, fairly worried, or not worried at all?"

The rank order of the countries on the proportion of respondents who say they are "very worried," . . . as Table 2 makes clear, . . . closely corresponds to the previous order on high disarmament inspection scores. Japan, which ranks high on favorableness toward disarmament inspection, also ranks high on the perception of threat of a world war; and Great Britain, which ranks low on favorableness toward disarmament inspection, also ranks low on the perception of threat of a world war.

TABLE 2. *Comparison of Rank Order of Six Selected Nations on High Disarmament Inspection Scores and on Perception of Threat of War*

Nation	*Rank Order on High Disarmament Inspection Scores*	*Rank Order on "Very Worried" about War*
Japan	1	1
West Germany	2	4
India	3	2
France	4	3
United States	5	6
Great Britain	6	5

Sociological Factors Associated with Attitudes Toward Disarmament

Apart from the social-psychological variable of the perception of threat of a world war, what is the relation of such sociological variables as occupation, sex, education, etc.—which locate people in different segments of the social structure—to attitudes toward disarmament and "Inspection by the People"? On theoretical grounds we should expect some of these variables to be related to attitudes toward disarmament inspection. However, since the six countries differ substantially in their systems of beliefs and patterns of social relationships, the effect of a particular variable on attitudes toward disarmament would not necessarily be uniform in all countries.

Of the seven social background questions asked in the poll, space permits an analysis of but three: sex, occupation, and party affiliation or vote in the last election. With respect to the first of these variables, sex differences in opinions about disarmament inspection are negligible in the United States and Great Britain . . . where it may be surmised that the sexes have moved farthest toward a position of relative social equality and a consequent convergence in opinions. . . . In France, Germany, and India, sex is correlated with attitudes toward inspection, with a higher proportion of males than females expressing readiness to report violations and having a high disarmament inspection score. This difference may be due to a more traditional relationship between the sexes in these countries; occupying a subordinate position in the family and in other areas of life, the woman is discouraged from venturing new opinions. The reluctance to express an opinion on a controversial issue is reflected in the higher proportion of "don't know" answers to Question 3 among women than among men in these countries. In Japan, on the other hand, a higher proportion of women than men approve of reporting violations and have a high disarmament inspection score. This is probably due to the fact that family obligations are more likely to take precedence over traditional, militaristic, and nationalistic obligations among women than among men.

. . .

The second sociological variable to be considered, occupation, is commonly found to correlate with social, political, and economic opinions. With the exception of France and Japan, a higher proportion of nonmanual workers than of manual workers is willing to report violations and has a high disarmament inspection score. . . . This may very well be due to such occupationally correlated factors as education and level of information, particularly with respect to the possible hazards of nuclear radiation. The reversal of this relationship in Japan may be accounted for by the fact that more than one half of the manual workers in the Japanese sample are fishermen—an occupational group which may be especially aware of the dangers of radioactive fall-out. In

France the reversal is probably due to the differential impact of the leftist parties on manual and nonmanual workers.

. . .

The attitudes of two specific occupational groups, engineers and scientists, toward disarmament inspection are particularly crucial, since these groups not only have access to the production and testing of nuclear weapons . . . but they also possess specialized knowledge which would enable them to identify clandestine production in violation of an international disarmament agreement. Hence, their disposition to comply with the duty to report violations is of great significance to the question of the feasibility of a disarmament inspection system in general and of "Inspection by the People" in particular. A [comparison of] . . . scientists and engineers in the six countries with all other respondents in these countries shows the former more willing to report violations to a world-wide inspection organization and more likely to have a high disarmament inspection score. Their direct role in the production of such weapons, combined with their knowledge of the destructive power of nuclear weapons, may give them a greater appreciation of the importance of an international disarmament agreement. In addition, the scientist's search for laws transcending time and space, and the need for communication across national boundaries, may be conducive to a supranational orientation.

The third sociological variable, party affiliation or vote in the last election, has relatively little bearing on attitudes toward disarmament inspection in four of the six nations. . . . In Germany and India, where leftist opposition parties have taken a strong stand on the cessation of nuclear testing, a higher proportion of respondents affiliated with leftist parties, as compared with other parties, both indicate willingness to report violations and have a high disarmament inspection score. In the other four countries, attitudes toward disarmament cut across party lines.

In contrast to the three sociological variables which correlate differently with attitudes toward disarmament in the six countries, the social-psychological variable of perception of threat of war correlates uniformly in all countries: the greater degree of "worry" about a world war, the higher the proportion of respondents who are willing to report violations and the higher the proportion of respondents who have a high disarmament inspection score (see Table 3). This finding suggests that the fear of nuclear war may prove to be a powerful force making for supranationalism.

. . .

CONCLUSIONS

The public opinion poll discussed above yields the surprising finding that [as of the time of the survey] the majority in all six countries supports the proposal for a disarmament agreement with a system of "Inspection by the People." Does this result provide us with a reliable prediction as to how people would behave if such an agreement were actually reached, and if an inspection system were established? This raises the general and critical question of the relation between attitudes and behavior or verbal behavior in the present and nonverbal behavior in the future.

Among the conditions making for a close correlation between attitude and behavior are the strength and importance of the attitudes expressed. The greater the strength and importance to a respondent of an opinion, the greater the likelihood that the opinion is predictive of his behavior. In the case of the disarmament questions of this poll, two (Questions 2 and 3) are fairly novel and hypothetical in character. Hence, we might conservatively infer that the strength and importance of the opinions expressed about them are relatively low. If this were so, we could not confidently take the high disarmament inspection scores as predictive of what people are likely to do in the event that an international agreement is reached, obligating citizens to report violations to an international inspection authority.

On the other hand, two factors argue in favor of the possible predictiveness of the attitudes reported in this paper, assuming, of course, that these attitudes are maintained in

TABLE 3. *Willingness to Report Violations and High Disarmament Inspection Scores by Perception of Threat of World War in Six Selected Nations*

	Willing To Report Violations						*Have a High Disarmament Inspection Score*					
	Very Worried		*Fairly Worried*		*Not at All Worried*		*Very Worried*		*Fairly Worried*		*Not at All Worried*	
Nation	%	N	%	N	%	N	%	N	%	N	%	N
United States	85	(228)	81	(675)	80	(658)	62	(228)	61	(675)	53	(658)
Great Britain	62	(154)	53	(387)	49	(345)	57	(54)	49	(387)	41	(345)
France	70	(142)	65	(76)	51	(45)	65	(142)	58	(76)	47	(45)
West Germany	79	(131)	75	(99)	68	(33)	79	(131)	74	(99)	64	(33)
India	82	(143)	64	(52)	36[a]	(11)	79	(143)	56	(52)	36[a]	(11)
Japan	87	(139)	79	(57)	25[a]	(4)	80	(139)	56	(57)	25[a]	(4)

[a] The N is too small for meaningful statistical inferences. However, the percentages are shown for general comparative purposes.

the future. First, the public opinion poll results in conjunction with the responses of the validation groups suggest that underlying the opinions expressed is a commitment to the values of peace and supranationalism. This indicates that the peoples of the countries that are parties to a disarmament agreement would probably comply with the provision to participate in a system of "Inspection by the People"—at least in the six countries in which the poll was conducted. Moreover, if we suppose that a clandestine system of production of nuclear weapons, or the practice of other large-scale evasions, requires a strong nationalistic orientation of a large segment of the population, then it is reasonable to predict that an effort to evade the agreement would not enjoy popular support in these countries.

A second consideration which enhances the prospects of action in line with expressed opinions is the fact that law generally legitimizes the commission or omission of an act. Since an international disarmament agreement would have the force of law in the signatory countries, it would encourage and facilitate the translation of favorable opinions about "Inspection by the People" into action. Following the establishment of such an agreement, the level of support for disarmament and "Inspection by the People"—barring government efforts to undermine the agreement—may even exceed that found in this poll. Such a response may be anticipated because of the finding by social scientists that after the enactment of a law there tends to be an increase of public opinion favorable to the law in question.

Another important result of this poll is that the variation in national climates of opinion regarding disarmament inspection within the six countries is correlated with the perception of threat of war. This helps to account for differences in favorable attitudes toward disarmament inspection: It suggests that if the fear of war increases, favorable attitudes towards disarmament and "Inspection by the People" will increase unless they are counterbalanced by an effort to achieve collective military security.

Yet another important finding is the relationship between occupation and attitudes toward disarmament: engineers and scientists, two strategic occupational groups, express more willingness to comply with a disarmament inspection agreement than non-engineers and non-scientists.

Finally, in an effort to explain the unexpected reversal in the pattern of responses to the three disarmament questions in the United States poll, it was found that obedience to law is highly valued by many respondents. Although commitment to the value of law-abidingness may vary from one country to another, it is highly probable that, like the value of peace, it too transcends national boundaries. Commitment to the values of peace and law-abidingness is a potential basis for the participation of individual citizens of the nations of the world in a new social institution: "Inspection by the People."

Part II

The Problem of the State

THE TERRITORIAL STATE IN INTERNATIONAL RELATIONS

John H. Herz

FROM TERRITORIALITY resulted the concepts and institutions which characterized the interrelations of sovereign units, the modern state system. Modern international law, for instance, could then develop. Like the international system that produced it, international law has often been considered inherently contradictory because of its claim to bind sovereign units. But whether or not we deny to it for this reason the name and character of genuine law, it is important to see it in its connection with the territorial nature of the state system that it served. Only then can it be understood as a system of rules not contrary to, but implementing, the sovereign independence of states. Only to the extent that it reflected their territoriality and took into account their sovereignty could international law develop in modern times. For its general rules and principles deal primarily with the delimitation of the jurisdiction of countries. It thus implements the *de facto* condition of territorial impenetrability by more closely defining unit, area, and conditions of impenetrability. Such a law must reflect, rather than regulate. As one author has rightly remarked, "International law really amounts to laying down the principle of national sovereignty and deducing the consequences."[1] It is not for this reason superfluous, for sovereign units must know in some detail where their jurisdictions end and those of other

Reprinted from "Rise and Demise of the Territorial State," *World Politics*, Vol. 9, No. 4 (July, 1957), pp. 480–493. (Some footnotes have been deleted.)

units begin; without such standards, nations would be involved in constant strife over the implementation of their independence.

But it was not only this mutual legal accommodation which rendered possible a relatively peaceful coexistence of nations. War itself, the very phenomenon which reflected, not the strength, but the limitations of impermeability, was of such a nature as to maintain at least the principle of territoriality. War was limited not only in conduct but also in objectives. It was not a process of physical or political annihilation but a contest of power and will in which the interests, but not the existence, of the contestants were at stake. Now that we approach the era of absolute exposure, without walls or moats, where penetration will mean not mere damage or change but utter annihilation of life and way of life, it may dawn on us that what has vanished with the age of sovereignty and "power politics" was not entirely adverse in nature and effects.

Among other "conservative" features of the classical system, we notice one only in passing: the balance of power. It is only recently that emphasis has shifted from a somewhat one-sided concern with the negative aspects of the balance—its uncertainty, its giving rise to unending conflicts and frequent wars, etc.—to its protective effect of preventing the expansionist capacity of power from destroying other power altogether.[2] But at the time of its perfection in statecraft and diplomacy, there were even theories (not lived up to in practice, of course) about the *legal* obligations of nations to form barriers against hegemony power in the common interest.[3]

More fundamental to the conservative structure of the old system was its character as a community. Forming a comparatively pacified whole, Europe was set off sharply against the world outside, a world beyond those lines which, by common agreement, separated a community based on territoriality and common heritage from anarchy, where the law of nature reigned and no standards of civilization applied. Only recently have the existence and role of so-called "amity lines" been rediscovered, lines which were drawn in the treaties of the early modern period and which separated European territories, where the rules of war and peace were to prevail, from overseas territories and areas.[4] There was to be "no place beyond the line"; that is, European powers, although possibly at peace in Europe, continued to be *homo homini lupus* abroad. This practice made it easier for the European family of nations to observe self-denying standards at home by providing them with an outlet in the vast realm discovered outside Europe. While the practice of drawing amity lines subsequently disappeared, one chief function of overseas expansion remained: a European balance of power could be maintained or adjusted because it was relatively easy to divert European conflicts into overseas directions and adjust them there. Thus the openness of the world contributed to the consolidation of the territorial system. The end of the "world frontier" and the resulting closedness of an interdependent world inevitably affected this system's effectiveness.

Another characteristic of the old system's protective nature may be seen in the almost complete absence of instances in which countries were wiped out in the course of wars or as a consequence of other power-political events. This, of course, refers to the territorial units at home only, not to the peoples and state units beyond the pale abroad; and to the complete destruction of a state's independent existence, not to mere loss of territory or similar changes, which obviously abounded in the age of power politics.

Evidence of this is to be found not only in a legal and political ideology that denied the permissibility of conquest at home while recognizing it as a title for the acquisition of territorial jurisdiction abroad.[5] For such a doctrine had its non-ideological foundation in the actual difference between European and non-European politics so far as their territoriality was concerned. European states were impermeable in the sense here outlined, while most of those overseas were easily penetrable by Europeans. In accordance with these circumstances, international politics in Europe knew only rare and exceptional instances of actual annihilation through conquest of similar forceful means.

Prior to the twentieth century, there were indeed the Napoleonic conquests, but I submit that this is a case where the exception confirms the rule. The Napoleonic system, as a hegemonial one, was devised to destroy the established system of territoriality and balanced power as such. Consequently, Napoleon and his policies appeared "demonic" to contemporaries,[6] as well as to a nineteenth century which experienced the restoration of the earlier system. During that century occurred Bismarck's annexations of some German units into Prussia in pursuance of German unification. As in Napoleon's case, they appeared abnormal to many of his contemporaries, although the issue of national unification tended to mitigate this impression.[7] Besides these, there was indeed the partition of Poland, and considering the lamentable and lasting impression and the universal bad conscience it produced even among the ruling nations in a century used to quite a bit of international skulduggery, again one may well claim an exceptional character for that event.[8]

What, in particular, accounts for this remarkable stability? Territoriality—the establishment of defensible units, internally pacified and hard-shell rimmed—may be called its foundation. On this foundation, two phenomena permitted the system to become more stable than might otherwise have been the case: the prevalence of the legitimacy principle and, subsequently, nationalism. Legitmacy implied that the dynasties ruling the territorial states of old Europe mutually recognized each other as rightful sovereigns. Depriving one sovereign of his rights by force could not but appear to destroy the very principle on which the rights of all of them rested.

With the rise of nationalism, we witness the personalization of the units as self-determining, national groups. Nationalism now made it appear as abhorrent to deprive a sovereign nation of its independence as to despoil a legitimate ruler had appeared before. States, of course, had first to become "nation-states," considering themselves as representing specific nationality groups, which explains why in the two regions of Europe where larger numbers of old units stood in the way of national unification their demise encountered little objection. In most instances, however, the rise of nationalism led to the emergence of *new* states, which split away from multinational or colonial empires. This meant the extension of the European principle of "non-obliteration" all over the world. It is perhaps significant that even in our century, and even after the turmoil of attempted world conquest and resulting world wars, a point has been made of restoring the most minute and inconsiderable of sovereignties, down to Luxembourg and Albania.[9]

This hypertrophy of nation-states presented new problems —above all, that of an improved system of protection. For by now it had become clear that the protective function of the old system was only a relative blessing after all. Continued existence of states as such was perhaps more or less guaranteed. But power and influence, status, frontiers, economic interests—in short, everything that constituted the life and interests of nations beyond bare existence—were always at the mercy of what power politics wrought. Furthermore, much of the relative stability and political equilibrium of the territorial states had been due to the extension of Western control over the world. When what could be penetrated had been subjugated, assimilated, or established as fellow "sovereign" states, the old old units were thrown back upon themselves. Hence the demand for a new system which would offer more security to old and new nations: collective security.

I propose to view collective security not as the extreme opposite of power politics, but as an attempt to maintain, and render more secure, the impermeability of what were still territorial states. To an age which took territoriality for granted, replacing power politics with collective security would indeed appear to be a radical departure. From the vantage point of the nuclear age, however, a plan to protect individual sovereignties by collective guarantees for continuing sovereignty appears questionable not because of its innovating, but because of its conservative, nature. Its conservatism lies in its basic objective: the protection of the hard-shell territorial structure of its members, or, as the core article of the Covenant of the League of Nations put it, its guarantee of their "territorial integrity and political independence" against external aggression. The beginning of air war and the increasing economic interdependence of nations had indicated by the end of World War I that the old-style military barriers might be by-passed. If territorial units were to be preserved in the future, it would be accomplished less by reliance on individual defense potentials than by marshaling collective power in order to preserve individual powers.

But since the idea of organizing a genuine supranational force—an international police force—was rejected, the League had to cling to classical arrangements insofar as the procedures of protection were concerned. The guarantee to the individual states was to be the formation of the "Grand Coalition" of all against the isolated aggressor, which presupposed the maintenance of a certain level of armed strength by the member states. A member without that minimum of military strength would be a liability rather than an asset to the organization—in Geneva parlance, a "consumer" and not a "producer" of security.[10] Thus classical concepts (the sovereignty and independence of nation-states) as well as classical institutions (in particular, hard-shell defensibility) were to be maintained under the new system.

Whether there ever was a chance for the system to be effective in practice is beside the point here. It is sufficient to realize how closely it was tied to the underlying structure as well as to the prevailing concepts and policies of the territorial age.

THE DECLINE OF THE TERRITORIAL STATE

Beginning with the nineteenth century, certain trends became visible which tended to endanger the functioning of the classical system. Directly or indirectly, all of them had a bearing upon that feature of the territorial state which was the strongest guarantee of its independent coexistence with

other states of like nature: its hard shell—that is, its defensibility in case of war.

Naturally, many of these trends concerned war itself and the way in which it was conducted. But they were not related to the shift from the limited, duel-type contests of the eighteenth century to the more or less unlimited wars that developed in the nineteenth century with conscription, "nations in arms," and increasing destructiveness of weapons. By themselves, these developments were not inconsistent with the classical function of war. Enhancing a nation's defensive capacity, instituting universal military service, putting the economy on a war footing, and similar measures tended to bolster the territorial state rather than to endanger it.

Total war in a quite different sense is tied up with developments in warfare which enable the belligerents to overleap or by-pass the traditional hard-shell defense of states. When this happens, the traditional relationship between war, on the one hand, and territorial power and sovereignty, on the other, is altered decisively. Arranged in order of increasing effectiveness, these new factors may be listed under the following headings: (a) possibility of economic blockade; (b) ideological-political penetration; (c) air warfare; and (d) atomic warfare.

(a) *Economic warfare.* It should be said from the outset that so far economic blockade has never enabled one belligerent to force another into surrender through starvation alone. Although in World War I Germany and her allies were seriously endangered when the Western allies cut them off from overseas supplies, a very real effort was still required to defeat them on the military fronts. The same thing applies to World War II. Blockade was an important contributing factor, however. Its importance for the present analysis lies in its unconventional nature, permitting belligerents to by-pass the hard shell of the enemy. Its effect is due to the changed economic status of industrialized nations.

Prior to the industrial age, the territorial state was largely self-contained economically. Although one of the customary means of conducting limited war was starving fortresses into surrender, this applied merely to these individual portions of the hard shell, and not to entire nations. Attempts to starve a belligerent nation in order to avoid having to breach the shell proved rather ineffective, as witness the Continental Blockade and its counterpart in the Napoleonic era. The Industrial Revolution made countries like Britain and Germany increasingly dependent on imports. In war, this meant that they could survive only by controlling areas larger than their own territory. In peacetime, economic dependency became one of the causes of a phenomenon which itself contributed to the transformation of the old state system: imperialism. Anticipating war, with its new danger of blockade, countries strove to become more self-sufficient through enlargement of their areas of control. To the extent that the industrialized nations lost self-sufficiency, they were driven into expansion in a (futile) effort to regain it. Today, if at all, only control of entire continents enables major nations to survive economically in major wars. This implies that hard-shell military defense must be a matter of defending more than a single nation; it must extend around half the world.

(b) *Psychological warfare,* the attempt to undermine the morale of an enemy population, or to subvert its loyalty, shares with economic warfare a by-passing effect on old-style territorial defensibility. It was formerly practiced, and practicable, only under quite exceptional circumstances. Short periods of genuine world revolutionary propaganda, such as the early stages of the French Revolution,[11] scarcely affected a general practice under which dynasties, and later governments, fought each other with little ideological involvement on the part of larger masses or classes. Only in rare cases—for instance, where national groups enclosed in and hostile to multinational empires could be appealed to—was there an opening wedge for "fifth column" strategies.

With the emergence of political belief-systems, however, nations became more susceptible to undermining from within. Although wars have not yet been won solely by subversion of loyalties, the threat involved has affected the inner coherence of the territorial state ever since the rise to power of a regime that claims to represent, not the cause of a particular nation, but that of mankind, or at least of its suppressed and exploited portions. Bolshevism from 1917 on has provided the second instance in modern history of world revolutionary propaganda. Communist penetration tactics subsequently were imitated by the Nazi and Fascist regimes and, eventually, by the democracies. In this way, new lines of division, cutting horizontally through state units instead of leaving them separated vertically from each other at their frontiers, have now become possible.

(c) *Air warfare* and (d) *nuclear warfare.* Of all the new developments, air warfare, up to the atomic age, has been the one that affected the territoriality of nations most radically. With its coming, the bottom dropped out—or, rather, the roof blew off—the relative security of the territorial state. True, even this new kind of warfare, up to and including the Second World War, did not by itself account for the defeat of a belligerent, as some of the more enthusiastic prophets of the air age had predicted it would. Undoubtedly, however, it had a massive contributory effect. And this effect was due to strategic action in the *hinterland* rather than to tactical use at the front. It came at least close to defeating one side by direct action against the "soft" interior of the country, by-passing outer defenses and thus foreshadowing the end of the frontier—that is, the demise of the traditional impermeability of even the militarily most powerful states. Warfare now changed "from a fight to a process of devastation."[12]

That air warfare was considered as something entirely unconventional is seen from the initial reaction to it. Revolutionary transition from an old to a new system has always affected moral standards. In the classical age of the modern state system, the "new morality" of shooting at human beings from a distance had finally come to be accepted, but the standards of the age clearly distinguished "lawful combatants" at the front or in fortifications from the civilian remainder of the population. When air war came, reactions thus differed significantly in the cases of air fighting at the front and of air war carried behind the front. City bombing was felt to constitute "illegitimate" warfare, and populations were inclined to treat airmen engaging in it as "war criminals."[13] This feeling continued into World War II, with its large-scale area bombing. Such sentiments reflected the general feeling of helplessness in the face of a war which threatened to render obsolete the concept of territorial power, together with its ancient implication of protection.

The process has now been completed with the advent of nuclear weapons. For it is more than doubtful that the processes of scientific invention and technological discovery, which not only have created and perfected the fission and fusion weapons themselves but have brought in their wake guided missiles with nuclear warheads, jet aircraft with intercontinental range and supersonic speed, and the prospect of nuclear-powered planes or rockets with unlimited range and with automatic guidance to specific targets anywhere in the world, can in any meaningful way be likened to previous new inventions, however revolutionary. These processes add up to an uncanny absoluteness of effect which previous innovations could not achieve. The latter might render power units of a certain type (for instance, castles or cities) obsolete and enlarge the realm of defensible power units from city-state to territorial state or even large-area empire. They might involve destruction, in war, of entire populations. But there still remained the seemingly inexhaustible reservoir of the rest of mankind. Today, when not even two halves of the globe remain impermeable, it can no longer be a question of enlarging an area of protection and of substituting one unit of security for another. Since we are inhabitants of a planet of limited (and, as it now seems, insufficient) size, we have reached the limit within which the effect of the means of destruction has become absolute. Whatever remained of the impermeability of states seems to have gone for good.

What has been lost can be seen from two statements by thinkers separated by thousands of years and half the world; both reflect the condition of territorial security. Mencius, in ancient China, when asked for guidance in matters of defense and foreign policy by the ruler of a small state, is said to have counseled: "Dig deeper your moats; build higher your walls; guard them along with your people." This remained the classical posture up to our age, when a Western sage, Bertrand Russell, in the interwar period could still define power as something radiating from one center and growing less with distance from that center until it finds an equilibrium with that of similar geographically anchored units. Now that power can destroy power from center to center, everything is different.

OUTLOOK AND CONCLUSION

It is beyond the compass of this article to ask what the change in the statehood of nations implies for present and future world relations; whether, indeed, international relations in the traditional sense of the term, dependent as they have been on a number of basic data (existence of the nation-state, measurable power, etc.) and interpreted as they were with the aid of certain concepts (sovereignty, independence, etc.), can survive at all; and, if not, what might take their place.[14] Suffice it to remark that this question is vastly complex. We cannot even be sure that one and only one set of conclusions derives from what has happened or is in the process of happening. For, in J. Robert Oppenheimer's words, one of the characteristics of the present is "the prevalence of newness, the changing scale and scope of change itself. . . ."[15] In the field of military policy, this means that since World War II half a dozen military innovations "have followed each other so rapidly that efforts at adaptation are hardly begun before they must be scrapped."[16] The scientific revolution has been "so fast-moving as to make almost impossible the task of military men whose responsibility it is to anticipate the future. Military planning cannot make the facts of this future stay long enough to analyze them.[17]

If this applies to military planning, it must apply equally to foreign policy planning, and, indeed, the newness of the new is perhaps the most significant and the most exasperating aspect of present world relations. Hardly has a bipolar world replaced the multipower world of classical territoriality than there loom new and unpredictable multipower constellations on the international horizon. However, the possible rise of new powers does not seem to affect bipolarity in the sense of a mere return to traditional multipower relations; since rising powers are likely to be nuclear powers, their effect must be an entirely novel one. What international relations would (or will) look like, once nuclear power is possessed by a larger number of power units, is not only extremely unpleasant to contemplate but almost impossible to anticipate, using any familiar concepts. Or, to use another example: We have hardly drawn the military and political conclusions from the new weapons developments, which at one point seemed to indicate the necessity of basing defense on the formation and maintenance of pacts like NATO and the establishment of a network of bases on allied territory from which to launch nuclear weapons "in case" (or whose existence was to deter the opponent from doing so on his part), and already further scientific and technological developments seem to render entire defense blocs, with all their new "hard shells" of bases and similar installations, obsolete.

To complicate matters even more, the change-over is not even uniform and unilinear. On the contrary, in concepts as well as in policies, we witness the juxtaposition of old and new (or several new) factors, a coexistence in theory and practice of conventional and new concepts, of traditional and new policies. Part of a nation's (or a bloc's) defense policy, then, may proceed on pre-atomic assumptions, while another part is based on the assumption of a preponderantly nuclear contest. And a compounding trouble is that the future depends on what the present anticipates, on what powers now think and how they intend to act on the basis of their present thinking; and on the fact that each of the actors on the scene must take into consideration the assumptions of the others.[18]

There then evolves the necessity of multilevel concepts and of multilevel policies in the new era. In this we have, perhaps, the chief cause of the confusion and bewilderment of countries and publics. A good deal in recent foreign policies, with their violent swings from one extreme to another, from appeasement or apathy to truculence and threats of war, and also much in internal policies, with their suspicions and hysterias, may be reflections of world-political uncertainties. Confusion, despair, or easy optimism have been rampant; desire to give in, keep out, or get it over with underlies advocacy of appeasement, neutralism, or preventive war; mutually exclusive attitudes follow each other in rapid succession.

One radical conclusion to be drawn from the new condition of permeability would seem to be that nothing short of global rule can utimately satisfy the security interest of any one power, and particularly any superpower. For only through elimination of the single competitor who really counts can one feel safe from the threat of annihilation. And since elimination without war is hardly imaginable, destruction of the other power by preventive war would therefore seem to be the logical objective of each superpower. But—and here the security dilemma encounters the other great dilemma of our time—such an aim is no longer practical. Since thermonuclear war would in all likelihood involve one's own destruction together with the opponent's, the means through which the end would have to be attained defeats the end itself. Pursuance of the "logical" security objective would result in mutual annihilation rather than in one unit's global control of a pacified world.

If this is so, the short-term objective must surely be mutual accommodation, a drawing of demarcation lines, geographical and otherwise, between East and West which would at least serve as a stopgap policy, a holding operation pending the creation of an atmosphere in which perhaps in consequence of a prolonged period of "cold peace," tensions may abate and the impact of the ideologies presently dividing the world diminish. May we then expect, or hope, that radically new attitudes, in accordance with a radically transformed structure of nationhood and international relations, may ultimately gain the upper hand over the inherited ones based on familiar concepts of old-style national security, power, and power competition? Until recently, advocacy of policies based on internationalism instead of power politics, on substituting the observance of universal interests for the prevalence of national interests, was considered utopian, and correctly so. National interests were still tied up with nation-states as units of power and with their security as impermeable units; internationalist ideals, while possibly recognized as ethically valid, ran counter to what nations were able to afford if they wanted to survive and prosper. But the dichotomy between "national self-interest" and "internationalist ideals" no longer fits a situation in which sovereignty and ever so absolute power cannot protect nations from annihilation.

What used to be a dichotomy of interests and ideals now emerges as a dichotomy between two sets of interests. For the former ideal has become a compelling interest itself. In former times, the lives of people, their goods and possessions, their hopes and their happiness, were tied up with the affairs of the country in which they lived, and interests thus centered around nation and national issues. Now that destruction threatens everybody, in every one of his most intimate, personal interests, national interests are bound to recede behind—or at least compete with—the common interest of all mankind in sheer survival. And if we add to this the universal interest in the common solution of other great world problems, such as those posed by the population-resources dilemma (exhaustion of vital resources coupled with the "population explosion" throughout the world), or, indeed, that of "peacetime" planetary pollution through radio-active fallout, it is perhaps not entirely utopian to expect the ultimate spread of an attitude of "universalism" through which a rational approach to world problems would at last become possible.

It may be fitting to conclude this article by quoting two men, one a contemporary scientist whose words on nuclear problems may well apply to other problems of world relations, the second a philosopher whose statement on the revolutionary impact of attitude changes seems as valid today as when it was first made:

It is a practical thing to recognize as a common responsibility, wholly incapable of unilateral solution, the complete common peril that atomic weapons constitute for the world, to recognize that only by a community of responsibility is there any hope of meeting the peril. It would seem to me visionary in the extreme, and not practical, to hope that methods which have so sadly failed in the past to avert war will succeed in the face of this far greater peril. It would in my opinion be most dangerous to regard, in these shattering times, a radical solution less practical than a conventional one.[19] . . .

And:

Thought achieves more in the world than practice; for, once the realm of imagination has been revolutionized, reality cannot resist.[20] . . .

TO INTERVENE OR NOT TO INTERVENE

Hans J. Morgenthau

I

INTERVENTION is as ancient and well-established an instrument of foreign policy as are diplomatic pressure, negotiations and war. From the time of the ancient Greeks to this day, some states have found it advantageous to intervene in the affairs of other states on behalf of their own interests and against the latters' will. Other states, in view of their interests, have opposed such interventions and have intervened on behalf of theirs.

It is only since the French Revolution of 1789 and the

Reprinted by special permission from *Foreign Affairs*, Vol. 45, No. 3 (April, 1967), pp. 425–436.

rise of the nation-state that the legitimacy of intervention has been questioned. Article 119 of the French Constitution of 1793 declared that the French people "do not interfere in the domestic affairs of other nations and will not tolerate interference by other nations in their affairs." This declaration ushered in a period of interventions by all concerned on the largest possible scale. For a century and a half afterwards, statesmen, lawyers and political writers tried in vain to formulate objective criteria by which to distinguish between legitimate and illegitimate intervention. The principle of nonintervention was incorporated into the textbooks of international law, and statesmen have never ceased to pay lip service to it. In December 1965, the United Nations General Assembly adopted a "Declaration on the Inadmissibility of Intervention in the Domestic Affairs of States and the Protection of their Independence and Sovereignty," according to which "no state has the right to intervene, directly or indirectly, for any reason whatever, in the internal or external affairs of any other state . . ." and "no state shall organize, assist, foment, finance, incite or tolerate subversive, terrorist or armed activities directed toward the violent overthrow of another state, or interfere in civil strife in another state." Yet again we are witnessing throughout the world activities violating all the rules laid down in this Declaration.

Both the legal commitments against intervention and the practice of intervention serve the political purposes of particular nations. The former serve to discredit the intervention of the other side and to justify one's own. Thus the principle of nonintervention, as formulated at the beginning of the nineteenth century, sought to protect the new nation-states from interference by the traditional monarchies of Europe. For the main instrument of the Holy Alliance, openly proclaimed in the treaty establishing it, was intervention. Thus, to give only two examples among many, Russia tried to intervene in Spain in 1820, and actually intervened in Hungary in 1848, in order to oppose liberal revolutions. Great Britain opposed these interventions because it was opposed to the expansion of Russian power. Yet it intervened on behalf of nationalism in Greece and on behalf of the conservative status quo in Portugal because its interests seemed to require it.

What we have witnessed since the end of the Second World War thus appears as a mere continuation of a tradition which was well established in the nineteenth century. There is nothing new either in the contemporary doctrine opposing intervention or in the pragmatic use of intervention on behalf of the interests of individual nations. What Great Britian and Russia were doing in the nineteenth century, the United States and the Soviet Union seem to be doing today. Thus, to cite again two spectacular examples among many, the Soviet Union intervened in Hungary in 1956 as Russia had done in 1848, and the United States intervened in Cuba at the beginning of the sixties as it had done in the first decades of the century. Yet there are fundamental differences between the interventions of the past and those of the present. Five such differences have significantly altered the techniques of contemporary intervention, have drastically reduced the traditional legal significance of the consent of the state intervened against, and have affected in a general way the peace and order of the world.

First, the process of decolonization, which started after the Second World War and is now almost completed, has more than doubled the number of sovereign nations. Many if not most of these new nations are not viable political, military and economic entities; they are lacking in some if not all of the prerequisites of nationhood. Their governments need regular outside support. Thus France subsidizes its former colonies in Africa; all the major industrial nations extend economic and financial aid to the new ones, and the United States, the Soviet Union and China do so on a competitive basis.

What makes this aid a lever for intervention is the fact that in most cases it is not just an advantage which the new nations can afford to take or leave, but a condition for their survival. The Indian economy, for example, would collapse without outside support, and in consequence the Indian state itself would probably disintegrate. Large masses of Egyptians would starve without the outside supply of food. What is true of these two ancient and relatively well developed nations is of course true of most of the new nations which are nations within their present boundaries only by virtue of the accidents of colonial policy: the supplier of foreign aid holds the power of life and death over them. If a foreign nation supplies aid it intervenes; if it does not supply aid it also intervenes. In the measure that the government must depend on foreign aid for its own and its nation's survival it is inevitably exposed to political pressures from the supplying government. Many of the recipient governments have been able to minimize or even neutralize these political pressures by keeping open alternative sources of foreign aid and by playing one supplying government against the other. Some nations, such as Egypt, have developed this technique into a fine and highly successful art.

Second, our age resembles the period of history after the Napoleonic Wars, when the theory of nonintervention and the practice of intervention flourished, in that it is a revolutionary age. Many nations, new and old, are threatened by revolution, or are at one time or another in the throes of it. A successful revolution frequently portends a new orientation in the country's foreign policy, as it did in the Congo, Cuba and Indonesia. Thus the great powers, expecting gains or fearing disadvantages from the revolution, are tempted to intervene on the side of the faction favoring them. This is particularly so when the revolution is committed to a communist or anti-communist position. Thus China has almost indiscriminately intervened throughout the world on behalf of subversive movements, very much in the manner in which the Bolshevist government under Lenin and Trotsky tried to promote world revolution. In many nations, the United States and the Soviet Union oppose each other surreptitiously through the intermediary of governments and political movements. It is at this point that the third new factor comes into play.

Of all the revolutionary changes that have occurred in world politics since the end of the Second World War, none has exerted a greater influence upon the conduct of foreign policy than the recognition on the part of the two superpowers, armed with a large arsenal of nuclear weapons, that a direct confrontation between them would entail unacceptable risks; for it could lead to their mutual destruction. Both have recognized that a nuclear war fought against each other would be a suicidal absurdity. Thus they have decided that they must avoid a direct confrontation. This is the real political and military meaning of the slogan of "peaceful coexistence."

Instead of confronting each other openly and directly, the United States and the Soviet Union have chosen to oppose and compete with each other surreptitiously through the intermediary of third parties. The internal weakness of most new and emerging nations requiring foreign support and the revolutionary situation in many of them give the great powers the opportunity of doing so. Thus, aside from competing for influence upon a particular government in the traditional ways, the United States and the Soviet Union have interjected their power into the domestic conflicts of weak nations, supporting the government or the opposition as the case may be. While one might think that on ideological grounds the United States would always intervene on the side of the government and the Soviet Union on the side of the opposition, it is characteristic of the interplay between ideology and power politics, to which we shall turn in a moment, that this has not always been so. Thus the Soviet Union intervened in Hungary in 1956 on the side of the government, and the United States has been intervening in Cuba on the side of the opposition. The Soviet slogan of support for "wars of national liberation" is in truth an ideological justification of Soviet support for that side in a civil conflict in which the Soviet Union happens to have an interest. In the Congo, the United States and the Soviet Union have switched their support from the government to the opposition and back again according to the fortunes of a succession of civil wars.

While contemporary interventions serving national power interests have sometimes been masked by the ideologies of communism and anti-communism, these ideologies have been an independent motivating force. This is the fourth factor which we must consider. The United States and the Soviet Union face each other not only as two great powers which in the traditional ways compete for advantage. They also face each other as the fountainheads of two hostile and incompatible ideologies, systems of government and ways of life, each trying to expand the reach of its respective political values and institutions and to prevent the expansion of the other. Thus the cold war has not only been a conflict between two world powers but also a contest between two secular religions. And like the religious wars of the seventeenth century, the war between communism and democracy does not respect national boundaries. It finds enemies and allies in all countries, opposing the one and supporting the other regardless of the niceties of international law. Here is the dynamic force which has led the two superpowers to intervene all over the globe, sometimes surreptitiously, sometimes openly, sometimes with the accepted methods of diplomatic prssure and propaganda, sometimes with the frowned-upon instruments of covert subversion and open force.

These four factors favoring intervention in our time are counteracted by a fifth one, which in a sense compensates for the weakness of the nations intervened in. Having just emerged from a colonial status or struggling to emerge from a semicolonial one, these nations react to their dependence on outside support with a fierce resistance to the threat of "neo-colonialism." While they cannot exist without support from stronger nations, they refuse to exchange their newly won independence for a new dependency. Hence their ambivalent reaction to outside intervention. They need it and they resent it. This ambivalence compels them to choose among several different courses of action. They can seek support from multiple outside sources, thereby canceling out dependence on one by dependence on the other. They can alternate among different sources of support, at one time relying on one, and at another time relying on another. Finally, they can choose between complete dependence and complete independence, either by becoming a client of one of the major powers or by forswearing outside support altogether.

This ambivalence of the weak nations imposes new techniques upon the intervening ones. Intervention must either be brutally direct in order to overcome resistance or it must be surreptitious in order to be acceptable, or the two extremes may be combined. Thus the United States intervened in Cuba in 1961 through the proxy of a refugee force, and the Soviet Union intervened in Hungary in 1956 by appointing a government which asked for its intervention.

II

What follows from this condition of intervention in our time for the foreign policies of the United States? Four basic conclusions can be drawn: the futility of the search for abstract principles, the error of anti-communist intervention per se, the self-defeating character of anti-revolutionary intervention per se, and the requirement of prudence.

First, it is futile to search for an abstract principle which would allow us to distinguish in a concrete case between legitimate and illegitimate intervention. This was so even in the nineteenth century when intervention for the purpose of colonial expansion was generally regarded to be legitimate and when the active players on the political stage were relatively self-sufficient nation-states, which not only were not in need of intervention but actually were opposed to it as a threat to their existence. If this was so then, it stands to reason that in an age where large segments of whole continents must choose between anarchy and intervention, intervention cannot be limited by abstract principles, let alone effectively outlawed by a United Nations resolution.

Let us suppose that nation A intervenes on behalf of the government of nation B by giving it military, economic and technical aid on the latter's request, and that the government of B becomes so completely dependent upon A as to act as the latter's satellite. Let us further suppose that the local opposition calls upon country C for support against the agents of a foreign oppressor and that C heeds that call. Which one of these interventions is legitimate? Country A will of course say that its own is and C's is not, and vice versa, and the ideologues on both sides will be kept busy justifying the one and damning the other. This ideological shadowboxing cannot affect the incidence of interventions. All nations will continue to be guided in their decisions to intervene and their choice of the means of intervention by what they regard as their respective national interests. There is indeed an urgent need for the governments of the great powers to abide by certain rules according to which the game of intervention is to be played. But these rules must be deduced not from abstract principles which are incapable of controlling the actions of governments, but from the interests of the nations concerned and from their practice of foreign policy reflecting those interests.

The failure to understand this distinction between abstract principles and national interests as guidance for a policy of intervention was in good measure responsible for the fiasco of the Bay of Pigs in 1961. The United States was resolved to intervene on behalf of its interests, but it was also resolved to intervene in such a way as not openly to violate the principle of nonintervention. Both resolutions were legitimate in terms of American interests. The United States had an interest in eliminating the political and military power of the Soviet Union, which used Cuba as a base from which to threaten the security interests of the United States in the Western Hemisphere. The United States also had an interest in avoiding whatever would jeopardize its standing in the new and emerging nations. The United States failed to assign priorities to these two interests. In order to minimize the loss of prestige, the United States jeopardized the success of the intervention. Instead of using concern for prestige as a datum among others in the political equation—that is, as an interest among others—it submitted to it as though it were an abstract principle imposing absolute limits upon the actions necessary to achieve success. In consequence, the United States failed thrice. The intervention did not succeed; in the attempt we suffered the temporary impairment of our standing among the new and emerging nations; and we lost much prestige as a great nation able to use its power successfully on behalf of its interests.

Had the United States approached the problem of intervening in Cuba in a rational fashion, it would have asked itself which was more important: to succeed in the intervention or to prevent a temporary loss of prestige among the new and emerging nations. Had it settled upon the latter alternative, it would have refrained from intervening altogether; had it chosen the former alternative, it would have taken all the measures necessary to make the intervention a success, regardless of unfavorable reactions in the rest of the world. Instead, it sought the best of both worlds and got the worst.

The Soviet Union's intervention in Hungary in 1956 is instructive in this respect. The Soviet Union put the success of the intervention above all other considerations, and succeeded. Its prestige throughout the world suffered drastically in consequence. But Hungary is today a communist state within the orbit of the Soviet Union, and Soviet prestige recovered quickly from the damage it suffered in 1956.

The interventions of the United States in Cuba, the Dominican Republic and Viet Nam, as well as others less spectacular, have been justified as reactions to communist intervention. This argument derives from the assumption that communism everywhere in the world is not only morally unacceptable and philosophically hostile to the United States, but is also detrimental to the national interests of the United States and must therefore be opposed on political as well as moral and philosophic grounds. I shall assume for the purposes of this discussion that, as a matter of fact, communist intervention actually preceded ours in all these instances, and shall raise the question as to whether our national interest required our counter-intervention.

Ten or twenty years ago, this question could have been answered in the positive without further examination. For then communism anywhere in the world was a mere extension of Soviet power, controlled and used for the purposes of that power. Since we were committed to the containment of the Soviet Union, we were also committed to the containment of communism anywhere in the world. However, today we are faced not with one monolithic communist bloc controlled and used by Soviet Union, but with a variety of communisms, whose relations with the Soviet Union and China change from country to country and from time to time and whose bearing upon the interests of the United States requires empirical examination in each concrete instance. Communism has become polycentric, that is to say, each communist government and movement, to a greater or lesser extent, pursues its own national interests within the common framework of communist ideology and institutions. The bearing which the pursuit of those interests has upon the interests of the United States must be determined in terms not of communist ideology but of the compatibility of those interests with the interests of the United States.

Subjecting our interventions in Cuba, the Dominican Republic and Viet Nam to this empirical test, one realizes the inadequacy of the simple slogan "stop communism" as the rationale of our interventions. While this slogan is popular at home and makes but minimal demands upon discriminating judgment, it inspires policies which do either too much or too little in opposing communism and can provide no yardstick for a policy which measures the degree of its opposition by the degree of the communist threat. Thus on the one hand, as part of the settlement of the missile crisis of 1962, we pledged ourselves not to intervene in Cuba, which is today a military and political outpost of the Soviet Union and the fountainhead of subversion and military intervention in the Western Hemisphere, and as such directly affects the interests of the United States. On the other hand, we have intervened massively in Viet Nam, even at the risk of a major war, although the communist threat to American interests from Viet Nam is at best remote and in any event is infinitely more remote than the communist threat emanating from Cuba.

As concerns the intervention in the Dominican Republic, even if one takes at face value the official assessment that the revolution of April 1965 was controlled by Cuban communists, it appears incongruous that we intervened massively in the Dominican Republic, whose revolution was, according to our government's assessment of the facts, a mere symptom of the disease, while the disease itself—that is, Cuban communism—is exempt from effective intervention altogether.

This type of intervention against communism per se naturally tends to blend into intervention against revolution per se. Thus we tend to intervene against all radical revolutionary movements because we are afraid lest they be taken over by communists, and conversely we tend to intervene on behalf of all governments and movements which are opposed to radical revolution, because they are also opposed to communism. Such a policy of intervention is unsound on intellectual grounds for the reason mentioned in our discussion of contemporary communism; it is also bound to fail in practice.

Many nations of Asia, Africa and Latin America are today in a pre-revolutionary stage, and it is likely to be only a matter of time until actual revolution will break out in one or another of these nations. The revolutionary movements which will then come to the fore are bound to have, to a greater or lesser degree, a communist component; that is, they risk being taken over by communism. Nothing is simpler, both in terms of intellectual effort and, at least initially, practical execution, than to trace all these revolutions to a common conspiratorial source, to equate all revolutionary movements with world communism, and to oppose them with indiscriminate fervor as uniformly hostile to our interests. The United States would then be forced to intervene against revolutions throughout the world because of the ever-present threat of a communist take-over, and would transform itself, in spite of its better insight and intentions, into an anti-revolutionary power per se.

Such a policy of intervention might succeed if it had to deal with nothing more than isolated revolutionary movements which could be smothered by force of arms. But it cannot succeed, since it is faced with revolutionary situations all over the world; for even the militarily most powerful nation does not have sufficient usable resources to deal simultaneously with a number of acute revolutions. Such a policy of indiscriminate intervention against revolution is bound to fail not only with regard to the individual revolution to which it is applied but also in terms of its own indiscriminate anti-communism. For the very logic which would make us appear as the anti-revolutionary power per se would surrender to communism the sponsorship or revolution everywhere. Thus anti-communist intervention achieves what it aims to prevent: the exploitation of the revolutions of the age by communism.

In truth, the choice before us is not between the status quo and revolution or even between communist and noncommunist revolution, but between a revolution hostile to the interests of the United States and a revolution which is not hostile to these interests. The United States, far from intervening against revolutions per se, has therefore to intervene in competition with the main instigators of revolution—the Soviet Union, Communist China and Cuba—on behalf of revolution. This intervention should serve two alternative aims: first, to protect the revolution from a communist takeover, and second, if we should fail in this, to prevent such a communist revolution from turning against the interests of the United States. Such a policy, substituting the yardstick of the American national interest for that of anti-communism, would obviously form a complete reversal of the positions which we have taken in recent years and of which our interventions in Viet Nam and the Dominican Republic are the recent prime examples.

If this analysis of our policy of intervention is correct, then we have intervened not wisely but too well. Our policy of intervention has been under the ideological spell of our opposition to communism and potentially communist-led revolutions. Yet while this ideological orientation has continued to determine our policy of intervention, the Soviet Union has continued to pay lip service to support for "wars of national liberation" but has in practice relegated these wars to a secondary place in the struggle for the world. This softening of the Soviet ideological position has become one of the points of contention in the ideological dispute between the Soviet Union and China. In a statement of June 14, 1963, the Chinese Communist Party declared that "the whole cause of the international proletarian revolution hinges on the outcome of revolutionary struggles" in the "vast areas of Asia, Africa and Latin America" that are today the "storm centers of world revolution dealing direct blows at imperialism." In their reply of July 14 of the same year, the Soviet leaders opposed the " 'new theory' according to which the decisive force in the struggle against imperialism . . . is not the world system of socialism, not the struggle of the international working class, but . . . the national liberation movement." The Soviet Union's recent practice of restraint in fomenting and supporting revolution has matched this theoretical position. This ideological "revisionism" has of course not prevented the Soviet Union from intervening, as in Syria and Somalia, when its national interest appeared to require intervention.

One factor which cannot have failed to influence the Soviet Union in toning down its ideological commitment to intervention has been the relative failure of ideological intervention. The United States, China and Cuba have joined the Soviet Union in the experience of that failure. The new and emerging nations have been eager to reap the benefits of intervention, but have also been very anxious not to be tied with ideological strings to the intervening nation. After making great efforts, expending considerable resources and running serious risks, the participants in this worldwide ideological competition are still approximately at the point from which they started: measured against their ambitions and expectations, the uncommitted third of the world is still by and large an ideological no-man's-land.

This experience of failure is particularly painful, and ought to be particularly instructive, for the United States. For we have intervened in the political, military and economic affairs of other countries to the tune of far in excess of $100 billion, and we are at present involved in a costly and risky war in order to build a nation in South Viet Nam. Only the enemies of the United States will question the generosity of these efforts, which have no parallel in history. But have these efforts been wise? Have the commitments made and risks taken been commensurate with the results to be expected and actually achieved? The answer must be in the negative. Our economic aid has been successful in supporting economies which were already in the process of development; it has been by and large unsuccessful in creating economic development where none existed before, largely because the moral and rational preconditions for such development were lacking. Learning from this failure, we have established the theoretical principle of concentrating aid upon the few nations which can use it rather than giving it to the many who need it. While this principle of selectivity is sound in theory, its consistent practical application has been thwarted by the harsh political and military realities which may require economic aid which is economically not justified, as well as by political and military considerations derived from the ideological concerns discussed above.

This principle of selectivity must be extended to the political and military sphere as well. We have come to overrate enormously what a nation can do for another nation by intervening in its affairs—even with the latter's consent. This overestimation of our power to intervene is a corollary of our ideological commitment, which by its very nature has no limit. Committed to intervening against communist aggression and subversion anywhere, we have come to assume that we have the power to do so successfully. But in truth, both the need for intervention and the chances for successful intervention are much more limited than we have been led to believe. Intervene we must where our national interest requires it and where our power gives us a chance to succeed. The choice of these occasions will be determined not by sweeping ideological commitments nor by blind reliance upon American power but by a careful calculation of the interests involved and the power available. If the United

States applies this standard, it will intervene less and succeed more.

THE GROWTH OF TRANSNATIONAL PARTICIPATION

Robert C. Angell

A FRUITFUL concept is one subsuming data that need to be held together if one is to make valid generalizations. This does not mean that the bundle of data thus held together always has the same consequences. Take the concept of bureaucracy, for instance. There has been much dispute about the effects of what we call bureaucracy, and we now believe that under certain conditions it has one set of effects, under other conditions another set. But few would deny that it is a useful concept because it puts together a cluster of relationships that is central to modern complex societies.

TRANSNATIONAL PARTICIPATION

Transnational participation is a concept that will probably have increasing fruitfulness as communication and transportation draw the world closer together. In trying to isolate the right set of phenomena to be conceptualized, the importance of the idea of crossing national borders is obvious; but it is not at all obvious what set of relationships among

Reprinted from *Journal of Social Issues,* Vol. 23, No. 1 (January, 1967), pp. 108–129. Adapted from *Peace on the March* by Robert C. Angell. (Three tables have been deleted.)

persons from different nations needs to be specified. The term participation is designed to draw upon the work of the social psychologists who have found that certain kinds of relationships have much more profound influence on the value-orientations of the actors than others. These relationships are of two sorts: (a) those in which there is necessary collaboration in achieving common objectives, and (b) those in which there is an intimate living together. In the former the participants have a specific, in the latter, a diffuse relationship. In both the interaction is close. If these relationships have been established voluntarily, the result is usually some convergence of the value-orientations of the participants. If, on the other hand, the participants find themselves together involuntarily, the consequence may be hostility and divergence. In either case the effect is profound. Thus, the concept of transnational participation draws together data on relationships across borders that are fateful one way or the other.

This definition of transnational participation excludes much that could be termed transnational experience. The brief and fleeting contacts of the tourist, for instance, are omitted. *A fortiori*, distance communication through the mass media or via school textbooks is not included. Even international trade is beyond the pale unless the traders are functioning in some non-contractual grouping. And if they are, it is that grouping, not their trade, that makes them transnational participants.

A concept is developed because it is useful in thinking about a problem—either practical or scientific. Transnational participation is useful for both reasons. It is relevant to the problem of attaining world peace, since it refers to the intimate connection for good or ill of citizens of the units that make war, the nation-states. It is significant scientifically because sociologists are becoming interested in intersystem relations at all levels—interinstitutional as well as intermetropolitan and intersocietal. Participation across system boundaries is therefore a phenomenon in need of conceptualization. Transnational participation can become a subconcept under the broader term intersystem participation.

From the standpoint of intersystem conflict or cooperation there are two central questions to be asked about any form of intersystem participation: (a) What are the effects on the connected systems? and (b) Is the participation growing or shrinking? I am investigating both of these questions for the transnational case, but I am here presenting material only on the second question. These data are, of course, inconclusive for both the practical problem of peace and the theoretical problem of intersystem accommodation without data on the first question, but as trend data they have interest because they describe what is going on in the world.

The six categories of transnational participation that follow are not the fruit of theoretical analysis but are simply those in which existing statistical series are gathered. One category that is important is not represented. This is residence abroad in military service. So far, we have been unable to unearth reliable figures on which trend analysis could be based. Since for several of the categories adequate statistics have only recently been tabulated, the trends are those of the last decade. The time span covered varies, but the figures for different categories are made comparable by computing the rate of increase compounded annually.

PARTICIPATION—BY RENEWING FAMILY TIES

Perhaps the oldest and the simplest form of transnational participation is the visiting of relatives and friends abroad. Human migration must always have been followed by the desire to renew old ties. With the explosion outward of European populations in the nineteenth century and the ability to pay for transportation in the twentieth this form of participation has mushroomed. The only adequate statistics on the subject, however, come from the United States. Fortunately they cover movement in both directions.

The Aviation Department of the Port of New York Authority made a study of all passengers departing for overseas from its international airport (then Idlewild) in 1956-57. The study was repeated in 1963-64. The data are broken down in two ways—by American or foreign residence of the passenger and by European or Bermuda-Latin American destination. We have chosen to utilize data on both American and foreign residents because transnational participation is a two-way street, but have utilized only the Europe-bound trips because we wished to adjust the figures to include those going by ship, and such figures are more reliable for transatlantic than for other voyages.

The adult passengers in a carefully designed sample of all outbound trips filled out questionnaires about themselves and their trips. They were asked the reasons for their journey and these were coded into eleven categories. One was visiting relatives and friends.

Since roughly two-thirds of all transatlantic flights from the United States originate in New York, we assume that the proportions of all transatlantic air travelers going to or returning from visits to relatives and friends will be much the same as those given by the Port of New York Authority. It is, of course, much more risky to assume that the same proportions hold for transatlantic passengers going by sea. Since, however, there are no data on the reasons for the sea voyages, we make that assumption as better than any other. The number of air and sea passages to Europe are compiled annually by the United States Immigration and Naturalization Service. It is unimportant that the Service distinguishes between Americans and foreigners on the basis of citizenship rather than residence (which was used by the Port of New York Authority).

The proportion of New York transatlantic departures of American residents for the purpose of visiting relatives and friends in 1956-57 was 28%. Of foreign residents returning from visits in the United States it was 15%. In 1963-64 the corresponding figures were 29% and 27%. . . .

The 112.3% increase in seven years for American citizens amounts to a yearly rate of increase of 14% (compounded). The greater increase for aliens of 398.1% for the same period yields a rate of increase of 25.8% per year. This rapid rise undoubtedly reflects the fact that the economic recovery of Europe is allowing older Europeans to visit relatives and friends in the United States who migrated before the onset of the Great Depression. Americans have been able to afford the reverse journey since World War II. Though the numbers visiting in Europe are still almost twice the numbers visiting in the United States, the disproportion is decreasing rapidly. If the trends shown were to continue (which is unlikely) the two movements would balance in the year of 1967. A point that is interesting, but irrelevant for our purposes, is that foreigners continue to use sea travel more than citizens of the United States.

PARTICIPATION—BY CONDUCTING BUSINESS

The second category of transnational participation on which we have data is sojourn abroad for business reasons. These data too are drawn from the two studies of the Port of New York Authority. We have attempted to include only sojourns that involve organic ties with business enterprises or businessmen abroad by omitting those who were coded as traveling to attend a convention or fair or those traveling for business and pleasure combined.

As in the case of visiting relatives and friends we have extrapolated the percentages for both Americans and foreigners leaving the New York International Airport to all those leaving by sea and air from the United States for Europe. These percentages were 19% for Americans and 30% for aliens in 1956-57. In 1963-64 the corresponding figures were 20.4% and 26.6%. . . .

In this case the rates of increase are quite similar in both directions, that for the United States citizens amounting to a compound increase of 11.9% a year and for the foreign citizens one of 13.5%. The volume of travel of the United States citizens is not very much greater than that of the foreigners. This is a little surprising in view of the much greater United States investments in Europe than of European countries in the United States. Perhaps it is explained, in part, by the employment of foreign nationals as managers by American companies operating abroad.

The term sojourn perhaps aptly describes what is involved

in most business trips. The stays are short. The involvement in the other country may be minor. It, therefore, becomes important to ask what are the trends so far as long periods of residence are concerned. Since the duration of actual stay in the case of foreigners returning home and of expected stay in the case of natives is recorded in the Port of New York Authority surveys, we have constructed Table 1 to show the trends in stays of less than and more than one year. Here we note that both types of stays for both United States and foreign citizens are increasing rapidly but that increase is most rapid for long-term stays of foreigners and least for long-term stays of Americans. If we call the long-term stays residence abroad in contrast to sojourn, the rates of increase per year are as follows:

Residence of Americans abroad:	11.6%
Sojourn of Americans abroad:	12.0%
Sojourn of foreigners in the United States:	13.2%
Residence of foreigners in the United States:	25.8%

Although the numbers involved in the residence of foreigners in the United States for business purposes are small, the rate of increase is surprisingly large. It is a curious fact that it is almost identical with the rate of foreigners visiting relatives and friends in this country. It would seem to be true that transatlantic transnational participation is becoming a more balanced process than it has been in the past.

A word of caution is in order about extending the findings on transatlantic visiting and business to the whole globe. Both series would undoubtedly show sharp increases in many parts of the world, but whether the rates would be increasing in all parts of the world as fast as they are across the Atlantic seems doubtful. Per capita income is not increasing as rapidly in most other parts of the world. Nor are there as many ties of relationship and business enterprise.

PARTICIPATION—BY STUDY ABROAD

For our third category of transnational participation—residence abroad for study—we do not have to rely on data

TABLE 1. *Duration of Trips of Transatlantic Travelers for Business Purposes*

Duration	*American Citizens Going to Europe*				*Foreign Citizens Returning from the United States*			
			Increase				*Increase*	
	1956-57	1963-64	*Number*	*Per Cent*	1956-57	1963-64	*Number*	*Per Cent*
Less than one year	97,881	216,377	118,496	121.1	70,445	168,088	97,643	138.6
More than one year	10,876	22,978	12,102	111.8	1,438	7,186	5,748	399.7
Total	108,757	239,355	130,598	120.1	71,883	175,274	103,391	143.8

from the United States alone, but can turn to the world data set forth in the UNESCO Statistical Yearbook for 1963. Unfortunately the data there are quite incomplete. For many countries the data on foreign students either have not been collected or have not been reported to UNESCO. Table 15, for instance, shows the total number of students in the institutions of the third level (higher education) for 125 countries, but Table 17, which records the number of foreign students, gives data for only 75 countries. And for only 45 of these 75 can good trend data be obtained; that is, a comparison of 1955 with 1961 (or in a few cases 1960).

Before looking at the trends for these 45 countries it is important to indicate to what degree they can be regarded as representative of the world trend. First, one can estimate roughly the percentage of all students studying abroad. From Table 15 we learn that in 1961 there were 13,012,996 students in the institutions of higher education of the 125 countries. More than 61% of these were in the 45 countries for which we have trend data. The other 80 countries in the table contributed under 39% of the total.

The most damaging omission from the standpoint of knowing the world picture is the Union of Soviet Socialist Republics. It had 2,639,900 students in its institutions of higher education in 1961, the second largest number for any country. Foreign students are perhaps 1% of this total, or 26,400. Other important omissions are the Chinese Peoples Republic and the Philippines, each with nearly 300,000 students in higher education, and Argentina with nearly 200,000. If the rate of increase in foreign students in these four countries is sharply different from that in the 45 countries for which we have trend data, the latter may be misleading.

Table 2 shows that the increase for the 45 countries over the six-year period is 78.4%. This is a yearly rate of increase of 10.0%. Although we cannot have great confidence in this figure as reflecting the world situation, it probably is based upon some 70% of the students in foreign institutions. Although the 45 countries included in this tabulation have only 61.5% of the students in 125 countries, their institutions tend to be the larger and better known ones and hence more attractive to students wishing to study abroad. We might guess, then, that there are some 270,000 foreign students in all countries.

TABLE 2. *Number of Foreign Students, 15 Countries*

			Per Cent Increase	
1955	*1961*	*Increase*	*1955-61*	*Per Year*
107,283	191,359	84,076	78.4	10.0

Though the world figures are the significant ones, it is interesting to compare them with the trends as shown by the departures from New York International Airport expanded to the total sea and air departures for Europe. Using the same techniques described for other forms of transnational participation, we find the compound yearly increase in travel for study and research is 16.6% for Americans leaving for Europe and 18.3% for foreign citizens returning home. These higher rates of increase shown for study abroad on the world level are somewhat surprising since one might have assumed that the United States, as a country long in the business of scholarly exchange, might not show as high rates of increase as more recently participating nations.

Beside data on trends in numbers, the UNESCO Statistical Yearbook gives, in Table 18, data on foreign students by country of origin, in fifteen countries for 1960, 1961 or 1962. Although we cannot derive trends from this table, it does make possible an analysis of the types of relationships that are being established—whether study abroad is mostly confined within ideological blocs, whether it is mostly a matter of students from developed countries going to other developed countries, or whether it is students from underdeveloped countries going to developed countries, and the like. Unfortunately again the fifteen countries are not well distributed over the several types. None of them is a Communist country.

Eight of them are Western European, and 10 of them are in the Western camp. The 15 nations are: Australia, Austria, Belgium, France, West Germany, Ireland, Italy, Japan, Mexico, Senegal, Switzerland, Syria, United Arab Republic, United Kingdom, United States. In view of their unrepresentative character we shall supplement the pattern of linkages shown by the recorded data by estimating the pattern of linkages for the countries with large numbers of foreign students not included in the 15, and then combine the two sets of data into an estimated world pattern.

In order to analyze the pattern of transnational participation through study abroad we will classify nations on two bases. One is ideological, the other concerns the degree of development. There are three categories in each: Western, uncommitted and Communist; and developed, semi-developed and underdeveloped. The ideological classification is the conventional one, though some difficult choices had to be made. Finland, Israel and Japan, for instance, were included among the Western nations. Yugoslavia and all the Latin American Countries except Cuba were classified as uncommitted.

The work of Harbison and Myers, *Education, Manpower and Economic Growth* (1964), was drawn upon for the developmental classifications. Gross national product per capita and their Composite Index of Human Resource Development were used as follows:

Developed Nations: at least $400 gross national product per capita and at least 53 or more on the Composite Index.
These criteria bring in all the Western nations given above except Spain, Portugal, Greece, and Turkey plus the following: Argentina, Uruguay, Soviet Union, Poland, East Germany, Czechoslovakia and Hungary.

Semideveloped Nations: those not qualifying as Developed, but that are above $200 gross national product per capita and above 20 on the Composite Index.
These criteria bring in the following nations: Mexico, Cuba, Costa Rica, Panama, Colombia, Venezuela, Brazil, Chile, Portugal, Spain, Yugoslavia, Rumania, Bulgaria, Albania, Greece, Turkey, Cyprus, Lebanon, South Africa and Malaysia.

Underdeveloped Nations: those not qualifying as either Developed or Semideveloped.

The ideological and developmental classifications yield a nine-fold table. In such a table there are 45 sorts of linkages including linkages of a country of a particular type with another country of the same type. To simplify matters we have combined cases like the following: the linkage of a Western developed country with an uncommitted semi-developed one, and the linkage of an uncommitted developed country with a Western semideveloped one. This reduces the types of linkage to 36. The situation is most easily expressed in terms of barriers crossed. Table 3 is drawn up in this manner. It will be noted how few linkages there are across the Communist barrier. This, of course, is because only students from Communist countries going to other countries for study could gain entrance into this table, since there is no Communist nation among the 15 comprising it to catch the reverse flow. Hence this table is almost worthless for considering the world situation.

As a basis for estimating the world situation there are two sets of relevant data in the UNESCO volume. Table 17 gives the number of foreign students in 1960 or 1961 for 29 nations in addition to the 45 for which comparisons can be made with 1955. Of these 74, full data are available on 15. An estimate of the numbers in various categories of countries-of-origin for the remaining 59 could be made; however, it hardly seems worth the effort for those having less than 500 foreign students. This cuts out 39. Left are the 20 for which we have established the types of countries from which their foreign students come. This has been done by examining the distributions in the countries that are near them geographically, or like them in either ideology or level of development. It is obvious that there are inadequate analogues for many of them.

The other set of relevant data is contained in the UNESCO Table 15 where the total number of students in 126 countries is given. By applying percentages of foreign students in countries known to be similar in certain respects, the percentage of all their students that are foreign can be estimated. Only 13 further countries were estimated to have more than 500 foreign students. For these 13, distributions have been estimated by the country of origin as in the case of those countries the number of whose foreign students is known. Table 4 gives the linkages for these 33 countries. Whereas Table 3 showed a large proportion studying abroad within the Western orbit, Table 4 shows about one-third studying abroad within the Communist bloc. This is only natural since the Communist countries of study did not appear in Table 3.

Table 5 is a composite of Tables 3 and 4. If any reliance can be placed at all on the estimates in Table 5, it would give some inkling of the world picture. Note first that it shows 254,000 students abroad, somewhat less than the 270,000 thought likely on the basis of world enrollments in higher education. Since, however, there are 78 of the 126 nations represented in UNESCO Table 15 that have not been included because they probably have less than 500 foreign students each, the original estimate may be not far from the truth. An average of 200 apiece would bring the total to 270,000.

It is no surprise to find the largest group of students are those linking the uncommitted, underdeveloped countries with the developed, Western countries. Next most important is the group from one Western developed country studying in another. At a much lower level is the Communist interchange of the same kind. If one looks at the columns that show the interchange with uncommitted countries it appears that there is a 7 to 1 advantage in favor of the Western as against the Communist nations.

Review of the data on study abroad indicates that this form of transnational participation is increasing steadily, though not so fast as visiting relatives and friends, and sojourn for business reasons. Study abroad, however, is linking nations of very different kinds and may well, therefore, have a more profound influence on future relationships in the world.

TABLE 3. *Number of Foreign Students in 15 Countries in Relation to Barriers*

	Both Western	*Both Uncommitted*	*Both Communist*	*One Western, One Uncommitted*	*One Western, One Communist*	*One Uncommitted, One Communist*	*Total*
Both developed	46,446			903	2,329		49,678
Both semideveloped		331		14		27	372
Both underdeveloped		7,238					7,323
One developed, one semideveloped	14,232	14		12,489	1,349		28,084
One developed, one underdeveloped	11,656	66		70,578			82,300
One semideveloped, one underdeveloped		1,136		84		4	1,224
Total	72,334	8,870	0	84,068	3,678	31	168,981

TABLE 4. *Number of Foreign Students (Estimated) in 33 Countries in Relation to Barriers*

	Both Western	*Both Uncommitted*	*Both Communist*	*One Western, One Uncommitted*	*One Western, One Communist*	*One Uncommitted, One Communist*	*Total*
Both developed	4,685	348	15,953	606	846	68	22,515
Both semideveloped	899	835	195	1,282	336	940	4,487
Both underdeveloped	74	6,530	2,494	632		2,787	12,517
One developed, one semideveloped	1,294	2,236	5,341	3,098	614	1,005	13,588
One developed, one underdeveloped	265	1,644	3,190	6,558	58	8,365	20,080
One semideveloped, one underdeveloped	37	5,209	310	5,563	84	837	12,040
Total	7,254	16,794	27,483	17,739	1,955	14,002	85,227

TABLE 5. *Number of Foreign Students (Estimated) in 48 Countries in Relation to Barriers*

	Both Western	*Both Uncommitted*	*Both Communist*	*One Western, One Uncommitted*	*One Western, One Communist*	*One Uncommitted, One Communist*	*Total*
Both developed	51,131	340	15,953	1,509	3,192	68	72,193
Both semideveloped	899	1,166	195	1,296	336	967	4,859
Both underdeveloped	74	13,853	2,494	632		2,787	19,840
One developed, one semideveloped	15,526	2,250	5,341	15,587	1,963	1,005	41,672
One developed, one underdeveloped	11,921	1,710	3,190	77,136	58	8,365	102,380
One semideveloped, one underdeveloped	37	6,345	310	5,647	84	841	13,264
Total	79,588	25,664	27,483	101,807	5,633	14,033	254,208

PARTICIPATION—BY OFFERING TECHNICAL ASSISTANCE

The fourth category of transnational participation is technical assistance. Both bilateral and multilateral assistance are included. For bilateral trends we have only United States data; for multilateral, the data from the United Nations.

The United States has had a succession of agencies in the technical assistance field—the Mutual Security Agency, The Technical Cooperation Administration and the Agency for International Development—but statistics on civilian personnel involved in foreign aid programs have been kept continuously. From 1958 to 1964 the statistics seem to have been gathered in identical categories. Table 6 gives information on American nationals abroad and foreign nationals brought to this country or sent to other countries for training, for the three years—1958, 1961 and 1964—because the former upward trend in personnel has been reversed of recent years. The figures for yearly increases in this situation are meaningless because they represent a combination of two trends. If the recent one persists the mean yearly increase will go to zero or even become negative. It is clear that United States Technical Assistance is not at present a source of increasing transnational participation.

The situation with respect to United Nations Technical Assistance is different. Both the regular programs of tech-

TABLE 6. *Transnational Participation in the United States Program of Technical Assistance*

	U.S. Nationals Abroad Paid from Regular Program Funds	*Foreign Nationals Training*		
		In the U.S.	*In Third Countries*	*Total*
1958	2926	5596	1746	7342
1961	3485	6915	2093	9008
1964	3431	6511	1703	8214
Increase 1958-64	505	915	(43)	872
% Increase	17.3	16.4	(2.5)	11.9

nical assistance of the several Specialized Agencies and the Expanded Program financed by the Economic and Social Council (often in cooperation with the Specialized Agencies) are steadily growing. . . . It is obvious that the Expanded Program, though growing slowly, is rapidly losing ground to the programs of the Specialized Agencies. This mirrors the fact that the Specialized Agencies, which originally performed mainly clearing-house functions in the field of technical assistance, have more lately been carrying out field projects. Thus, there is more decentralization of the programs.

The overall rates of increase of the number of experts and of the holders of fellowships for training are modest but significant. It is apparent that even if bilateral technical assistance declines, as that of the United States seems likely to do, the multilateral programs are likely to grow and take over a large share of the total effort.

PARTICIPATION—BY WORKING FOR INTERNATIONAL ORGANIZATIONS

The fifth sort of transnational participation to be examined is that connected with international nongovernmental organizations. These bring people from different countries together in a multilateral fashion to achieve common objectives. For their study the *Yearbook of International Organizations* published by the Union of International Associations is essential. Here we will analyze the trends as shown in the 1956-57 and 1962-63 editions.

The *Yearbook* includes both intergovernmental and nongovernmental organizations. In the analysis to follow 177 intergovernmental organizations in the 1962-63 edition are excluded. Such are the units of the United Nations, the official bodies of the European Community, those of the Communist bloc, and technical organizations resulting from treaties like the International Wheat Council. This leaves 1,570 governmental organizations.

Table 7 shows the comparison of 1962-63 with 1956-57 in mere numbers of such organizations, classified according to

TABLE 7. *Number of International Nongovernmental Organizations*

	World-Wide	*Particularistic*	*Regional*	*Data Insufficient to Classify*	*Total*
1956-57	503	246	191	13	953
1962-63	677	312	555	26	1,570
Increase	174	68	364		617
% Increase	34.6	26.8	190.6		64.7
Compound Yearly % Increase	5.1	4.1	19.6		8.7

whether they are regional in name or in fact, whether they have a religious, ideological or ethnic limitation though otherwise potentially world-wide in scope (particularistic), or whether they are potentially world-wide and actually more than regional. The much higher rate of increase for regional organizations is largely due to the great proliferation of groups formed within the Common Market after that was established in 1958. Almost two-thirds of the growth in this category is accounted for by the 223 such organizations. But this would have been the fastest growing category in any case. One reason for this may be the resentment by the less developed countries of the dominance of Europeans in world-wide international organizations. Of all the organizations in the 1962-63 *Yearbook,* more than 85% had their headquarters in Europe and more than 75% of their directors and offices were from Europe.

The rate of growth for all types of organization of 8.77% certainly underrepresents the rate at which new people are becoming involved in this form of transnational participation, since the existing organizations are growing at the same time that new ones are being added. Although we cannot obtain any data on individual activity in connection with nongovernmental organizations we can obtain data on how many involvements of countries there are in particular organizations. For this purpose, involvement of Americans in the activities of any nongovernmental organization would count as one involvement for the United States. We have not analyzed this matter for all the organizations but we have done so for a selected group of "globally oriented" ones. These are of three types: those whose aim is to strengthen political ties among nations, those that are in fact participating in a nonpolitical world system, like organizations of meteorologists and those whose main purpose is international understanding. Table 8 gives the number of involvements in such organizations in 1956-57 and 1962-63.

It is clear from the data presented that, not only is the number of these globally oriented organizations growing, but the number of countries involved in each is doing so. For those existing at the beginning and end of the six-year span the mean yearly increase is 6.3%.

TABLE 8. *Number of Country Involvements in Globally Oriented International Nongovernmental Organizations*

	Number of Involvements 1956-57	*Number of Involvements 1962-63*	*Increase Per Cent*
12 organizations 1956-57 edition, not in 1962-63 edition	250		
151 organizations in both editions	4,529	6,534	44.3
33 organizations in 1962-63 edition, not in 1956-57 edition		874	
Total	4,779	7,408	55.0

We can show the increasing participation in these organizations in still another way: by analyzing involvement in relation to the barriers discussed in connection with study abroad. The same three classes of ideological position and the same three classes of development are used in reaching the conclusions set forth in Table 9. Here we see that only 5

TABLE 9. *Coverage of Different Types of Countries by 150 Globally Oriented International Nongovernmental Organizations*

	With Respect to Ideology			
With Respect to Development	*Less in 1962-63 than in 1956-57*	*Same in 1962-63 as in 1956-57*	*More in 1962-63 than in 1956-57*	*Total*
Less in 1962-63 than in 1956-57	1	1	0	2
Same in 1962-63 as in 1956-57	3	114	17	134
More in 1962-63 than in 1956-57	0	8	6	14
Total	4	123	23	150

organizations have gone backward in coverage, either ideologically or in terms of the development spectrum; 31 have increased their coverage. From Table 8 we learned that these organizations involved 44% more countries in 1962-63 than in 1956-57. It is evident that the net gain of 26 organizations with broader coverage among 150 organizations (17%) means that about two-fifths of the expansion in involvement carries these organizations across barriers.

Our discussion of nongovernmental organizations can be summed up in three statements: (a) the number of such organizations is growing at almost 9% per year; (b) their involvement of countries is growing at 6.3% per year; and (c) both ideological and developmental barriers are being progressively breached.

PARTICIPATION—BY BEING A MEMBER OF THE U.N.

The last kind of transnational participation to be considered is membership in United Nations secretariats. These consist of the headquarters in New York plus its branches in other parts of the world and the headquarters of the twelve Specialized Agencies and their branches. Members of delegations from member countries to these bodies are not here considered, both for practical and theoretical reasons. Information on the numbers who have served on delegations at different points in time is not easily available. More

TABLE 10. *Established Posts in the United Nations and Its Specialized Agencies*

	All Established Posts	*Established Posts Not Related to Technical Assistance*
1956	8,370	7,821
1963	13,165	11,299
Increase	4,795	3,478
% increase	57.3	45.8
Compound yearly % increase	6.7	5.5

important, it is doubtful whether such service should be included under the concept of transnational participation. Instructed delegates hardly participate in the solution of common problems in a way that changes them fundamentally. They tend to interact on a formal level, and they do not live intimately together. It is for the same reason that we have excluded other intergovernmental organizations from consideration while including nongovernmental organizations.

The Annexes to the Official Records of the United Nations General Assembly give figures each year on the number of established posts in the various agencies of the United Nations system. These are given in Table 10. Since these engaged on the Regular Programs in Technical Assistance as contrasted with the Expanded Program are holders of established posts, . . . we also show here the growth in established posts minus technical assistance personnel. The figures show that the technical assistance work has been growing somewhat faster than the other work of the several agencies, but both rates of increases are modest.

The six sorts of transnational participation that have been examined all show increases. Where we have some inkling of the world-wide situation, as in study abroad, multilateral technical assistance, international nongovernmental organizations and secretariats of the United Nations system, there seems to be a growth rate of between 5% and 10% a year. If this trend continues for a decade or more the results will almost certainly be important. But whether for good or ill will depend upon knowledge of the effects of the growing participation. Unfortunately, sociologists have carried out few studies of these effects.

Part III

The Problem of the Economy

ALTERNATIVES TO DEFENSE PRODUCTION

Emile Benoit

THE STORY is told of Rosie the Riveter, working in a West Coast shipyard in World War II, who, during a luncheon break, expressed decided reservations about the then Pope. When challenged, she explained that she and all her family had been unemployed for years, until the defense boom had suddenly provided them with well-paying jobs. She said she found it hard to understand how the Pope, who was supposed to be a good Christian, could be praying right out in public for peace.

To the noneconomist, the process by which new jobs are created to take the place of old ones appears both mysterious and unreliable. The economists, on the other hand, have sometimes attributed too much to the reallocative virtues of the free market. While the market is a superb instrument for reallocating displaced resources in relatively small doses, provided the level of aggregate demand is sustained, it is less effective if the amount of displaced resources becomes indigestibly large, or when there is a slump in the level of aggregate demand.

In fact, our economy has a second mechanism for directing and redirecting resources, which, while not as important as the free market, plays an essential role in a modern private enterprise economy. This is the mechanism of the government budget, which enables the government to redirect

Reprinted from Emile Benoit and Kenneth E. Boulding, eds., *Disarmament and the Economy* (New York: Harper & Row, Publishers, Incorporated, 1963), pp. 203–220. **(Footnotes have been deleted.)**

resources from one government use to another or from one group of citizens to another, or by net cuts in government purchases to free resources for nongovernment uses. If the cuts are made without corresponding cuts in taxes then the resources freed from government use and not positively directed to other uses may not readily find re-employment. On the other hand, if there are parallel tax cuts as expenditures are reduced, resources are not only freed by the government, but positively directed toward the groups of taxpayers who are left with larger disposable incomes. . . .

The widely-expressed fear that tax cuts would *not* raise the expenditures of the individuals and businesses that receive them has little apparent justification. The percentage of personal disposable income which is spent by consumers is one of the more stable of economic phenomena. Since 1950, the annual rate has varied only between 92 and 94 per cent; and in no quarter has the ratio dropped below 91 per cent. We know less about the percentage of *additions* to disposable income that will be used for consumption, but budget studies suggest that at least two dollars out of three will be spent. . . .

. . . Business propensity to invest out of cash flow is more variable than personal propensity to consume: it was 55 per cent in 1950, 81 per cent in 1952, and under 62 per cent in 1961. Even so, except in depressions, one can count on it to be over 50 per cent, and if we could raise aggregate demand and eliminate excess capacity, we should be able to attain again the 75 per cent average achieved in the 1951–1957 period. Moreover, nearly a third (31 per cent) of cash flow was distributed in dividends during the fifties —and dividends, in turn, affect both personal consumption and personal investment. Thus, cuts in corporate taxes will raise aggregate demand. . . .

Apparently, then, . . . redundant defense resources may be shifted either to other government programs by changes in the pattern of budget expenditures or to private use by tax reductions. Many persons, however, . . . have the general impression that there is nothing of any urgency left to do which could justify or motivate additional expenditure. It may be helpful, therefore, to consider a variety of high-priority needs to which unutilized resources could be shifted. . . .

. . . No claim is here made as to the objective validity of the following list of "needs" and expenditure programs. It is presented simply as a summary of what well-informed students of current social and economic conditions consider desirable and appropriate uses of additional resources. Most of these programs have been set forth as national objectives in an official United States document sent to the United Nations. . . .

CONSUMPTION AND INVESTMENT

While the American standard of living is by far the highest in the world, . . . a great many Americans do not enjoy that standard. Per capita personal income after taxes had not yet reached $40 a week in 1962, and many families live on far smaller amounts. In 1960, 3.33 million families, predominantly city families, had an average income *per family* of only $23.50 a week, and there were nearly 4 million individuals, living alone, with an average income of less than $20 a week. To raise this poverty-stricken one-eighth of American households even to a hardly tolerable level of $40 a week per household would require an increase in annual consumer expenditures of $6.4 billion. There will be need of another extra $6.6 billion a year merely to keep up with population growth, even if average income levels do not rise. . . .

Growth in consumption will undoubtedly have to derive mainly from increases in the number of persons employed and from wage increases. . . . But an effective attack on severe poverty in the lowest income group would also require special programs, emphasizing health services, education, rehabilitation and retraining programs, psychiatric and social counseling, and special youth assistance and employment programs, as well as more generous social security benefits and relief payments. Resources released from defense uses could be channeled to these uses by expanded federal welfare programs, including federal welfare grants to states and localities.

For general stimulation of consumption, the simple expedient of a general reduction of personal income taxes is available. Because of the comparatively broad base of this tax today, across-the-board reductions would benefit a large majority of the population, and would stimulate consumption in the broad middle-income group of households with incomes between $5,000 and $15,000, which now includes half of all families, and about 60 per cent of all taxable income.

Consumption increases in the long run can be sustained only out of current production; therefore, a high priority must attach to the strengthening of our capital equipment and to the further improvement of our education, vocational training, and R&D programs, upon which our future productivity and welfare will most vitally depend.

. . . Our need to modernize and expand our industrial plant in order to remain internationally competitive is becoming a matter of serious concern to well-informed people. We will need to speed up our annual plant and equipment outlays during this decade by about $16.3 billion over the 1961 level if we want to maintain full use of capacity and the high average ratio of new investment to corporate cash flow achieved from 1951 to 1957.

RESIDENTIAL CONSTRUCTION

Housing in this country barely meets our present needs. Current vacancy rates are 1.2 per cent of home-owner units and 7.7 per cent of rental units. Over 3 million of these total units are in a dilapidated condition. To keep pace with the growing population and to insure that every American household can be adequately accommodated by the end of this decade, we should be building 2 million units a year by 1970, at a cost of $25 billion (1961 dollars)—an $8.8 billion increase over 1961 levels. . . . Present projections indicate that effective demand will probably fall short of the level required to purchase this much housing, and low-income groups will clearly require housing subsidies. . . .

URBAN NEEDS

The explosive growth of our metropolitan areas will be one of the major domestic problems of this decade, during which the urban population is expected to increase by about thirty-six million. . . . Over two-thirds of our population now live in big urban areas. The revitalization of the older cities in these areas, and the expansion of the newer ones, will call for vast expenditures for improvement, modernization, and rebuilding. Approximately $2 billion of federal grant authorization has been reserved for urban renewal projects, exclusive of the $2 billion earmarked for new projects by the Housing Act of 1961. Obviously, such sums only scratch the surface of the problems, and must be viewed as preliminaries to much larger programs.

The problems of urban transportation and traffic congestion are becoming almost terrifying in magnitude and complexity. With only a 75 per cent population increase in urban areas between 1935 and 1959, transit rides declined by 20 per cent but automobile travel increased by 180 per cent. One transportation specialist estimated that an additional $1 billion a year will be needed to obtain satisfactory urban transit and suburban railroad facilities during the decade. The Housing Act of 1961 authorized $25 million of grants just to make studies of the problem.

With a rapidly expanding population, the need for more water and sewer facilities is becoming acute. . . . On the basis of estimated present and potential needs, we shall soon have to be spending about $5 billion a year for these purposes. Our cities also confront a growing problem of solid-waste disposal. Current total national expenditures for urban collection and disposal are approximately $2 billion annually. This figure will have to be raised by about 50 per cent to meet increasing needs.

There are many other community needs in these urban areas—recreational facilities, police and fire stations, the solution of air pollution problems, etc.—that are growing rapidly along with the increasing population, increasing automobile traffic, and increasing congestion. It is difficult to obtain any precise notion of the cost of obtaining and maintaining adequate programs in these fields, but we do know that such programs usually cost more than can be foreseen and that the costs of delay may be even higher.

NATURAL RESOURCES

The United States is richly endowed with natural resources, but positive programs are needed to conserve and develop them to keep pace with our growing requirements. Our margin of safety in some fields, especially with regard to water, is uncomfortably narrow. Periodic serious water shortages have already appeared in many communities. The 1961 report of the Senate Select Committee on National Water Resources points out that . . . our daily water requirements, . . . by the year 2000, . . . will absorb more than 80 per cent of the total streamflow. To achieve this, along with some associated programs for navigation, flood control, power generation, irrigation, water supply and waste disposal, recreation, wildlife and fisheries protection, as well as some for urban water and sewage disposal, will require average expenditures of around $5.5 billion a year.

A tentative estimate of the Department of the Interior, for the cost of a program of reforestation, reseeding, forest recreational area development, watershed and erosion control on forest land, and public land acquisition, sets the total at $3.6 billion during a period of ten years. The Department of Agriculture has outlined a ten-year forestry development program, costing more than $2.5 billion; and the Bureau of Public Roads calls for the construction of public highways through national forests at a cost of $2.7 billion by 1971. A ten-year program for soil and watershed conservation would involve expenditures of $4.6 billion. . . . A program for the conservation of federal range lands would require the expenditure of $1.2 billion over a ten-year period.

. . .

Altogether, the total federal costs of . . . proposed programs for the conservation and development of national resources would be about $40 billion over a ten-year period—$16 billion more than the current rate. State, local, and industrial programs for water development, estimated to cost about $8 billion annually, are not included in this figure.

EDUCATIONAL NEEDS

By 1970, school enrollments in kindergarten through the twelfth grade will require annual expenditures of $10 billion more than the 1960–1961 expenditures. . . . Institutions of higher learning, giving degrees, will require expenditures by 1970 of $10 billion above present levels to accommodate the prospective growth in the student body. . . . But $10 billion would do little more than maintain the present standards of education, and American life in the 1970's will make considerably greater demands on education than it is currently doing. The labor force will require more skill and technical know-how, and the accelerating rate of additions to knowledge . . . will call for more extended study by larger numbers of educated people. . . . The National Science Foundation estimates that to maintain our present world position in science, we will have to double the number of persons receiving Ph.D's in science and engineering by 1970. The added annual cost of the necessary facilities would average $1.6 billion during this decade.

HEALTH SERVICES

. . . In 1959–1960, 5.4 per cent of our gross national product was devoted to public health, personal health services, construction of medical facilities, and medical research. However, there are still many Americans who cannot afford, and do not obtain, a satisfactory amount and quality of medical services. . . .

. . .

In 1960 there were 140 physicians for every 100,000 of the population, but this ratio, while insufficient, is declining. In the case of dentists, the decline is even more rapid and has continued steadily since 1940. To maintain even the existing ratios of physicians and dentists to the population would require an additional expenditure of $1 billion (at present prices) by 1970 to expand existing medical and dental schools and to set up new ones.

During the next decade, 23,000 additional hospital beds each year will be required to maintain the current ratio of 7.7 beds per 1,000 population. To provide even a slight improvement in this ratio—to replace, renovate, and modernize hospital plants, to maintain outpatient care facilities, and to increase rehabilitation facilities—would require the expenditure over the next decade of at least $6 billion above present levels.

About 6 per cent of our population live in counties with no organized local tax-supported health services, often because of limitations in staff and financial resources. To provide adequate public health services by official state and local health agencies, it has been estimated that a minimum expenditure of at least $4 per capita is required. To achieve this would require that present levels of annual expenditures be increased by $383 million.

The dangers of air pollution are becoming widely recognized as a serious health hazard in many urban communities. At present we are spending about $300–$400 million per year in an effort to control it. To provide proper protection we will need at least to double this amount by 1970.

The reports of two expert groups have suggested that by 1970, personnel and other resources will be available to justify an expenditure of $3.0 billion a year on health research, with incalculable potention benefits to the nation's health. This research could be rapidly stepped up if the research facilities and personnel now devoted to defense activities could be released.

OTHER SOCIAL SERVICES

. . . Social insurance protection . . . remains incomplete and the level of benefits in relation to income continues to shrink. Since 1940, benefits under the national Old Age, Survivors, and Disability Insurance program have risen less than a third as much as increases in general wage levels. To relate such benefits to increases in productivity, it would be necessary to increase the annual outlays by more than $11 billion before 1970. Private pension benefits (now running at close to $2 billion annually) also require improvement: Very few of them are adjusted to changing price or wage levels. . . .

In 1960, only $0.8 billion was paid out under public and private sickness insurance programs despite the very wide coverage already existing for these programs. If there had been a nationwide system of sickness insurance, covering all wage and salary workers in private industry and providing benefits equal to two-thirds of weekly wage loss after a one-week waiting period, the benefits paid would have amounted to $2.2 billion in 1960. A program such as this would require benefit payments in 1970 of $3.3 billion (in 1960 prices).

Payments for wage loss and medical benefits under the state and federal workmen's compensation laws amounted to $1.3 billion in 1960. These payments replaced less than two-fifths of the wage loss in the average temporary disability case, and an even smaller proportion in fatalities or permanent injuries. . . . A system which provided medical care for the duration of the disability, replacement of two-thirds of wage loss (after a one-week waiting period), and survivors' benefits to widows for life, and to children to the age of eighteen, would have cost, it is estimated, an additional $700 million in 1960. Such a system would provide an important attack on the problem of poverty in the United States, which is frequently tied up with injury or death of a breadwinner.

The 7 million persons in the United States who are currently receiving public assistance under one program or another, and the 7 million persons who might also receive assistance in 1970, require an additional $1 billion a year to assure reasonable levels of living, according to a 1958 study.

In the field of community and social services there is a need . . . for expansion in the services of public and private agencies to meet the needs of a complex and growing urban economy. For example, vocational rehabilitation services are currently helping 100,000 disabled people back to work, but there are 275,000 persons disabled annually who without rehabilitation services will not be able to work. Public expenditures for existing child welfare services amounted to $211 million in 1960, but could usefully be doubled by 1970, with an additional $60 million for expansion of day care services for children.

Most of the benefits of increased social expenditure will be obtained only if they are guided by improved research and administered by effective administrators and social workers. This research, and the training of the necessary personnel, could usefully absorb some of the resources released by defense cuts.

FOREIGN ASSISTANCE

. . . It should never be forgotten . . . that the severity of our material needs is small in comparison with those of the larger part of mankind. We are led by feelings of compassion and moral obligation, as well as by alleged considerations of long-term self-interest, to devote a small part of our annual savings to foreign development assistance. Between 1957 and 1961, it amounted to about 5 per cent of gross national savings.

I suspect we do not yet know enough about the marginal productivity of such aid to justify the elaborate calculations frequently made in estimating how much more aid is required to enable developing nations to achieve self-sustaining growth. . . . Factors other than external capital availabilities may be decisive. In any case, the effective limits on United States economic aid to underdeveloped countries would appear to be set by quite different considerations: (1) With respect to the private part, it would be the net profitability of investment in underdeveloped countries relative to that in industrial countries, discounted by the heavier political risks; and (2) with respect to the public part, the willingness of legislatures to make such appropriations, taking into account the balance of public sentiment on the question and the visible evidence as to whether or not past programs have been effectively administered and have served a useful purpose. . . .

If disarmament is achieved, we would eliminate $1 billion a year of foreign military expenditure—or more if, by that time, the United States government had not succeeded in the very difficult task of cutting it down to that level. We would also eliminate defense-related economic aid, which now costs in the neighborhood of $300 million. It would be relatively easy and natural to devote these savings to increased regular foreign aid. . . .

An increase of this size ($1.3 billion) added to the 1961 level of United States development assistance of $4.6 billion would bring the total only $400 million short of what was required to comprise 1 per cent of the probable GNP in the mid-sixties and, thus, to conform to the minimum standard which has sometimes been urged in international discussions and has been recommended by, e.g., Jean Monnet's Action Committee for a United States of Europe. . . . If it is achieved, we would be spending around $6.3 billion a year by the mid-sixties, about $2.4 billion more than in 1960. An assistance figure tied to such a formula would, moreover, rise by about $300 million a year and reach $7.5 billion by the end of the decade. Over the decade as a whole, such a program implies an annual figure some $2 billion over the 1960 level.

. . . Much larger amounts could probably be arranged with the right type of cooperation between the industrial and the underdeveloped countries. I have elsewhere proposed "economic development treaties," which would commit the

United States to supply specified quantities of assistance (private and public) over a decade, in exchange for all-out cooperation by a developing country in achieving ambitious (and clearly defined) growth objectives agreed upon in advance. A mechanism of this sort might mobilize a great deal more assistance by providing concrete goals against which the success of the effort being made could be measured and the deficiencies identified and eliminated. . . .

RESEARCH AND DEVELOPMENT

The National Science Foundation has urged an expanded program of basic research in the 1960's that would involve additional expenditures averaging $900 million a year.

The expansion in the civilian space program has been so embroiled in controversy that the rate of build-up during the decade is hard to predict. In the READ model, the expansion in the expenditures of NASA and of the civilian side of the AEC (which does some work for NASA under contract) was estimated at something short of $7 billion, i.e., from an annual rate of $0.9 billion in 1960 to an annual rate of $7.9 billion by 1971. The build-up has been going faster than projected in the READ model, but the relevant question of how much expansion will occur between 1965 and 1977 is not necessarily affected by this. *Total* expenditures in the NASA program during the 12 years are estimated at $80 billion, which would appear to be a fairly ambitious figure. Nevertheless, some opportunities for further expansion may seem worth taking.

In the event of disarmament, enough military R&D might be demobilized in the latter part of the 1960's, not only to meet the expansion requirements of NASA and the AEC, but to create something of a glut in the R&D market. . . . The surplus could sooner or later all be reabsorbed by industrial R&D in private enterprise. Whether it is wise to wait until this happens may be questioned. Even a temporary slack in the demand for R&D could have unfortunate, even dangerous, consequences. . . . The lead time in this area is so long that even a temporary letdown can be most difficult to make up. We are already falling behind, and there is some evidence of a slackening in the rate of adoptions of science and engineering courses, which require a high level of ability and more effort than many other courses of study leading to better-remunerated employment.

I also believe that there are important positive advantages in preserving some of the working scientist-technician-management teams and organizations now functioning in the defense effort, and utilizing their outstanding skills and expert knowledge in seeking solutions to fundamental problems of national importance. . . .

The above makes no allowances for the continued expansion in industrial R&D, upon which our future productivity gains and product improvements in most of our industry will heavily rely. The step-up in new investment discussed earlier in this chapter would presumably require, by itself, a rise of about $0.5 billion in the annual rate of R&D expenditures in the coming decade.

The various programs presented in this chapter . . . total . . . around $66 billion a year during the 1960's—exclusive of the very large amounts that may be called for in the space program and other special R&D programs of national importance. Because of the rather broad terms in which most of these estimates have been defined, the total is not too meaningful, but it does signify that probably more than twice the estimated resources released by disarmament would have high-priority alternative uses. . . . The problem then will not be to find important alternative uses for resources released from the defense effort: It will be to achieve a consensus on priorities, and to endow the chosen programs with enough purchasing power to make them effectively able to bid for and absorb the released resources. . . .

NONECONOMIC FACTORS IN THE INSTITUTIONALIZATION OF THE COLD WAR

Irving Louis Horowitz

WHENEVER the question of the costs or benefits of the arms race arises, there is a common propensity to deal with the matter in economic terms. Perhaps this is as it should be, since monetary and fiscal considerations do seem to determine what can be done to alter an industrial apparatus of incredible complexity tooled up for a quarter of a century to handle military assignments. But even more knowledgeable economists have clearly indicated that the 10 per cent of the national budget directly allocated to arms production is not a "necessity" from an economic viewpoint.[1] Even though exact knowledge on the phasing time, economic costs, and manpower shifts of any transition to peacetime production is available, the prospects for such a momentous industrial and commercial retooling remain dim because of social and political considerations. Why should it be the case that, in the midst of this intellectual know-how, there is such a paucity of activity oriented toward the realization of that long-postponed and ephemeral phenomenon—a peacetime economy?

This is obviously an extremely difficult problem, one which can only be tentatively answered. In order to confront this major issue directly, I shall outline each issue separately and then indicate recommendations which could reduce the amount of expenditures for military and paramilitary purposes at a minimal *social* cost. What follows is predicated

Reprinted from *Annals of the American Academy of Political and Social Science,* Vol. 351 (January, 1964), pp. 110–120. (The first paragraph of this article has been omitted.)

on two premises, one ethical and the other political. My first premise is that the chief task confronting Americans is disarmament and not deterrence—that is, a peace based on the institutionalization of world law and juridical limits to sovereignty as well as weaponry and not a peace grounded on a presumed "delicate balance of terror."[2] The second premise is that bilateral settlement between East and West, specifically between the United States and the Soviet Union, is now eminently possible, and even imminent.[3] Such bilateral negotiations cut through the fog of rhetoric introduced into the situation by unilateralists on one side and by the still more menacing new civilian militarists on the other. Neither moralism nor gamesmanship is relevant in the present context.

UNAWARENESS OF DANGER

The first point which must be considered, and one so obvious as often to be overlooked, is the simple absence of consciousness that an economy on a permanent war footing carries with it menacing possibilities. The plain fact is that many Americans imbibe the economic benefits of the arms race in the form of steady work, good living and working conditions, high wages, and often professional standing. Indeed, the study of international conflicts has itself been professionalized and institutionalized to an amazing degree. It does not require an economic determinist to realize that such benefits drown out the over-all need for a reduction of tension through a reduction in arms production. Taken in its broadest sense, arms production covers military personnel, operations and maintenance of the war industries, as well as military hardware as such. The arms industries present a pattern of high growth combined with sales risk—which makes resistance to change quite understandable. The following reveals the pattern of this growth:

> Expenditures of the Department of Defense have risen from $19.8 billion in fiscal year 1951 to $43 billion in 1961, or by over 100 per cent, a growth rate far in excess of that of any other major area of the American economy. At the present time,

Defense Department purchases of goods and services are equal to almost one-tenth of the gross national product. The proportion reached peaks of 48 per cent during World War II and 12 per cent during the Korean War, but was, of course, lower during the interwar period of the cold war. An abrupt change in the nature of the external threat would probably cause another major shift in the proportion of the country's resources devoted to armaments.[4]

The problem with most business enterprises presently engaged in direct or subsidiary forms of arms production is not that they are fearful of an economic retooling, or even that they fear their survival possibilities in a peacetime economy, but simply that no thought has been given to remobilization of the economy in a nonmilitary direction. Peaceful production is not a felt need because the syndrome of high wages and solid profits has essentially remained unbroken in the American economy ever since 1939, when the nation first went on a partial defense mobilization. And when "recessions" did take place, such as the one of 1949, the Korean war—and the rise in some spending—mitigated its economic effects.

In a major survey of defense industry planning for the future, Philip Shabecoff and Joseph Lelyveld were compelled by the evidence to conclude that most defense contractors "have no idea at present of how to plan for a sharp reduction in defense spending. A few companies are confident they would be able to make a smooth transition to civilian business. Fewer still report that they have actually done some long range planning in this area."[5] The general consensus among military producers and contractors is that no arms reduction will take place and that, if it did, the problem could be met pragmatically—meaning through yet further government help. There is, in short, a profound inability of defense contractors such as Lockheed Aircraft, General Dynamics, Boeing Company, North American Aviation, to mention only a few, to take seriously their own faith in the private-enterprise system. What they have become used to is government subsidization of private profits—something radically different than the confrontation of buyers and sellers in a symbolic market place. Thus, the unconsciousness of the need to disarm is reinforced by the absence of competitive capitalism!

The basic correctives for this institutional unconsciousness require, at the outset, a clear separation of issues. National interests must be distinguished from commercial interests. In this way, it might be made plain that the policy of the United States is dictated by considerations larger than those motivating defense contractors. This would spark an interest in conversion, if for no other reason than that entepreneurial survival would once again become a real factor. Where this has been done, where federal cutbacks on military hardware have been effected, the business establishment has proven most resourceful in maintaining high productive levels and full employment after a relatively brief crisis period.

ARMS REDUCTION

Senator George McGovern has proposed a five billion dollar cutback in arms spending. But, more important, he indicated ways in which the effects of this cutback could be mitigated and overcome. First, he proposed that all industries having more than 25 per cent of their production in defense contracts be required to establish an operating conversion committee to prepare for possible alternatives in the event of a loss in military contracts. Second, he proposed a government board which would have as its main task assisting businesses in the process of considering reconversion. What makes such conversion relatively simple is the concentration of defense contracts in the very large corporations and in engineering firms which perform specialized services. This would make it possible to have conversion to a peacetime economy without any over-all disruption to the social fabric. One economist has seen the problem as a short-run effort to shift $22 billions now allocated for defense purposes to the larger civilian economy.[6]

One contribution of the new civilian militarists to the present unconscious state of industrialists has been the oft-repeated statement that "arms control will not cut defense cost"[7] but what is neglected is the possibility that a policy of *disarmament* would indeed cut such costs. This reinforces the decision-makers in the war industries who view any policy other than arms control as dangerous to their continued welfare. This, coupled with a fear that marketing commercial products would be unprofitable, has made defense contractors perhaps the most conservative force in American society. What is needed to unfreeze these attitudes is first a clear-cut federal policy indicating that arms control is only the first phase of arms reduction. This done, the federal administration must assist in the opening up of certain highly monopolized peacetime enterprises, such as the automobile and electronics industries. There is a need for new capital investment in old industries no less than for the creation of new types of commercial production.

Federal initiative in planning would enable defense contractors to consider the larger implications of converting their plants to peacetime uses. A temporary downward adjustment need not lead to industrial calamaties or financial bankruptcies. And even the extent of such a downward turn in the short run is problematic, since economists are now in a position carefully to "phase in" peacetime production with a minimum amount of disruption. One thing is not possible: for defense contractors to lobby against federal spending for civilian purposes while at the same time urging increased federal contracts for defense purposes. To call one kind of spending socialistic and the other patriotic is simply to confuse the ineluctable fact of federal direction of the economy with the tentative forms of such direction through monetary allocation.[8]

CONVERSION REQUIRES PLANNING

A second problem in defense spending is that many new industries have emerged as a result of the Cold War, so that the problem for General Electric might be reconversion but for General Dynamics it is simple conversion for *the first time* to peaceful production. The war industries have no built-in agencies for unguided conversion. And since this is true for many firms doing military work on contract, the traditional arguments against federal planning are largely obsolete and meaningless.

A subsidiary argument employed in defense of high military budgets is that such spending stimulates discovery and the application of discovery. The one strong point in this line of reasoning is that the process of application of scientific invention is often an unprofitable venture, one which cannot be maintained without heavy federal subsidization. But the conclusion drawn, that peacetime production would involve a cutback not only in military production but in scientific technology as well, simply does not follow. For what would be involved is not a withdrawal or retrenchment in federal spending per se but simply the reallocation of funds for nonmilitary purposes.

What must be made clear is that the argument for peacetime uses of industry does not imply a nineteenth-century neomercantilist view of balancing the budget. Indeed, it might conceivably be the case that a real adjustment of the company may entail higher rather than lower, more and not fewer federal outlays. Highway construction, foreign assistance, space exploration, civilian uses of energy sources may be applied for war or peace. But the application in one direction or another is something quite apart from the quantity of federal expenditures or even taxation.

The problem is ideological in character. Americans are accustomed to government spending being paired with military requisitions, because they view the military establishment as intrinsically national in character. But, if any conversion is to be successful, an entirely novel concept—in American ideology at least—must be institutionalized—namely, the infusion and intrusion of government planning of commercial and industrial enterprises. Without becoming tendentious, it is plain that the Tennessee Valley Authority (TVA) and the Missouri Valley Authority (MVA) are just as legitimate allocations of federal funds as aircraft or rocket production. The argument that "to try any large part of a conversion process centrally would raise severe problems"[9] mistakes the nature of democratic polity. This is not a plea for increased management of individuals but a recognition that there remains a need to increase the management of things. This, at any rate, is a likely consequence of any serious reconversion of scientific and industrial initiative.

A FALSE "NATIONAL PURPOSE"

A third major obstacle to conversion and reconversion is the directly ideological notion of having a "national purpose." The manifest function of such a search is to define the goals for Americans at midpassage: to determine the American posture toward the Communist-bloc nations, toward newly emerging nation-states, and, above all, toward our own future aims and ambitions. The latent function of such a frenetic search, doomed to failure by the very nature of a pluralistic society exhibiting contrasting goals and instrumentalities, is to provide what Durkheim called the "collective conscience" with a sense of cohesion. It has become clear even to the rhetoricians of the Cold War that anticommunism is itself a negative response with built-in boomerang effects. Without a positive program, Americans entered the present decade immunized to a considerable degree from Cold War policies, and this led to fractionalized public opinion. A feeling that everything was done from the top down and that the "little man" counted for naught translated itself into negative attitudes toward armed service, civil defense, and other citizen-participation activities. But, instead of making adjustments, policy-making tended to become increasingly strident, making for a reinforcement of the rhetoric of oversimplification.

Both as participants and as leaders, members of the corporate structure adhered to policies calculated to retain a cold-war consensus, rather than alter the character of this consensus. The Cold War, which has functioned as an exclusive mode of expression of American political leadership in the postwar period, had succeeded in institutionalizing itself. To dislodge the Cold War from its gray eminence required the sort of broad-scale political reorientation that defense contractors were least suited to carry forth and those best suited, such as labor organizations and voluntary associations, least able to carry forth. The concept of anticommunism, negative and frustrating though it may be, is at least a political cement. The Communist menace served to justify resistance to all kinds of social innovation. As one anthropologist has recently observed, "The view of the Soviet Union as a deadly adversary that at any moment may destroy us also makes real disarmament unlikely; and suggests that instead of getting rid of our arms we will merely rest on them."[10] That this carries within itself a paralyzing and narcotizing effect on significant action was held to be less important than the preservation of the ideology of Cold War. That in the process of combating erosion, through a self-conscious definition of national purpose, Americans have subjected themselves to a still deeper erosion, a fear of the consequences of unsanctioned change, is only now being recognized—and, even now, in private pronouncements rather than in public policies.

The comment by David Riesman on this quest for a singular purpose deserves serious attention:[11]

> There is something oddly regressive in the spectacle of the United States reducing itself to the size of a new nation that needs a manifest destiny. . . . Affluence ought to mean abundance of purposes, and intense exploration and discovery of new ones, both individual and collective. It might mean a stronger concern for the purposes of others who have not yet reached the dilemmas of abundance.

But this narrowing-down process, this search for ideological uniformity disguised as a commonly inspected and arrived at social consensus, is indicative of widespread fear that only a monolith can overcome a monolith, that only a bureaucratized state can defeat another bureaucratized state. The strength of our conservatism stems from the same psychological sources as the strength of communism in the developing regions: a fear that democratic-process consensus structures are indeed weaker than totalitarian command structures. The war industries, the military establishment, the defense-department engineers turned strategists thus underwrite this fear—since they have moved policy-making out of the public political arena and mimetically reproduced elitist modes of operating on the body politic. The only problem is that this produces a boomerang effect.

By thoroughly dulling the sense of mass participation in political life, it leads to a form of "privatization" that seeks gratifications in a personal and egotistic fashion—not only without regard to the consequences of such behavior for an anticipated "enemy" but, more profoundly, without due regard to the human consequences for one's own family, community, or nation. The reconversion of industry to peacetime uses should have as its essential by-product a corresponding rise in public participation in public affairs—and only those who are profoundly hostile to democratic norms could find such an outcome objectionable.

SECRECY AND COERCION

The fourth point to be noted is the internal system of secrecy and coercion which has become legitimated. If we assume—and I daresay this is more than an assumption—that any society tooled up for "spontaneous" outbreak of thermonuclear warfare requires a significant quantum of coercion and the institutionalization of this coercion in the form of police, federal investigators, congressional investigators, and the like, then it can be seen that the maintenance of a high military budget directly affects the lives of many people who are described as dissidents in relation to the Cold War. It can only be considered Pollyannish to hold that an invisible consensual blanket alone guarantees active participation in the Cold War. The element of coercion, while more sharply limited in the United States by countervailing veto groups and by historical and juridical limitations than in the Soviet Union, is nonetheless present.[12]

The armaments industry, with its emphasis on clearance, surveillance, and security, legitimates coercive intervention in the lives of private citizens. Since the "next war" will be between arms and arms, rather than men and men, this stress on secrecy generates a growth in the command mechanisms. This is still more apparent in the Soviet Union, where munitions production is the responsibility not of the military establishment but of economic agencies. Since the mid thirties, planning agencies specialized to this end.[13] Thus, such policing agencies, whether from the East or West, have a vested interest in the maintenance of a huge armaments industry.

This is a matter which cuts both ways. It is a relatively stable law of organizational behavior that a bureaucracy attempts to maximize its power and to retain this power beyond the point of external necessity. Organizations do not vanish because their need has been obviated—they simply search out new rationalizations for their perpetuation. A number of press reports have indicated a frantic interaction between corporation lobbies and the military establishment to sway senatorial sentiment away from the test-ban treaty.[14] It may be gathered, in view of the minimal basis of the test-ban treaty, that far more powerful forces would be mobilized in the event of any bilateral treaty which would entail actual arms reductions in its provisions.

What is urgently required is the widest sort of public education about the problems of transition to peace, for the current tendencies to maximize the coercive apparatus pose a genuine threat to American democracy. A wide exercise of political rights is far less of a risk than an uncritical commitment to a society of secret agents. The increased demand of nuclear scientists for freedom of movement and less secrecy is an indication that one major veto group is cognizant of the relation between secrecy and coercion.

Substantive arguments against an excess of coercion in a cold-war atmosphere are: first, it is difficult to differentiate or to limit coercion so that it does not become terroristic; second, the secret society is inhibiting to traditional American rights of communication and transportation; third, it inhibits the growth of science—which requires the widest access to information and verification of data. On this point, it is now clear that the institutionalization of the Cold War, far from stimulating scientific progress, actually serves to inhibit it, by creating an atmosphere of closure about information and the exchange of ideas. Thus, the over-all consequence of the reduction in arms spending would be a general liberation from the world of secrecy. As long as the arms race continues, the most that can be hoped for is an enlightened leadership that is willing and ready to smother its critics with a consensual blanket.

It is not a simplistic question of America's "will" to fight for freedom, or the Soviet Union's "will" to fight for communism. It is a question of a higher will to survive despite differences. Once the threads of the Cold War start coming apart, the entire garment is subject to discard.[15] The struggle now is thus between those desiring to patch up traditional alliances and those seeking a *détente* with the Soviets. Political decisions will ultimately determine the rate at which the Cold War will be converted into a peaceful competition of social systems. One significant feature of the Kennedy Administration is the belief within its higher echelons that such a peaceful struggle can be won; the assumption is that "time" is on the "side" of capitalist America, rather than on the side of Communist Russia. Whether this optimism is warranted or not, its very permeation of administrative policy bodies serves to increase the possibilities that conversion and reconversion of the industrial base are in the offing.

DEFENDING THE STATUS QUO

The fifth point that requires attention is the relationship between what Kenneth Boulding has aptly termed "the world war industry" and foreign affairs. In some measure, although to what extent it is difficult to say, the world-war industry is an inhibiting factor on social change. Armaments reinforce regimes with which the United States and Soviet Union respectively have working relations and thus draw the nations of the world into the bipolarization which has obtained since the close of the Second World War. This monopolization of military hardware serves to make the world dependent on the leading powers to a degree which cannot be described as healthy. The argument adduced by some to the effect that we have "allies" while the Soviets have "captives"[16] simply ignores the social function of military establishments in Latin America no less than in Eastern

Europe—a function of maintaining a *status quo* which can hardly be said to constitute a popular will.

The political argument runs that to reduce investments in armaments is to invite chaos around the world—particularly in developing areas. But this argument is strictly political in character. From an economic standpoint, in the General Agreement on Trade and Tariffs (GATT) report on *Measures for the Economic Development of Under-Developed Countries*, the developing regions have needs of such enormous proportions that they alone could absorb the 10 per cent of the gross national product siphoned off for military spending.[17] Import requirements of these areas will double—from $27 billion in 1960 to 43 billion by 1970—even if it is assumed that the growth rate in these areas remains what it now is—at present levels. The needs in these areas for American consumer goods, the need of American technical manpower in all sorts of projects, from land clearing to dam-building, would likewise grow. But the purely economic standpoint is inoperative while such political considerations as the character of the social structure and political agencies in these countries are subject to constant scrutiny and veto by Washington or by Moscow. Thus, the external aspects of the heavy armaments industry operate to keep change at a minimum. If every social change in Latin America, Asia, or Africa is to be greeted by the war cry of treason, then the actual economic redistribution of production will be seriously handicapped.

It is a vicious circle. The world-war industry prevents any real dramatic shifts in the social structure, and then the "backwardness" of foreign areas is used as an argument to prove that a political crisis would flow from any release of production from armaments towards production for consumption. The statement by Roger Hagan on the reasons for the polarizing simplicity of the Cold War helps to explain why such an undue faith in military hardware continues to blunt the implementation of broad-scale reform programs that would be based on principles of relative equality.[18]

So much has the political career of much of Congress come to depend on anti-Communist hoop-la that one can almost infer that the fight against subtlety has become a matter of survival for vast elements of our society. For behind the Congressmen are millions of Americans whose style of life, whose sense of meaning, and whose manner of economic endeavor and personal encounter have come to depend upon being publicly patriotic and firm. In a society outdistancing its roots and values and trying to fill the gap with the public virtues of boosterism, the Cold War has become Babbittry gone mad, and it is impossible to be optimistic about the chances for altering the image of Soviet aggressiveness sufficiently to erode the bed-rock argument against nuclear parity.

In such a context, all of the economic arguments for conversion and reconversion away from the "milorg" (military organization) to the "firm" (nonwar industry) come upon this bedrock of an oversimplified image of *Realpolitik*. What may disrupt the present equilibrium is the bifurcation going on in the Socialist bloc which may compel a reappraisal of present alignments and alliances and which may open the possibilities for at least a pragmatic settlement of East-West differences. This will take place if by no other device than a redefinition of just who and what is East and who is West. But, without such an over-all *political* settlement, the chances that the economics of armament production will be reduced in its capabilities and capacities are severely limited.

GAINS FROM CONVERSION

One final problem which remains knotty is that the bulk of Americans remain "economic determinists." They more readily see the results of large arms budgets in advantageous terms than in disadvantageous terms. The need is to gain a public awareness of the broad psychosocial consequences of the large output for armaments. A modest beginning has been made by the United Nations—which has emphasized a number of basic sociological advantages to a conversion of the international economy to peacetime production. First, the general level of living would rise, since federal agencies would begin to devote far more attention to matters of social welfare, health, and education. Second, a reduction in the armaments industry would accelerate the tendency towards the shorter work week, experimentation in types of work habitats, and also in new forms of planning automation without social disruption. Third, a conversion to peacetime production would decrease the sort of tensions which lead to privatization and a general fear that there are no tomorrows. Personal planning would take on meaning, and the frenetic behavior characteristic of the younger generation could be expected to diminish. Fourth, distinctions between have and have-not nations would be alleviated at least in terms of invidious comparison in the military sphere. A by-product of this would be a lower expenditure on non-profitable and rapidly obsolete military hardware and a higher expenditure on commodity production. Fifth, the value system itself would undergo transformation. The faith in raw power could be expected to give way to negotiation and tension management through rational and juridical means. Sixth, cultural contacts would increase and also the possibility that deeper understanding would open yet newer horizons for settlements. Perhaps we will know that a basic change has taken place by the slogans of nations. When peaceful competition gives way to peace co-operation, then the possibility of strengthening a *de facto* settlement by social and personal feelings of kinship will itself become a factor in securing a more perfect machinery of conflict resolution.[19]

Before long, let us hope, resources which are now allocated to the maintenance of military establishment can be released. This very process will create the basis for beneficent social uses of natural and human resources.[20] The breakup of the Communist bloc as a monolithic unit has moved with surprising speed—especially when it is considered that the hegemony of the capitalist democracies was maintained for a far longer time, for centuries and not just decades. New forms of social behavior and political organization are being released. In this way, the fear of totalitarian *coups d'etat* can be considerably mitigated. It is highly questionable that any amount of military build-up can successfully cope with world communism in a frontal assault. The lesson of Korea, South Vietnam, and Germany indicates that direct military confrontations are now, at best, ambiguous, indecisive, and incapable of victory, but it is quite possible that the new *Realpolitik* will involve arms reduction and arms elimination and, in this form, institutionalize free choice and democratic norms.

PEACE MUST BE INSTITUTIONALIZED

From a pragmatic point of view, police actions, counterinsurgency guerrilla actions, and volunteer Hessians have failed, each in its turn. The first failed in Korea, the second failed in South Vietnam, and the third failed in Cuba. The age of "winning" a global conflict, after the spread of nuclear weaponry to more than one country, has decisively ended. Logically, the age of defeat has also ended. Hence, if all future military actions must result in settlement, it seems eminently reasonable to suggest that agencies for settlement can be institutionalized without recourse to the symbolic, and now largely vacuous, threat of extermination.

There is no day of peace. A secure peace comes closer to realization as sensitivity to the needs of social development increases. There is no perfect planning for World War Three because the contingencies cannot be accounted for. Likewise, there is no perfect plan for phasing in industrial conversion to nonmilitary production. On the other hand, the prima-facie priority which planning for peace has over planning for war is that war in our age, like peace, is largely a matter of impetus and impulse. The trajectory to be ridden—reconversion of industrial production on one side or continued military production on the other—may well prove decisive in pushing us toward the stars, co-operatively, or toward the abyss, collectively. The element of risk cannot be eliminated—no more by exponents of disarmament than by those urging continued arms spending. The question really is not *how much* but *just what* are the Americans and Soviets willing to risk?

Part IV

The Problem of Confrontation

STUDIES OF INTERPERSONAL BARGAINING

Morton Deutsch and Robert M. Krauss

INTRODUCTION

A BARGAIN is defined in Webster's Unabridged Dictionary as "an agreement between parties settling what each shall give and receive in a transaction between them"; it is further specified that a bargain is "an agreement or compact viewed as advantageous or the reverse." When the term "agreement" is broadened to include tacit, informal agreements as well as explicit agreements, it is evident that bargains and the processes involved in arriving at bargains ("bargaining") are pervasive characteristics of social life.

The definition of "bargain" fits under sociological definitions of the term "social norm." In this light, it may be seen that the experimental study of the bargaining process and of bargaining outcomes provides a means for the laboratory study of the development of certain types of social norms. It is well to recognize, however, that bargaining situations have certain distinctive features which, unlike many other types of social situations, make it relevant to consider the conditions which determine whether or not a social norm will develop as well as to consider the conditions which determine the nature of the social norm if it develops. Bargaining situations highlight for the investigator the need to be sensitive to the possibility that, even where cooperation would be mutually advantageous, shared purposes may not

Reprinted from *The Journal of Conflict Resolution*, Vol. 6, No. 1 (March, 1962), pp. 57–76. (All footnotes and references have been deleted.)

develop, agreement may not be reached, interaction may be regulated antagonistically rather than normatively.

The essential features of a bargaining situation exist when:

1. both parties perceive that there is the possibility of reaching an agreement in which each party would be better off, or no worse off, than if no agreement is reached;
2. both parties perceive that there is more than one such agreement which could be reached; and
3. both parties perceive each other to have conflicting preferences or opposed interests with regard to the different agreements which might be reached.

Everyday examples of a bargaining situation include such situations as: the buyer-seller relationship when the price is not fixed; the husband and wife who want to spend and evening out together but have conflicting preferences about where to go; union-management negotiations; drivers who meet at an intersection when there is no clear right of way; disarmament negotiations.

From our description of the essential features of a bargaining situation it can be seen that . . . it is a situation in which the participants have mixed motives toward one another: on the one hand, each has interest in cooperating so that they reach an agreement; on the other hand, they have competitive interests with regard to the nature of the agreement they reach. In effect, to reach agreement the cooperative interest of the bargainers must be strong enough to overcome their competitive interests. However, agreement is not only contingent upon the *motivational* balances of cooperative to competitive interests but also upon the situational and *cognitive* factors which would facilitate or hinder the recognition or invention of a bargaining agreement that reduces the opposition of interest and enhances the mutuality of interest.

The discussion of the preceding paragraph leads to the formulation of two general, closely related propositions about the likelihood that a bargaining agreement will be reached.

1. Bargainers are more likely to reach an agreement, the stronger are their cooperative interests in comparison with their competitive interests in relationship to each other.

2. Bargainers are more likely to reach an agreement, the more resources they have available for the recognition or invention of potential bargaining agreements and the more resources they have for communication to one another once a potential agreement has been recognized or invented.

From these two basic propositions and additional hypotheses concerning the conditions which determine the strengths of the cooperative and competitive interests and the amount of available resources, we believe it is possible to explain the ease or difficulty of arriving at a bargaining agreement. We shall not present a full statement of these hypotheses here but shall instead turn to a description of a series of experiments that relate to Proposition 1.

EXPERIMENT I

The first experiment to be reported here was concerned with the effect of the availability of threat upon bargaining in a two-person experimental bargaining game we have devised. Threat is defined as the expression of an intention to do something which is detrimental to the interests of another. Our experiment was guided by two assumptions about threat:

1. If there is a conflict of interest and a means of threatening the other person exists, there will be a tendency to use the threat in an attempt to force the other person to yield. This tendency will be stronger, the more irreconcilable the conflict is perceived to be.

2. If threat is used in an attempt to intimidate another, the threatened person (if he considers himself to be of equal or superior status) will feel hostility toward the threatener and will tend to respond with counterthreat and/or increased resistance to yielding. We qualify this assumption by stating that the tendency to resist will be greater, the greater the perceived probability and magnitude of

detriment to the other and the lesser the percived probability and magnitude of detriment to the potential resistor from the anticipated resistance to yielding.

The second assumption is based upon the view that to allow oneself to be intimidated, particularly by someone who does not have the right to expect deferential behavior, is (when resistance is not seen to be suicidal or useless) to suffer a loss of social face and, hence, of self-esteem; and that the culturally defined way of maintaining self-esteem in the face of attempted intimidation is to engage in a contest for supremacy *vis-à-vis* the power to intimidate or, minimally, to resist intimidation. Thus, in effect, it can be seen that the use of threat (and if it is available to be used, there will be a tendency to use it) should strengthen the competitive interests of the bargainers in relationship to one another by introducing or enhancing the competitive struggle for self-esteem. Hence, from Proposition 1, it follows that the availability of a means of threat should make it more difficult for the bargainers to reach agreement (providing that the threatened person has some means of resisting the threat). . . . For several reasons, it seems likely that a situation of bilateral threat is less conducive to agreement than is a condition of unilateral threat. First, the sheer likelihood that a threat will be made is greater when two people rather than one have the means of making the threat. Secondly, once a threat is made in the bilateral case, it is likely to evoke counterthreat. Withdrawal of threat in the face of counterthreat probably involves more loss of face . . . than does withdrawal of threat in the face of resistance to threat. Finally, in the unilateral case, although the person without the threat potential can resist and not yield to the threat, his position *vis-à-vis* the other is not so strong as the position of the threatened person in the bilateral case. In the unilateral case, the threatened person may have a worse outcome than the other whether he resists or yields; while in the bilateral case, the threatened person is sure to have a worse outcome if he yields but he may insure that he does not have a worse outcome if he does not yield.

Method

Subjects (Ss) were asked to imagine that they were in charge of a trucking company, carrying merchandise over a road to a destination. For each trip they completed they made $.60, minus their operating expenses. Operating expenses were calculated at the rate of one cent per second. So, for example, if it took thirty-seven seconds to complete a particular trip, the player's profit would be $ .60 – $ .37 or a net profit of $ .23 for that particular trip.

Each subject was assigned a name, Acme or Bolt. As the "road map" (see Figure 1) indicates, both players start from separate points and go to separate destinations. At one point their paths coincide. This is the section of road labeled "one-lane road." This section of road is only one lane wide; this means that two trucks, heading in opposite directions, could not pass each other. If one backs up the other can go forward, or both can back up, or both can sit there head-on without moving.

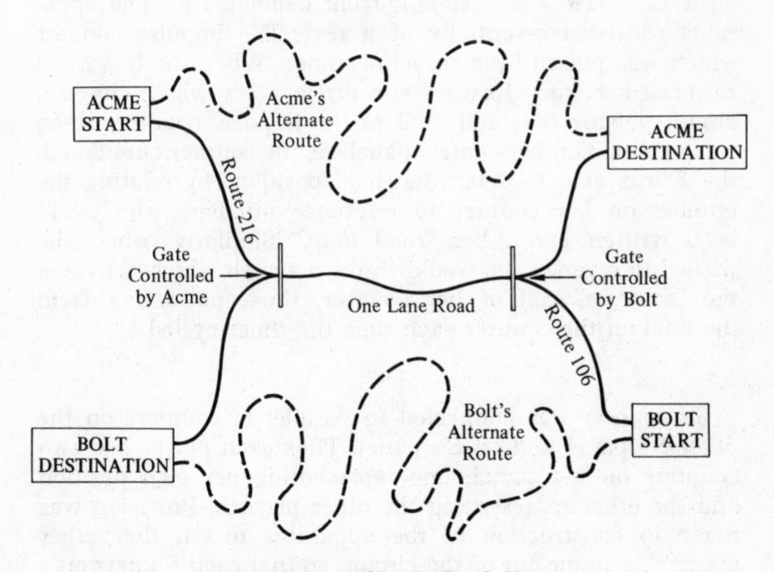

FIGURE 1. *Subject's Road Map*

There is another way for each subject to reach the destination on the map and this is labeled the "alternate route." The two players' paths do not cross on this route, but the alternate is 56 per cent longer than the main route. Subjects were told that they could expect to lose at least $.10 each time they used the alternate route.

At either end of the one-lane section there is a gate which is under the control of the player to whose starting point it is closest. By closing the gate, one player can prevent the other from traveling over that section of the main route. It is the use of the gate which we will call the threat potential in this game. In the bilateral threat potential condition (*Two gates*) both players had gates under their control. In a second condition of unilateral threat (*One Gate*) Acme had control of a gate but Bolt did not. In a third condition (*No Gates*) neither player controlled a gate.

Subjects played the game seated in separate booths positioned so that they could not see each other but both could see the experimenter. Each *S* had a "control panel" mounted on a 12″ × 18″ × 12″ sloping-front cabinet. . . . The apparatus consisted essentially of a reversible impulse counter which was pulsed by a recycling timer. When the *S* wanted to move her truck forward she threw a key which closed a circuit pulsing the "add" coil of the impulse counter which was mounted on her control panel. As the counter cumulated, the *S* was able to determine her "position" by relating the number on her counter to reference numbers which had been written in on her "road map." Similarly, when she wished to reverse, she would throw a switch which activated the "subtract" coil of her counter, thus subtracting from the total on the counter each time the timer cycled.

. . .

S's counter was connected in parallel to counters on the other *S*'s panel and on *E*'s panel. Thus each player had two counters on her panel, one representing her own position and the other representing the other player's. Provision was made in construction of the apparatus to cut the "other player's" counter out of the circuit, so that each *S* knew only the position of her own truck. This was done in the present experiments.

The only time one player definitely knew the other player's position was when they had met head-on on the one-way section of road. This was indicated by a traffic light mounted on the panel. When this light was on, neither player could move forward unless the other moved back. The gates were controlled by toggle switches; panel-mounted indicator lights showed, for both subjects, whether each gate was open or closed.

The following "rules of the game" were stated to the *S*s:

1. A player who started out on one route and wished to switch to the other route could do so only after first reversing and going back to the start position. Direct transfer from one route to the other was not permitted except at the start position.

2. In the conditions where *S*s had gates, they were permitted to close the gates only when they were traveling on the main route. (That is, they were not permitted to close the gate while on the alternate route or after having reached their destinations.) However, *S*s were permitted to open their gates at any point in the game.

*S*s were taken through a number of practice exercises to familiarize them with the game. In the first trial they were made to meet head-on on the one-lane path; Acme was then told to back up until she was just off the one-lane path and Bolt was told to go forward. After Bolt had gone through the one-lane path, Acme was told to go forward. Each continued going forward until each arrived at her destination. The second practice trial was the same as the first except that Bolt rather than Acme backed up after meeting head-on. In the next practice trial, one of the players was made to wait just before the one-way path while the other traversed it and then was allowed to continue. In the next practice trial, one player was made to take the alternate route and the other was made to take the main route. Finally, in the Bilateral and Unilateral Threat conditions the use of the gate was illustrated (by having the player get on the main route, close the gate, and then go back and take the alternate route). The *S*s were told explicitly with emphasis that they did *not* have to use the gate. Before each trial in the game the gate or gates were in the open position.

The instructions stressed an individualistic motivational orientation. *S*s were told to try to earn as much money for themselves as possible and to have no interest in whether the other player made money or lost money. They were given $4.00 in poker chips to represent their working capital and told that after each trial they would be given "money" if they made a profit or that "money" would be taken from them if they lost (i.e., took more than 60 seconds to complete their trip). The profit or loss of each *S* was annonuced so that both *S*s could hear the announcement after each trial. Each pair of subjects played a total of twenty trials; on all trials, they started off together. In other words, each trial presented a repetition of the same bargaining problem. In cases where subjects lost their working capital before the twenty trials were completed, additional chips were given them. Subjects were aware that their monetary winnings and losses were to be imaginary and that no money would change hands as a result of the experiment.

Sixteen pairs of subjects were used in each of the three experimental conditions. The *S*s were female clerical and supervisory personnel of the New Jersey Bell Telephone Company who volunteered to participate during their working day. Their ages ranged from 20 to 39, with a mean of 26.2. All were naive to the purpose of the experiment. By staggering the arrival times and choosing girls from different locations, we were able to insure that our subjects did not know with whom they were playing.

Results

The best single measure of the difficulty experienced by the bargainers in reaching an agreement is the sum of each pair's profits (or losses) on a given trial. The higher the sum of the payoffs to the two players on a given trial, the less time it took them to arrive at a procedure for sharing the one-lane path of the main route. (It was, of course,

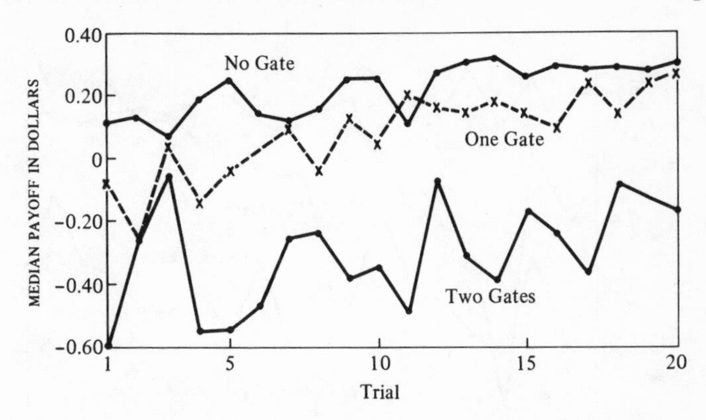

FIGURE 2. *Median Joint Payoff (Acme + Bolt) over Trials*

possible for one or both of the players to decide to take the alternate route so as to avoid a protracted stalemate during the process of bargaining. This, however, always resulted in at least a \$.20 smaller joint payoff if only one player took the alternate route, than an optimally arrived at agreement concerning the use of the one-way path.) Figure 2 presents

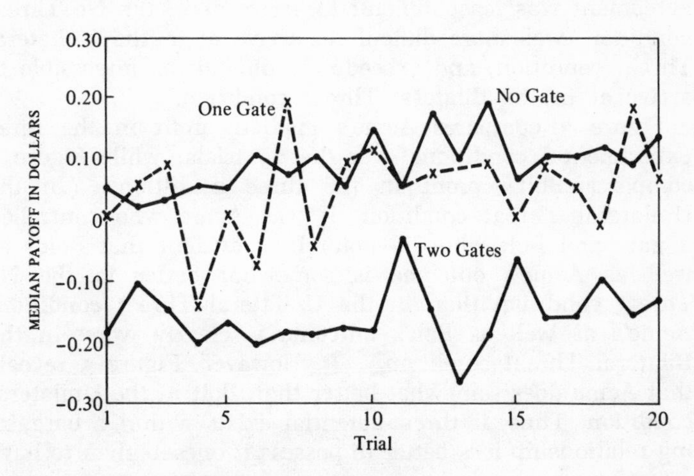

FIGURE 3. *Acme's Median Payoff*

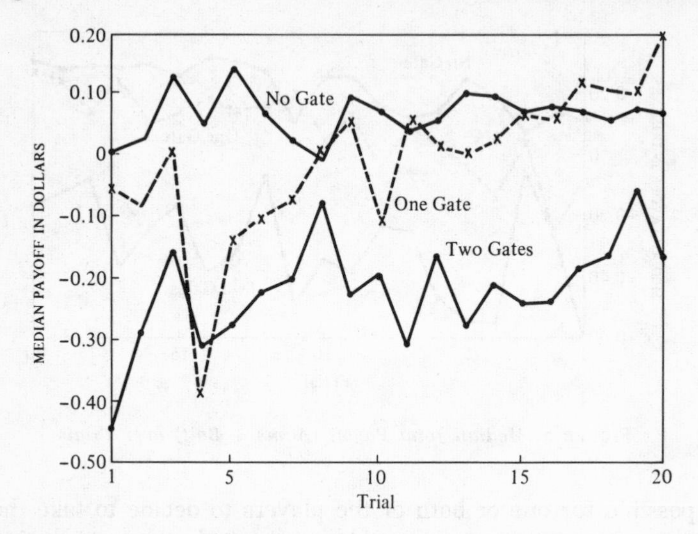

FIGURE 4. ***Bolt's Median Payoff***

the medians of the summed payoffs (i.e., Acme's plus Bolt's) for all pairs in each of the three experimental conditions over the twenty trials. These results indicate that agreement was least difficult to arrive at in the No Threat condition, was more difficult to arrive at in the Unilateral Threat condition, and exceedingly difficult or impossible to arrive at in the Bilateral Threat condition. . . .

Figure 3 compares Acme's median profit in the three experimental conditions over the 20 trials; while Figure 4 compares Bolt's profit in the three conditions. (In the Unilateral Threat condition, it was Acme who controlled a gate and Bolt who did not.) It is evident that Bolt's as well as Acme's outcome is somewhat better in the No Threat condition than in the Unilateral Threat condition; Acme's as well as Bolt's outcome is clearly worst in the Bilateral Threat condition. . . . However, Figure 5 reveals that Acme does somewhat better than Bolt in the Unilateral condition. Thus, if threat-potential exists within a bargaining relationship it is better to possess it oneself than to have

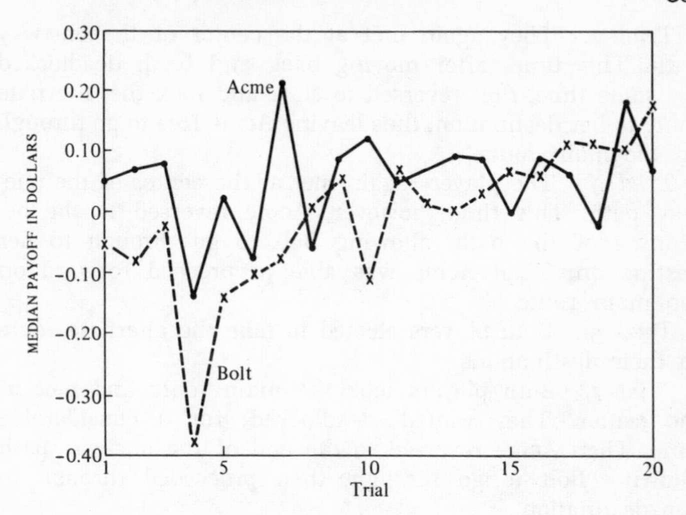

FIGURE 5. *Acme's and Bolt's Median Payoff in Unilateral Threat Condition*

the other party possess it. However, it is even better for neither party to possess it. Moreover, from Figure 4, it is evident that Bolt is better off not having than having a gate even when Acme has a gate: Bolt tends to do better in the Unilateral Threat condition than in the Bilateral Threat condition.

. . .

To provide the reader with a more detailed description of what went on during the bargaining game, we present a synopsis of the game for one pair in each of the three experimental treatments.

No Threat Condition

Trial 1. The players met in the center of the one-way section. After some back-and-forth movement Bolt reversed to the end of the one-way section, allowing Acme to pass through, and then proceeded forward herself.

Trial 2. They again met at the center of the one-way path. This time, after moving back and forth deadlocked for some time, Bolt reversed to start and took the alternate route to her destination, thus leaving Acme free to go through on the main route.

Trial 3. The players again met at the center of the one-way path. This time, however, Acme reversed to the beginning of the path, allowing Bolt to go through to her destination. Then Acme was able to proceed forward on the main route.

Trial 5. Both players elected to take the alternate route to their destinations.

Trial 7. Both players took the main route and met in the center. They waited, deadlocked, for a considerable time. Then Acme reversed to the end of the one-way path allowing Bolt to go through, then proceeded through to her destination.

Trials 10 through 20. Acme and Bolt fall into a pattern of alternating who is to go first on the one-way section. There is no deviation from this pattern.

The only other pattern which emerges in this condition is one in which one player dominates the other. That is, one player consistently goes first on the one-way section and the other player consistently yields.

Unilateral Threat Condition

Trial 1. Both players took the main route and met in the center of it. Acme immediately closed the gate, reversed to "start" and took the alternate route to her destination. Bolt waited for a few seconds, at the closed gate, then reversed and took the alternate route.

Trial 2. Both players took the main route and met in the center. After moving back and forth deadlocked for about fifteen seconds, Bolt reversed to the beginning of the one-way path, allowed Acme to pass, and then proceeded forward to her destination.

Trial 3. Both players started out on the main route, meeting in the center. After moving back and forth deadlocked for a while, Acme closed her gate, reversed to "start" and took the alternate route. Bolt, meanwhile, waited at the closed gate. When Acme arrived at her destination she opened the gate, and Bolt went through to complete her trip.

Trial 5. Both players took the main route, meeting at the center of the one-way section. Acme immediately closed her gate, reversed and took the alternate route. Bolt waited at the gate for about ten seconds, then reversed and took the alternate route to her destination.

Trial 10. Both players took the main route and met in the center. Acme closed her gate, reversed and took the alternate route. Bolt remained waiting at the closed gate. After Acme arrived at her destination, she opened the gate and Bolt completed her trip.

Trial 15. Acme took the main route to her destination and Bolt took the alternate route.

Trials 17, 18, 19 and 20. Both players took the main route and met in the center. Bolt waited a few seconds, then reversed to the end of the one-way section allowing Acme to go through. Then Bolt proceeded forward to her destination.

Other typical patterns which developed in this experimental condition included an alternating pattern similar to that described in the No Threat condition, a dominating pattern in which Bolt would select the alternate route leaving Acme free to use the main route unobstructed, and a pattern in which Acme would close her gate and then take the alternate route, also forcing Bolt to take the alternate route.

Bilateral Threat Condition

Trial 1. Acme took the main route and Bolt took the alternate route.

Trial 2. Both players took the main route and met head-on. Bolt closed her gate. Acme waited a few seconds, then closed her gate, reversed to "start," then went forward again to the closed gate. Acme reversed and took the alternate route. Bolt again reversed, then started on the alternate route. Acme opened her gate and Bolt reversed to start and went to her destination on the main route.

Trial 3. Acme took the alternate route to her destination. Bolt took the main route and closed her gate before entering the one-way section.

Trial 5. Both players took the main route and met head-on. After about ten seconds spent backing up and going forward, Acme closed her gate, reversed and took the alternate route. After waiting a few seconds, Bolt did the same.

Trials 8, 9, 10. Both players started out on the main route, immediately closed their gates, reversed to start and took the alternate route to their destinations.

Trial 15. Both players started out on the main route and met head-on. After some jockeying for position, Acme closed her gate, reversed and took the alternate route to her destination. After waiting at the gate for a few seconds, Bolt reversed to start and took the alternate route to her destination.

Trials 19, 20. Both players started out on the main route, immediately closed their gates, reversed to start and took the alternate routes to their destinations.

Other patterns which emerged in the Bilateral Threat condition included alternating first use of the one-way section, one player's dominating the other on first use of the one-way section, and another dominating pattern in which one player consistently took the main route while the other consistently took the alternate route.

Discussion

The results of Experiment I clearly indicate that the availability of a threat potential in our experimental bargaining situation adversely affects the player's ability to reach effective agreements. In terms of our introductory analysis of bargaining as a mixed motive situation (i.e., one in which both competitive and cooperative motivations are acting upon the participants), we can interpret these results as indicating that the existence of threat enhances the competitive aspects of interaction.

These results, we believe, reflect psychological tendencies which are not confined to our bargaining situation: the tendency to use threat (if a means for threatening is available) in an attempt to force the other person to yield when he is seen as an obstruction; the tendency to respond with counter-threat or increased resistance to attempts at intimidation. How general are these tendencies? What are the conditions likely to elicit them? Answers to these questions are necessary before our results can be generalized to other situations. . . .

EXPERIMENT II

Our discussion thus far has suggested that the psychological factors which operate in our experimental bargaining game are to be found in many real-life bargaining situations. However, it is well to point out an important unique feature of our experimental game: namely, that the bargainers had no opportunity to communicate verbally with one another. Prior research on the role of communication in trust . . . suggests that the opportunity for communication would ameliorate the difficulty bargainers experience in reaching agreement. This possibility was expressed spontaneously by a number of our subjects in a post-experimental interview. It should be noted, however, that the same research cited above . . . indicates that communication may not be effective between competitively oriented bargainers.

To test the effect of communication upon bargaining, we undertook an experiment in which subjects were permitted to talk over an intercom hookup. It was further decided to differentiate Bilateral Communication (both parties permitted to talk) from Unilateral Communication (only one party is permitted to talk.)

Method

The experimental apparatus, instructions to the *S*s and training procedures here were the same as described in Experiment I. In addition, each *S* was equipped with a headset (earphones and microphone) hooked into an intercom system. The intercom was so constructed that *E* could control the direction of *S*s' communication. This was necessary so that in the Unilateral Communication condition one

S was prevented from talking to the other, but both were able to talk to *E* when necessary. A filter, built into the intercom's amplification system, distorted voice quality sufficiently to make it unlikely that *S*s would recognize one another's voices even if they were previously acquainted, without significantly impairing intelligibility. *S*s received the following instructions on communication:

> During the game, when your trucks are en route, you may communicate with each other . . . (Here Ss received instructions on operating the intercom system) . . . In talking to the other player you may say anything you want; or if you don't want to talk you don't have to. You may talk about the game, about what you'd like to happen in the game, what you're going to do, what you'd like the other player to do, or anything else that comes to mind. What you talk about—or whether you decide to talk or not—is up to you.

These instructions were modified in the Unilateral Communication condition to indicate that only one player (Acme) would be permitted to talk. Communication was not allowed between trials; only during the actual "trip" were *S*s permitted to talk.

The two levels of our communication variable (bilateral and unilateral) were combined with the three levels of threat employed in the previous study to produce a 2×3 factorial experiment. It was necessary to employ such a design to test the possibility that communication might be differentially effective under different conditions of threat.

Five pairs of *S*s were centered randomly into each of six treatment conditions. All were female clerical and secretarial employees of the Bell Telephone Laboratories and were, in most respects, comparable to the New Jersey Bell Telephone employees used in Experiment I. Again, *S*s were selected from different work areas and arrival times were staggered to prevent *S*s from knowing their partner's identity.

Results

An analysis of variance of Experiment II indicates that our communication variable had no effect on the players' ability to reach effective agreements; however the "threat" variable, as in the first experiment, had a significant effect. It should also be noted that the results of this experiment are not significantly different from the findings of Experiment I, where no communication was permitted. For economy of presentation these cross-experiment comparisons will be included with the results of Experiment III below.

Product-moment correlations were computed between frequency of communication for each pair (the number of trials out of twenty in which one or both *S*s spoke) and joint payoff. Both over-all and within the threat conditions no significant relation was observed between frequency of communication and payoff. As will be discussed below, only a minimum of communication did occur and quite likely frequency of communication in this situation was determined by characteristics of the *S*s which were irrelevant to the achievement of agreement in the bargaining situation.

An additional finding of interest: it will be recalled that in the Unilateral Threat condition Acme was the player possessing the threat potential. Similarly, in the Unilateral Communication condition, it was Acme who was allowed to talk. To ascertain the effect of this double asymmetry we ran an additional five pairs of *S*s in a Unilateral Threat–Unilateral Communication condition in which Bolt was given the opportunity to talk, while Acme still possessed the threat potential. A comparison of this group with the standard Unilateral Threat–Unilateral Communication condition revealed no significant differences between them.

. . .

We can also examine the gross frequency of talking in the three threat conditions. Each pair of *S*s received a score based upon the number of trials on which one or both players spoke to the other. . . . Most talking occurs in the No Threat condition; the rate of talking in the Unilateral and Bilateral Threat conditions is approximately equal. However, these differences, when tested by a one-way analysis of variance, are not large enough to permit a rejection of the null hypothesis. If we examine frequency of talking in the Unilateral vs. Bilateral Communication conditions we find that, in accordance with expectation, significantly more talk occurs in the bilateral condition. . . .

. . .

In a post-experimental questionnaire and interview we questioned *S*s closely in an attempt to ascertain the reason for the paucity of communication. Most of our *S*s were at a loss to explain why they did not talk, although almost all acknowledged that they were less than normally talkative. With some probing on *E*'s part, a frequent comment concerned "the difficulty of talking to someone you don't know." Possibly, the communication process normally involves a system of reciprocal expectations by which a speaker has some idea of the effect his words will have on a listener. Even in an encounter between strangers these expectations may be partly derived from such visual cues as appearance, dress, facial expression, etc. All of these cues were absent in the communication between our *S*s. Interestingly enough, when *S*s were introduced after the experimental session, a great deal of spontaneous chatter ensued. . . .

Discussion

It is obvious from the results of Experiment II that the opportunity to communicate does not necessarily result in an amelioration of conflict in our experimental bargaining situation. Indeed, it should be stated that the *opportunity* to communicate does not necessarily result in communication at all. . . .

. . . Apparently the competitive orientation induced by the threat potential in our situation was sufficiently strong to overcome any possible ameliorating effects of communication. In the No Threat condition, where competitiveness is at a minimum, the advantage gained by the use of communication to coordinate effort was offset by the time consumed by talking. It would seem that the coordination problem posed for the *S*s by our experimental game was sufficiently simple to be solvable without communication, given the existence of an appropriate motivational orientation. This

will be considered further in our discussion of Experiment III.

EXPERIMENT III

. . . One may speculate that had our Ss in fact communicated, the outcome of Experiment II might have been quite different. Studies of collective bargaining procedures suggest one of their important values lies in their ability to prevent disputants from breaking off communication. . . . Experiment III was undertaken to test the effect of forced, or compulsory, communication.

Method

The experimental apparatus, instructions to the Ss, and training procedures employed here were the same as in Experiment II. Ss received the following instructions on communication (the italicized portions are those which differ from the instructions used in Experiment II):

> During the game, when your trucks are enroute, you *both will be required* to communicate with each other . . . (Here Ss received instructions on operating the intercom system) . . . In talking to the other player you may say anything you want. You may talk about the game, about what you'd like to happen in the game, what you're going to do, what you'd like the other player to do, or anything else that comes to mind. What you talk about is up to you. *But remember, you must say something to the other player on every trip.*

In Experiment III only a Bilateral Communication condition was run, again under three levels of threat potential. On trials where either *S* failed to talk, they were reminded by *E* at the conclusion of the trial of the requirement that they talk to the other player on every trial. In no group was it necessary to make this reminder on more than four trials.

Ten pairs of Ss were entered randomly into each of the three treatment conditions. Ss were drawn from the same pool used in Experiment II; however, none of the Ss in this experiment had served in the previous one.

Results

We will refer to the form of communication utilized in Experiment II as Permissive Communication; communication in Experiment III will be called Compulsory Communication; in Experiment I, No Communication was involved. Since in Experiment II no differences were found between our Bilateral and Unilateral Communication treatments, we have combined these two categories to increase the *N* of the Permissive Communication group.

Figure 6 presents the mean joint payoffs (summarized as the averages of four-trial blocks for convenience) for all three experiments. . . . The effectiveness of the Compulsory Communication variable is seen in comparison of groups in the Unilateral Threat condition. Here alone, of all the conditions in which gates are present, does performance approach that of *S*s in the No Threat condition. In the Bilateral Threat condition the competitive motivation

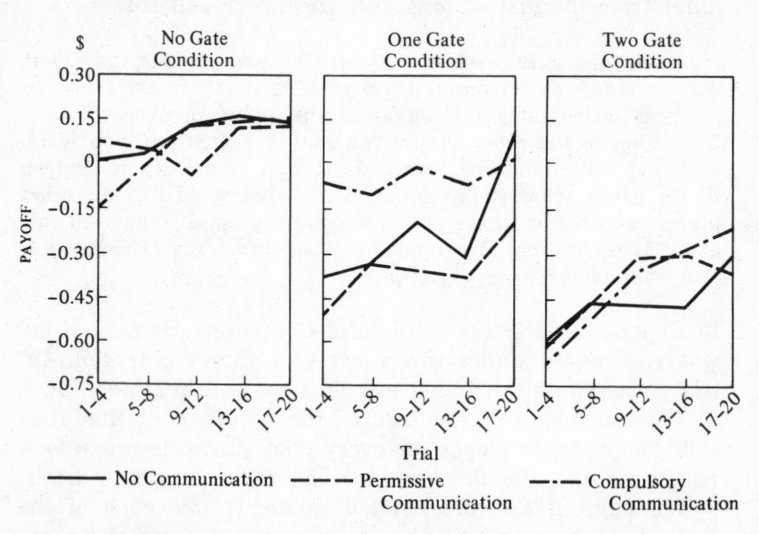

Figure 6. ***Mean Joint Payoffs (Acme + Bolt) in the Communication Conditions Across the Three Threat Conditions***

present seems too great to be overcome, even by the compulsory Communication treatment. As was noted above, in the No Threat condition coordination was sufficiently simple that communication failed to produce any visible effect.

. . .

We can examine more closely performance in the Unilateral Threat condition. For example, it is possible that the effectiveness of Compulsory Communication as reflected in the joint payoff data is due to an increase in the payoff to Acme (the player possessing a threat potential), without a corresponding increase in Bolt's payoff. In other words, it is possible that Compulsory Communication acts to increase the advantaged player's bargaining power in an asymmetrical situation. Figure 7 breaks down the payoffs of Acme and Bolt in the three communication conditions. Although in all conditions Acme does better than Bolt, the margin of discrepancy does not vary substantially in the three conditions.

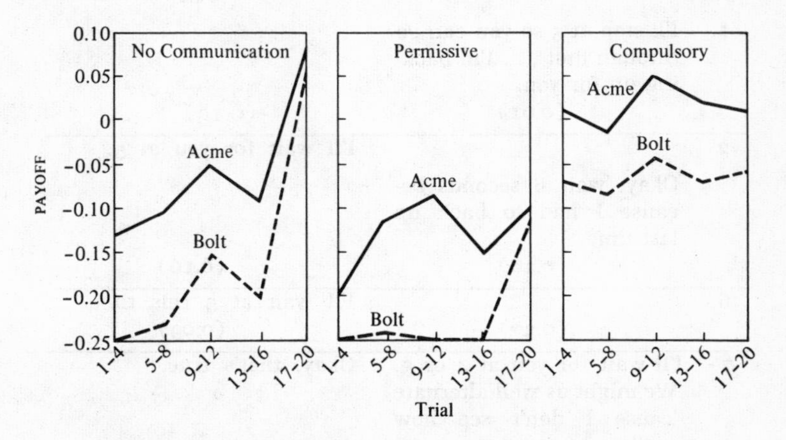

Figure 7. ***Acme's and Bolt's Mean Payoffs in the Unilateral Threat Condition Across the Three Communication Conditions***

An analysis of trend over trials . . . was performed on the data of the three experiments. Over-all, a significant linear component was present, as Figure 6 indicates; however, there were no differences in trend resulting from a partitioning of Ss by the two independent variables or their interactions. This result held true when the analysis was based on the joint payoff scores and on Acme's and Bolt's scores analyzed separately.

. . . In Experiment III we were . . . successful in obtaining complete recordings of a small number of our Ss' conversations. . . .We present below a transcript for selected trials of three pairs of Ss, one in each of the threat conditions, which were judged to be relatively typical. The numbers in parentheses below each conversation represent the payoff to each player on that trial (in imaginary dollars). Positive numbers represent winnings and negative numbers are losses.

No Threat Condition

Trial	*Acme*	*Bolt*
1	I'll stop at 5 so you can go through first . . . I'm backing up for you. (0.01)	(0.19)
2	Okay, wait 6 seconds because I had to back up last time. (0.26)	I'll wait for you at 5. (0.10)
6	(0.27)	I'll wait at 5 this time. (0.09)
7	I'll wait for you at 4 or 5. We might as well alternate 'cause I don't see how we'll make any money any other way. (0.03)	Okay, that's true. (0.25)

Trial	*Acme*	*Bolt*
12	Is it my turn to wait for you?	I'll wait for you this time at 5.
	Okay, I couldn't remember whose turn it was. . . . (counting) 13, 14, 15.	Let me know when you reach 15.
	(0.27)	(0.09)
13	I'll wait for you.	All right. I'll let you know at 15.
	Okay. I didn't go on break this morning and boy, am I hungry!	You can start now.
	I'll make 9 cents and you'll make 27. I started a few seconds too late.	
	(0.07)	(0.26)
16		I'll wait at 5 this time and let me know at 13 also.
	Okay. I'll count up so you know. 13, 14, 15.	Okay. Thank you.
	There's no way to make money except by compromising this way.	No, that's the only way and it comes out even that way, usually.
	Except for the first few times.	Yuh.
	(0.27)	(0.09)
17	I'll wait at 5.	Okay. You'll make 9 cents, I'll make 27.
	Yeah. Are you from around here?	Yuh, Summit [a local town]. . . . (counting) 13, 14, 15.
	Thank you. I won't ask you any more because I don't know you.	Okay. No.
	(0.08)	(0.26)
20		I'll wait for you this time.
	Okay. Do you have a watch on?	Yeah.

Trial	*Acme*	*Bolt*
	What time is it?	Twenty-five after eleven. What number are you on now?
	Twelve.	Okay, (counting) 13, 14.
	(counting) 14, 15. You're such a cooperative partner.	What?
	Nice working for such a cooperative partner.	Oh, nice to work with you, too.
	(0.26)	(0.09)

Unilateral Threat Condition

Trial	*Acme*	*Bolt*
1	Do you intend to take the main route?	Um . . . I'm taking it, but I've stopped.
		Are you going to close the gate?
	I've closed it already. I'm going to open it.	
		You finish yet?
	Yes, I have.	
	(0.26)	(0.05)
2		Are you on the main road?
	Yes, I am. I think we're going to meet again. I guess we've met, uh, I'm going to back up.	Where are you?
	I'm backing up.	What number are you on?
	Now I'm on 4.	Oh, all right. I'll go forward.
	I think we met again.	
	(–0.17)	(0.00)
5	My gate's closed.	Uh huh. I noticed.
	It's open now. Oh, we met?	Yes.

Trial	*Acme*	*Bolt*
	I'm going to reverse.	We met?
	Yes.	Go now.
	I can go?	We'll try.
	No.	No? (laughs)
	Wait a sec. I'll back up some more Okay. You must almost be there.	
	(–0.12)	(0.06)
6	My gate's closed.	Uh huh. Are you gonna leave it closed?
	No, it's open now. You go . . . . Oh. Oh, we met.	I'll go back.
	Okay.	Try it now.
	Okay, I'm there already.	
	(0.21)	(–0.03)
9	I'll back up.	Okay. I'm there.
	Oh, you're there? You beat me by a hair. I'm only halfway there.	I keep forgetting to push this thing down [probably a reference to switch on intercom].
	Oh.	
	(–0.06)	(0.11)
10	My gate's closed	Are you there?
	Yes.	All right. You beat me by seven, eight.
	(0.26)	(0.10)
13		Are you there?
	Yeah.	Are you gonna . . . oh, it's open.
	It's open.	
	(0.26)	(0.05)
14	I'll back up.	Try going forward.
	Okay. No.	Not yet?

Trial	*Acme*	*Bolt*
	You keep coming now.	What, go forward?
	Yeah.	On 15, 16, okay.
	I wonder how many times we're going to play this.	
	(–0.07)	(0.09)
19		Are you going back?
	Yes, are you going forward?	Yes.
	I'm back. There.	Um, no.
	Oh.	
	(0.01)	(0.18)
20		You going forward?
	Uh huh.	What number are you on?
	(counting) 10, 11.	10?
	Okay.	You there?
	Yeah, no, we're blocked.	Oh, I'll go back.
	Are you stopped or going back?	I'm going forward.
	Oh, now you're going forward. Oh, I guess we're okay now.	I'm on 9; are you there?
	Yeah.	I think I'm glad I'm not a truck driver.
	(0.20)	(–0.01)

Bilateral Threat Condition

Trial	*Acme*	*Bolt*
1	You decide on your route?	I'm taking the main route.
	I am, too.	Oh, we're stopped. What happens now?
	What did you say?	Did you stop?

Trial	*Acme*	*Bolt*
	Yeah, the lane is blocked completely.	Well, who's going to back up?
	Well, I don't know. You gonna back up this time?	All right. I'll back up.
	All right.	Your gate is locked.
	I know it's locked.	That wasn't very fair.
	Anything's fair.	Well, what are you going to do?
	I don't have to do anything. I'm going to my destination.	This is not funny.
	(laughs)	At your destination?
	No!	I'll never reach mine at this point.
	I've reached mine.	Well?
	Sit tight.	Planned your next route?
	No, have you?	I've got some ideas.
	Thanks a lot.	I'm getting there slowly but surely.
	(laughs)	
	(−0.95)	(−1.87)
2		I've got my plan.
	I've got mine, too.	How're you doing?
	Fine. How are you doing?	Oh, I'm fine. I'm not getting any place fast, though.
	This doesn't move very quick.	Slow trucking.
	That makes two of us.	Where are you now?
	Twenty-seven [on alternate route]. Where are you?	Twenty-four (both laugh). Looks like we both don't trust each other. I'll lose money this game.
	(−0.44)	(−0.54)

Trial	*Acme*	*Bolt*
5	We're stopped. What are we going to do now?	Oh, I backed up the first time. Now it's your turn.
	All right. What are you going to do?	I'm going to take the alternate route.
	Go right ahead.	Are you going to open your gate?
	No.	What are you going to do now?
	I've got to at least make the loss even.	I hear only one ticking [a reference to noise made by the apparatus].
	(–1.02)	(–0.75)
7		You've got yours closed, too.
	We're both stopped.	Are you going to open your gate?
	Why should I?	I'll do the same next time.
	Is that a threat?	You playing tricks?
	No.	I'll lose five dollars this trip because of you.
	(–1.33)	(–0.75)
9	I see you've got your gate closed. What route are you on?	Why should I tell you?
	Okay, if that's the way you want to play.	No, I'll tell you where I am if you tell me where you are.
	I asked you first.	So am I [sic]. . . . At 17. . . . How far are you?
	I don't believe you.	Have it your way.
	(–1.33)	(–0.75)
13	(Unintelligible)	You had yours closed.
	I think that's my business.	Why don't you open your gate?
	Don't have time.	I'm not getting any place.
	(–0.60)	(–0.23)

Trial	*Acme*	*Bolt*
14	You have yours shut, too.	What?
	You never let me through.	Let's open our gates as long as we're going the other way.
	I know you are (sarcastically).	
	(−0.20)	(−0.22)
18	What route are you taking?	(no answer)
	I think we both are going bankrupt.	They [sic] just don't trust each other, right?
	(−0.39)	(−0.50)
20		Your gate's closed again.
	So is yours, so that means you must have taken the alternate route.	Why? What gives you that idea?
	Well, you wouldn't be crazy enough to go to the main route with my gate closed.	Well, maybe I think I can persuade you to open it.
	You know better than that.	Do I? . . . I get the use of these gates all mixed up. I shut mine when I don't want to and, oh, . . .
	If I go into the trucking business I'm not going to have gates.	
	(−0.21)	(−0.22)

Discussion

In the introduction, we presented our view of bargaining as a situation in which both cooperative and competitive tendencies are present and acting upon the individual. From this point of view, it is relevant to inquire as to the conditions under which a stable agreement of any form will develop. However, implicit in most models of bargaining

. . . is the assumption that the cooperative interests of the bargainers will be sufficiently strong to insure that some form of mutually satisfactory agreement will be reached. For this reason, such models have focused upon the form of the agreement reached by the bargainers. Siegel and Fouraker . . . report a series of bargaining experiments quite different in structure from ours in which only one of many pairs of subjects was unable to reach agreement. . . .

. . .

In our experimental bargaining situation, the availability of threat clearly made it more difficult for bargainers to reach a mutually profitable agreement. Indeed, Bilateral Threat presents a situation so conflict-fraught that no amount of communication seems to have an ameliorating effect. These tendencies we believe are not confined to our experimental situation. The "affront–offense–punitive behavior sequence" to which Siegel and Fouraker refer, and which we have observed in our experiment, are common attributes of everyday interpersonal conflict. The processes which underlie them have long been of interest to social scientists and an imposing set of theoretical constructs have been employed to explain them.

. . . There seems to be little reason to doubt that the use of threat is a frequent reaction to interpersonal impasses. However, everyday observation indicates that threat does not inevitably occur when there is an interpersonal impasse. We would speculate that it is most likely to occur when the threatener has no positive interest in the other person's welfare (he is either egocentrically or competitively related to the other); when the threatener believes that the other has no positive interest in his welfare; and when the threatener anticipates either that his threat will be effective or, if ineffective, will not worsen his situation because he expects the worst to happen if he does not use his threat. We suggest that these conditions were operative in our experiment; the subjects were either egocentrically or competitively oriented to one another and they felt that they would not be worse off by the use of threat.

Everyday observation suggests that the tendency to respond with counterthreat or increased resistance to attempts at intimidation is also a common occurrence. It is our belief that the introduction of threat into a bargaining situation affects the meaning of yielding. . . .

. . .

. . . Why then did the subjects' reactions differ so markedly as a function of the availability of threat? The explanation for this lies, we believe, in the cultural interpretation of yielding (to a peer or subordinate) under duress, as compared to giving in without duress. The former, we believe, is perceived as a negatively valued form of behavior, with negative implications for the self-image of the individual who so behaves. At least partly, this is so because the locus of causality is perceived to be outside the voluntary control of the individual. No such evaluation, however, need be placed on the behavior of one who "gives in" in a situation where no threat or duress is a factor. Rather, we should expect the culturally defined evaluation of such an individual's behavior to be one of "reasonableness" or "maturity." Again, this may be because the cause of the individual's behavior is perceived to lie within the individual.

One special feature of our experimental game is worthy of note: the passage of time, without coming to an agreement, is costly to the players. There are, of course, bargaining situations in which the lack of agreement may simply preserve the *status quo* without any worsening of the bargainers' respective positions. This is the case in the typical bilateral monopoly case, where the buyer and seller are unable to agree upon a price. . . . In other sorts of bargaining situations, however (e.g., labor-management negotiations during a strike; inter-nation negotiations during an expensive cold war), the passage of time may play an important role. In our experiment, we received the impression that the meaning of time changed as time passed without the bargainers reaching an agreement. Initially, the passage of time seemed to pressure the players to come to an agreement before their costs mounted sufficiently to destroy their profit. With the continued passage of time, however, their mounting losses strengthened their resolution not to yield to the other player. They comment: "I've lost so much, I'll be damned if I give in now. At least I'll have the satisfaction of doing better than she does." The mounting losses and continued deadlock seemed to change the game from a mixed motive into a predominantly competitive situation.

The results of Experiments II and III justify, we believe, a reconsideration of the role of communication in the bargaining process. Typically, communication is perceived as a means whereby the bargainers coordinate effort (e.g., exchange bids, indicate positions, etc.). Usually, little emphasis is given to interaction of communication with motivational orientation. Certainly the coordination function of communication is important. However, as Siegel and Fouraker . . . point out, free communication may also be used to convey information (e.g., threats, insults, etc.) which may intensify the competitive aspects of the situation.

It should be emphasized here that the "solution" of our bargaining problem (i.e., alternating first use of the one-lane section of the main route) is a simple and rather obvious one. Indeed, the sort of coordination of effort required by the game is sufficiently simple to be readily achievable without the aid of communication. (Note that *Ss* in the No Threat–No Communication conditions did as well as *Ss* in the two No Threat conditions with communication.) More important than this coordinating function, however, is the capacity of communication to expedite the development of agreements. In this context, agreements serve a function similar to that ascribed by Thibaut and Kelley to the social norm; that is, "they serve as substitutes for the exercise of personal influence and produce more economically and efficiently certain consequences otherwise dependent upon personal influence processes." . . . Effective communication, by this line of reasoning, would be aimed at the development of agreements or, to state it another way, at a resolution of the competitive orientation which produces conflict in the bargaining situation.

One must grant that our *Ss* were relatively unsophisticated in the techniques of developing agreements under the stress of competition. Possibly persons who deal regularly with problems of conflict resolution (e.g., marriage counselors, labor-management arbitrators, diplomats, etc.) would have little difficulty in reaching agreement, even under our Bilateral Threat condition.

Another barrier to effective communication lies in the reticence of our Ss. As we noted above, our Ss found talking to an unknown partner a strange and rather uncomfortable experience. This factor alone would limit the possibility of any communication, let alone communication which was effective.

. . .

It is, of course, hazardous to generalize from a set of laboratory experiments to the problems of the real world. But our experiment and the theoretical ideas which underlie them can perhaps serve to emphasize some notions which, otherwise, have some intrinsic plausibility. In brief, these are the following: (1) There is more safety in cooperative than in competitive coexistence. (2) The mere existence of channels of communication is no guarantee that communication will indeed take place; and the greater the competitive orientation of the parties *vis-à-vis* each other, the less likely will they be to use such channels as do exist. (3) Where barriers to communication exist, a situation in which the parties are compelled to communicate will be more effective than one in which the choice to talk or not is put on a voluntary basis. (4) If the bargainers' primary orientation is competitive, communication which is not directed at changing this orientation is unlikely to be effective. (5) It is dangerous for bargainers to have weapons at their disposal. (6) Possibly, it is more dangerous for a bargainer to have the capacity to retaliate in kind than for him not to have this capacity, when the other bargainer has a weapon. This last statement assumes that the one who yields has more of his values preserved by accepting the agreement preferred by the other than by extended conflict Of course, in some bargaining situations in the real world the loss incurred by yielding may exceed the loss due to extended conflict.

THE ANALYSIS OF SOCIAL CONFLICT—TOWARD AN OVERVIEW AND SYNTHESIS

Raymond W. Mack and Richard C. Snyder

INTRODUCTION

. . .

[A VAST literature on social conflict has accumulated. . . .]

Despite the accumulation of experience and writing, certain basic queries remain unanswered. Only a few need be set forth here. Why do serious situations sometimes *not* develop into violent conflict while not so serious ones do? Why do some conflicts rather quickly run a natural course while others do not? What kinds of group attachments to which men are susceptible (in particular situations) are closely related to well-delineated lines of cleavage in society? What is the effect of size of groups on intergroup conflict? Does increased social mobility increase or decrease social conflict? Is desire to convert others to a set of beliefs more conducive to intense conflict than desire for scarce resources? Do differing value commitments have greater conflict potential when the corresponding behavior patterns are not brought into fact-to-face confrontation than when they are? Under what conditions are psychological mechanisms crucial to the emergence of conflict? Why do some forms of group identification accompany intergroup conflict while others do not? Under what conditions do differing needs, demands,

Reprinted from *The Journal of Conflict Resolution*, Vol. 1, No. 2 (1957), pp. 212–248. (One footnote has been deleted.)

and aspirations, combined with appraisals of interaction situations, produce conflict behavior? Such questions suggest either gaps in knowledge and/or the ineffective organization of existing knowledge.

For the foregoing reasons, we wish to argue the need for further intellectual stocktaking—for a propositional survey and assessment and for more precise conceptualization. We shall only attempt to suggest in simplified form the general lines along which this might be carried out. . . . Needless to say, the acquisition of new knowledge will depend primarily on empirical research. . . .

BASIC PROPOSITIONS

A reasonably thorough scanning of the literature reveals that the materials for an orderly and general index of propositions on social conflict are available. . . .

. . . Why is a propositional survey useful, and what are the necessary rules for constructing it? To begin with, it is universally recognized that a body of knowledge about anything consists primarily of a set of existential propositions which are in varying degrees verified. A necessary step in stocktaking is, therefore, the pinpointing of major generalizations. Once they are made explicit and rendered in propositional form, critical assessment is possible. A series of questions can and should be put to any set of propositions: What evidence can be mobilized in support or disproof? Which are educated guesses? Which are generally agreed to or disagreed from by qualified experts? Which need further testing and/or reformulation? Which represent cumulative, consistent observations?

In order to avoid an almost infinite list of propositions based on indiscriminate choice, criteria are required. Williams . . . suggests three: (1) those of potential importance for understanding social conflict and for application to policy problems; (2) those which offer the most promise of fruitfully guiding empirical research; and (3) those of most probable validity. These criteria direct initial attention to propositions which are of sufficient generality to provide a framework for more particular propositions (lower order of generality), which highlight the necessary and sufficient causes of social conflict, which provide a basis for linking different kinds of social conflict (e.g., industrial and international), and which can be ordered into a theory having explanatory and predictive power.

Some examples (paraphrased) drawn from the literature will illustrate, omitting for the moment the question of verification and qualification:

PROPOSITION 1: *Intragroup harmony tends to reduce intergroup friction* (industrial relations). . . .

PROPOSITION 2: *Certain personality characteristics germane to particular national groups are conflict-instigating* (international relations). . . .

PROPOSITION 3: *The more totalitarian a group, organization, or society, the greater the likelihood that its leaders will be aggressive* (general). . . .

PROPOSITION 4: *The more compartmentalized and restricted are the claims of a particular faith to define and regulate religious values, the less likely is religious group membership to be divisive* (religious conflict). . . .

PROPOSITION 5: *The more fixed the size of the "pie" to be divided, the more intense the conflict* (industrial relations). . . .

PROPOSITION 6: *Violence is more likely when a minority group is not content to accept the designation of low rank by majority groups and when it attempts to redefine the situation to permit its assimilation or equal ranking* (racial conflict). . . .

PROPOSITION 7: *The main source of persistence of intergroup hostility is the interlocking and mutual reinforcement of realistic and unrealistic conflict elements* (general). . . .

PROPOSITION 8: *As unions gain power, the duration of strikes decreases* (industrial relations). . . .

PROPOSITION 9: *Conflict with outgroups increases internal cohesion* (general). . . .

PROPOSITION 10: *Warlike attitudes may be expressions of deep-lying personality factors laid down in child-rearing* (international relations). . . .

PROPOSITION 11: *If the power of two parties is not grossly unequal, agreement is more likely when both are least rigid in their positions* (industrial and international relations). . . .

PROPOSITION 12: *The major source of international tension resides between, rather than within, nations* (international relations). . . .

PROPOSITION 13: *Far from being necessarily dysfunctional, a certain degree of conflict is an essential element in group formation and the persistence of group life* (general). . . .

PROPOSITION 14: *Religious conflict persists because of the need to preserve or protect one's power position* (religious conflict). . . .

PROPOSITION 15: *Conflict between groups becomes institutionalized* (general). . . .

These fifteen propositions, drawn more or less randomly from a larger sample, differ markedly from one another. Nevertheless, they are all focused on social conflict, and, to the extent that they are sustained by adequate evidence, they are not trivial. On the other hand, if the list were increased tenfold, the resulting revelation would be counterbalanced by an impression of confusion and incompleteness. For as soon as the process of ordering and evaluating the propositions began, it would be noticed that no explicit scheme of classification is present beyond the mere reference to the social conflict arena to which each was originally applied, that essential terms are undefined, and that the conditions under which the various propositions are alleged to hold true are not specified. Also the crucial question of relevant, acceptable, and sufficient evidence of proof or disproof is ignored. It is our contention that these problems, together with the application of Williams' criteria, are not susceptible of self-evident solutions. Propositions stated as they are above are literally imbedded in an invisible context.

There are, of course, a number of classification devices which might be employed, among them . . . the one implied by the identifications in parentheses following each proposition above (industrial, racial, religious, etc.). Williams classifies his propositions roughly according to conflict types, sources, and responses. [A] UNESCO study . . . discusses research findings in terms of two broad classes of approaches—the sociological and the psychological. However, there may be advantages in considering a somewhat different kind of classificatory scheme. One advantage is that of juxtaposing propositions drawn from observations in different areas of social conflict. If certain propositions on, say, industrial relations and international relations remain in completely separate categories, possible connections (logical and empirical) may be overlooked. Or if aspects of conflict analysis are not distinguished, propositions cannot be ordered and examined effectively.

Classification is one problem. Another is definition. Proposition 7, for example, hinges significantly on the respective definitions of realistic and unrealistic conflict. In Proposition 11, what does "power of two parties" actually mean? What is involved in the institutionalization of conflict as stated in Proposition 15? Does conflict itself have a common meaning throughout? Still another problem is the condition under which the propositions hold true. One implication of Proposition 4 is that persons of certain faiths may have a minimal involvement in their religion and that they may share non-religious values with others whose religious values conflict with their own, offsetting religious-value conflict. Proposition 2 seems to imply either that citizens exert a great deal of influence on war decisions or that policy-makers all share certain general personality characteristics.

Propositions must also be compared and related to one another. Often propositions are flatly contradictory—or so it seems. Two pairs of examples drawn from international and religious conflict will illustrate:

PROPOSITION 16: *Ideational and symbological conflicts are more important than economic or political conflicts in straining international relations. . . .*

PROPOSITION 17: *Change in the relative power position of nations is the source of tension leading to conflict. . . .*

PROPOSITION 18: *Religious intergroup conflict is most likely to develop when there are no cross-pressures at work within the individual. . . .*

PROPOSITION 19: *Intensity of positions taken in religious conflict is a function of guilt and insecurity feelings over having taken such positions. . . .*

Obviously, sufficient pertinent data would be needed to judge the relative validity of these competing propositions or to reconcile them. But, more than that, it would be necessary to probe the fundamental nature of conflict as well as types of conflict and conflict situations.

Knowledge is advanced by linking propositions. Here are three propositions which may be integrated into a more inclusive one:

PROPOSITION 20: *Social conflicts are primarily realistic conflicts of power. . . .*

PROPOSITION 14: *Religious conflict persists because of the need to preserve or protect one's power position. . . .*

PROPOSITION 17: *Change in the relative power position of nations is the source of tension leading to conflict. . . .*

PROPOSITION 21 (combining 20, 14, 17): *Social conflict is normally accompanied by a felt or actual discrepancy in the power relations of the parties.*

Many of the propositions which are current in the literature of a particular field ought to be analyzed to discover whether in fact, they have greater generality. . . . Take these propositions:

PROPOSITION 22: *If an adversary's strength could be measured prior to engagement in conflict, antagonistic interests might be adjusted without conflict.*

Does this apply to *all* kinds of social conflict?

PROPOSITION 23: *Misunderstandings and misuse of words often contribute to lessening conflict between labor and management. . . .*

If this is true, and, to the extent that it is true, would it hold for international conflict? Again it should be emphasized that more than empirical data is needed to answer these questions. Some way of putting industrial and international conflict on a comparable basis for the purposes at hand is also required.

THE PROBLEM OF CONCEPTUALIZATION AND CHOICES OF MAJOR VARIABLES

Having argued that the classification, ordering, and evaluation of basic propositions require prior intellectual operations, we shall now explore a tentative framework of analysis which might aid in these pursuits.

Definitions and Distinctions

Unless the phenomena denoted by the term "conflict" are limited and differentiated, the concept becomes too inclusive. On the whole, it is easier to begin by specifying what is not considered to be conflict. A review of the literature reveals certain distinctions which are apparently agreed upon or at least commonly made. *Competition* is not regarded as conflict or a form of conflict, though it may be an important source of the latter. . . . Competition involves striving for scarce objects (a prize or a resource usually "awarded" by a third party) according to established rules which strictly limit what the competitors can do to each other in the course of striving; the chief objective is the scarce object, not the injury or destruction of an opponent per se. A football game played normally according to the rules is competition *until* one or more players begin to assault one another in a manner forbidden by the rules; then it becomes a conflict.

Though closely related to conflict, the following are also considered differentiable: *antagonistic interests* . . . ; *misunderstandings* . . . ; *aggressiveness* . . .; *hostility or hostile sentiments* . . . ; *desire or intention to oppose* . . . ; *social cleavages* (e.g., along class lines) . . . ; *logical irreconcilability of goals or interests* . . . ; *tensions* . . . ; and *rivalry*. . . . The attitudes, behaviors, and states of affairs signified by these terms *may* be among the underlying sources of conflict. Or such factors *may* accompany or intensify conflict. But it seems generally agreed that none of the terms is a proper synonym for conflict, nor are the factors denoted singly or in combination sufficient preconditions of social conflict. However, there is no general agreement as to whether any one or more is a necessary precondition for conflict to arise or continue. On the other hand, the potential relevance of the factors is clear. These problems can be clarified by confronting the nature, sources, and conditions of conflict.

Properties of Conflictful Behaviors and Conflict Relationships

We shall not attempt a formal definition of conflict. Rather, a set of properties will be suggested which *in toto* will constitute a model for identifying and characterizing conflict phenomena and situations. Without claiming to be exhaustive, we shall insist that the essential elements are included and that conflict does not exist if the empirical conditions implied by properties 1–5 are not present. . . .

1. *Conflict requires at least two parties or two analytically distinct units or entities* (i.e., actor, organism, group, individual, collectivity, etc.).
   a) Social conflict is, by definition, an interaction relationship between two or more parties.
   b) One-party conflict (intrapersonal or individual conflict) may be viewed as *either* individual-environment or actor-nature conflict (in which case the parties may be human and non-human entities), *or* the individual in conflict with himself (conflict of two or more needs and values).
   c) "Games against nature" as provided in some formulations of game theory can be regarded as social conflict, but other forms of one-party conflict can be regarded as socially significant non-social conflict.
   d) A minimum "contact" (not necessarily face-to-face) and "visibility" are implied. . . .
2. *Conflict arises from "position scarcity" and "resource scarcity."* . . .
   a) Position scarcity is a condition in which an object cannot occupy two places at the same time, an object

cannot simultaneously serve two different functions, a role cannot be simultaneously occupied or performed by two or more actors, and different prescribed behaviors cannot be carried out simultaneously.

b) Resource scarcity is a condition in which the supply of desired objects (or states of affairs) is limited so that parties cannot have *all* they want of anything.

c) Different underlying value judgments may condition the demand or need for scarce resources and positions.

d) Hence mutually exclusive and/or mutually incompatible values and opposed values are inevitable characteristics of conflict.

3. *Conflictful behaviors are those designed to destroy, injure, thwart, or otherwise control another party or other parties, and a conflict relationship is one in which the parties can gain (relatively) only at each other's expense. . . .*

a) The key is the intent of action and the object of action.

b) Gains for one party result either from a net loss to the other party or from one party's having less of what he wants than he would have had in the absence of opposition.

c) Many tactics and techniques may be manifest in conflictful behaviors which are not necessarily always identified with conflict per se.

d) Expressive behaviors, such as anger, hostility, shouting, aggressiveness, may or may not accompany conflictful behavior.

4. *Conflict requires interaction among parties in which actions and counteractions are mutually opposed. . . .*

a) Conflict cannot exist without action.

b) The action-reaction-action sequence must embody the pursuit of exclusive or incompatible values.

c) Threats are actions.

5. *Conflict relations always involve attempts to gain control of scarce resources and positions or to influence behavior in certain directions; hence a conflict relationship always involves the attempt to acquire or exercise power or the actual acquisition of power. . . .*

a) Power is defined as control over decisions (i.e., disposition of scarce resources and positions) and as the basis of reciprocal influence between or among parties (i.e., control over behaviors).

b) Conflict reflects power strains (i.e., the need or desire to achieve or change control), and opposed actions are directed to changing or preserving existing power relations (i.e., control over objects and behaviors).

6. *Conflict relations constitute a fundamental social-interaction process having important consequences. . . .*

a) Conflict is not a breakdown or cessation of social interaction.

b) The conflict process has important functions for the parties and for the larger social system of which it is a part.

c) Conflict has a cost dimension.

7. *A conflict process or relation represents a temporary tendency toward disjunction in the interaction flow between parties. . . .*

a) Disjunction results from the presence of mutually incompatible tendencies which disrupt the normal or persistent patterns of behavior, norms, and expectations of the parties and their responses to each other.

8. *Conflict relations do not represent a breakdown in regulated conduct but rather a shift in the governing norms and expectations.*

a) Disjunctive tendencies do not continue to the point where the interaction is completely disrupted because the conflict is subject to its own rules and limits.

. . . Thus far we have indicated that there must be *parties* and *a particular kind of interactional relationship between parties*. But there are kinds and forms of conflict relations; there are sources of conflict; various conditions affect the nature and duration of conflict; conflict has certain functions or consequences; and, finally, conflict always occurs in an environmental context which transcends the conflict relationship itself.

Types of Conflict

We shall mention some major distinctions only briefly. One obvious distinction is implied in Postulate 1: conflict *within* persons (intraparty) and conflict *between* persons or groups. Both meet the criteria set forth, and respective analogies can be pursued usefully. For example, persons undergoing psychotic conflict can quite literally destroy themselves. . . . Perhaps the most significant question is the impact of intrapersonal conflict on social conflict. . . .

An important and familiar distinction is between *realistic* and *non-realistic* conflict. . . . Realistic conflict is characterized by opposed means and ends, by incompatibility of values and interests. Non-realistic conflict arises from the need for tension release, from deflected hostility, from historical tradition, and from ignorance or error. The two types differ in origin and in the ultimate motivation behind opposed action. In realistic conflict, wants and needs seem to be, or become, incompatible because of other factors, that is, resource and position scarcity. But non-realistic conflict, for example, would be continued opposed action between nations whose actual conflicting interests had long since been reconciled. Propositions 2 and 16, listed above, clearly are based on the alleged existence of much non-realistic conflict among nations. Proposition 7 states a relation between the two types—an important generalization which might be lost in the absence of the distinction. . . .

An implicit distinction is usually drawn between *institutionalized* and *non-institutionalized* conflict. The former is characterized by explicit rules, predictable behavior, and continuity, as in the case of collective bargaining. Most racial conflict is, on the other hand, non-institutionalized. *Disorganized* conflict, as in the case of a riot, . . . may take place within an institutional framework or not, the former being illustrated by an unauthorized, partially supported strike. Organized conflict, such as a war between armies, is obviously different from a spontaneous border clash between irregular armed units. *Extreme* . . . , *aggressive* . . . , and *violent* . . . conflict are also differentiated from *nonviolent, "diplomatic"* conflict—chiefly on the basis of coercive means versus persuasive means and on the assumption that, in the former, destruction or crippling of one of the parties is highly possible.

It appears useful to separate *primary, face-to-face conflicts* from *secondary, mediated conflicts*. Generally speaking, the rank and file of labor and the rank and file of management do not face each other in a conflict relation. Rather, chosen representatives speak for well-organized collectivities. On the other hand, in a town meeting or a legislature or in racial or ethnic contacts, conflict relations are, for the most part, direct. Closely related is another set of opposite types: *personal subjective conflict* and *impersonal objective* conflict. A conflict between husband and wife would fit the first category, and a conflict between two lawyers, each representing a client, would fit the second. A difference between *conflicts of right* and *conflicts of interest* may be noted. A conflict or right concerns the application of agreed standards to specified actions; a conflict of interest concerns the changing of old standards or the introduction of new standards—roughly, the distinction is between judicial and legislative conflict. This distinction applies to industrial, international, racial, and ethnic conflict.

Opposed values have been specified as inevitable concomitants of conflict, but any preliminary typology should include mention of types of conflict which are predominantly value conflicts per se. *Ideological conflict* is characterized by a clash of "conceptions of the desirable" . . . and prescriptive norms and beliefs which do or should govern particular behaviors. For purposes of this analysis, ideologies can be classified as relatively open and relatively closed in terms of the extent to which alien or opposed values and belief can or will be accommodated or absorbed. Ideological conflict can be further classified according to the significance of the clash of absolute values, i.e., no "higher values" exist to mediate "lower values," and thus one set must triumph, or there must be benevolent neutrality. Conflict of religious dogmas exemplifies this, as well as certain political ideologies. Religious conflict is likely to be intense where conversion from one faith to another is required or where one faith regards another as "infidel"; but the same would hold true of non-religious ideologies.

Cultural conflict is a term used so broadly that it often includes all other types and even subsumes "social." Presumably, of course, conflicts between cultures, depending on the nature of the contacts, might well include conflicting ideologies, religions, interests, rights, and all the other types suggested above. A breakdown of cultural conflict into component elements, then, would be facilitated by a typology and by the basic conceptualization of conflict. . . . Initial contacts between races and cultures are essentially biological. . . . At this stage, conflict is biological in the sense that the two parties do not regard each other as human; no common moral order prevails to restrain conduct or otherwise regulate behavior. It seems likely in view of wide differences in the circumstances under which racial and cultural contacts lead to intermarriage and general acculturation that there is a primitive psychological factor at work too. At any rate, the analysis of contemporary conflict between races and cultures ought to recognize the fundamental importance of initial psychobiological contacts and the persistent attitudes which they generate. . . .

. . .

Underlying Sources of Conflict

Properties 1–5 set forth above may be viewed as a set of analytic preconditions of conflict, but, as formulated, they say nothing about the empirical content in particular cases. For example, position and resource scarcity is one of the necessary preconditions of conflict; yet we have to look elsewhere for the factors which produce, or account for, a specific pattern of scarcity. Underlying sources are those empirical phenomena which may result in the existence of the five preconditions of conflict. Perhaps the line between sources and preconditions will seem arbitrary and difficult to draw. The distinction seems required, nonetheless, because the presence or persistence of underlying source factors does not necessarily mean that conflict, as defined, will arise. An observer is often embarrassed to discover that conflict does not arise despite the apparent indication of important source factors effectively at work in the social situation. Or conflict may arise in the absence of certain source factors. If the parties cannot "reach" each other by opposed action or if initiative is not assumed by at least one of the parties, a conflict interaction is impossible. Conversely, the decisions of one or more parties may, in effect, define a position or resource scarcity which an observer would find did not exist by his objective standards.

Most social scientists now accept the principle of multiple causality; hence there is no one basic source of conflict. . . . So far as particular areas of conflict are concerned, underlying sources have been rather thoroughly catalogued. It is fairly easy merely to list the most significant sources of, say, war. . . . The central problem is, of course, to determine the particular combination of underlying source factors in a given situation which does result in the analytic preconditions. In general, the catalogues of conflict sources which are available do not, for the most part, provide the observer with more than a list of alternative possibilities which he would want to explore in any single instance. Above all, there is little guidance as to patterns of combination which produce conflict and to the conditions under which they are formed. The latter point suggests that difficulties are further compounded because the combination of sources and the translation of these into the preconditions may be influenced by non-source factors, which is one reason why we shall discuss conditions of conflict in the next section.

Emphasis on the sources of conflict has not been due solely to the scientist's attempt to answer the question of why conflict arises. Because of preoccupation with conflict as a costly social problem, sources are natural foci for reforms and changes which will supposedly reduce or eliminate conflict. If the source of conflict is a psychological state called "tension," tension reduction is an indicated strategy. If the source is ignorance, as in the case of some non-realistic conflict, education will eliminate or minimize the "cause" of such conflict. And so on. Now here is impressive evidence that a direct approach to the removal or adaptation of sources per se is not necessarily an effective way to curb conflict. . . . Race itself may not be the "proper first object" of concern in controlling racial conflict; . . . the key may be in the behavioral patterns exhibited in the *generic* phenomena of conflict—which means putting racial conflict in a broader framework of the sort being outlined here. . . .

While it is true that the specific sources of, say, industrial conflict and international conflict are quite different, it is also true that generalized sources and types of sources may be identified. A generalized source is one which is not peculiar to any one arena or kind of conflict. Insofar as "tensions" are, in fact, a source of conflict, they may be either general personality conditions which can be focused on a range of particular situations, or they can be closely connected with only certain interaction relationships. Tensions between unions and managements may arise from the shrinking pie to be divided between them, or tensions from other sources may induce the demands which are made upon the existing pie. Presumably, the latter might also be expressed in ethnic or religious or other intergroup confiict. The search for underlying sources in the first case carries one only as far as the size of the pie; in the second, it requires a much wider range of inquiry. Two qestions arise. First, how deep should the search for underlying factors (this usually involves personality dynamies) be pushed? Second, are there certain basic motive patterns or facts of social life which might serve to account partially for a variety of conflict relations? Some explanations of conflict are based on the alleged consequences of what might be called "psychoanalytic mechanisms," such as Proposition 1 cited earlier. . . . Some are somewhat closer to the surface, as it were, being rooted in psychological variables, such as inferiority feelings or hostility and the like. . . . Still others are more sociological in nature, i.e., discontents over income, job conditions. . . . More or less in accord with these three levels of sources, two writers . . . have asserted that three primary motives underlie intergroup conflict: (*a*) desire for acquisition of scarce values (political or power conflict); (*b*) desire to convert others (ideological conflict); and (*c*) desire to prevent contact with inferiors (racist conflict). On the surface at least, there is no common agreement on the first question, namely, Should the search for source factors be pushed to the psychoanalytic level? But the lack of agreement is due partly to the failure to make consistent distinctions among types of, and parties to, conflict and to link sources explicitly with conditions and contexts. Furthermore, the problem of psychological and sociological levels of explanation should not obscure an integrative question: Under what social conditions do psychological mechanisms operate as sources of conflict?

On the second question, it seems generally agreed that scarcity of desired objects, states of affairs, and resources in nature and culture, the division of labor in organized society, and social differentiation lead inevitably to potentially conflictful cleavages and antagonistic interests. It is (or seems to be) further agreed that these factors, as well as more deeply psychological ones, contribute to a reservoir of "free-floating" aggression, hostility, and tension which, in turn, *may* lead to conflictful behaviors. This is illustrated by the mechanisms of projection and displacement which may be focused on any object or group (industrial, international, ethnic, etc.) in a conflict situation. Hence two general categories of sources emerge: those centering on interactional relationships, e.g., a conflict over land between cattle grazers, and those centering on certain internal characteristics of parties or intrapersonal (personality dynamics) factors, e.g., the frustration-aggression hypothesis. Propositions embodying explanations for the rise of conflict, which can be grouped according to these two categories, will be discussed in the next two sections. One utility of the distinction between realistic and non-realistic conflict now becomes clear. Realistic conflicts are presumed to have their origin primarily in interactional factors; non-realistic conflicts are presumed to be accountable for primarily in terms of non-interactional factors. Thus industrial conflict is inherent in the institutional situation in which labor and management interact: both cannot make the same decisions separately, their roles give rise to different values, total income from a given business is limited and cannot satisfy maximum demands by each side, and so on. . . . Religious conflict, in contrast, is inherent in the private nature of religious experience, in the nature of religious values as substitutes for other social values, and in the manner of transmission of religious beliefs. . . .

Concern over the origins of conflict draws attention to potential responses to conflict situations and to the decisions which result in moving from a desire to oppose to acts of opposition. In ascertaining why some situations lead to actual conflict interaction while others do not, it is necessary to identify certain crucial foci of analysis. Responses or decisions may result in the origination of conflict interaction, in withdrawal from a potential conflict situation, in a change from non-violent or extreme conflict, or in accommodation to a stable conflict relationship. These outcomes, more often than not, depend on choices. Therefore, the conditions which affect such choices must be probed, and similar cases which have different outcomes must be compared. Two possible foci will be mentioned here. First, in the case of secondary, mediated intergroup conflict. Deutsch's decision-making and communications approach would seem particularly useful. His approach suggests, for example, that a central question concerning the outbreak of war is: Under what conditions do foreign policy-makers decide, in effect, that all viable alternatives have been reduced to one? Is it possible to identify a "point of no return" in a conflict relation progressing toward war? What effect do the nature, flow, and interpretation of information have on the foreclosure of alternatives? Analyzing war decisions along these lines represents a much more fundamental approach than the listing of causes of war or the attribution of single, overpowering motives to nations. A second focus of analysis is more appropriate for individual responses to primary, immediated intergroup conflict. One lead is supplied by the cross-pressures hypothesis (Proposition 18), which indicates that conflict potential is dampened if individuals are pulled in opposite directions by their group affiliations or incompatible values. On the other hand, one of two contradictory pulls may triumph over the other. Thus Brown's approach-avoidance analysis may yield some hypotheses regarding the circumstances under which conflicting stimuli will produce either of two responses. . . . Individuals are not necessarily prevented from discriminatory acts against minorities by their religious values which prescribe the Golden Rule. Clearly, in this situation the minority member does not represent an ambigious stimulus—as would be true if the discriminatory individual saw him as both an undesirable inferior and a human being deserving of equal treatment. The converse of the cross-pressures hypothesis is that group conflicts are more likely to develop and to be intense when there is no conflict within the individual. Basically, in this situation the stimulus is unambiguous, and the "approach" response tendency is the stronger.

It is noteworthy that these two general approaches—and there are others which focus on decisions and responses—require simultaneous attention to psychological and sociological variables. The behavior of decision-makers is to be viewed as a resultant of such factors as individual perceptions and institutionalized information flows. The behavior of individuals responding to conflict or possible conflict is to be viewed as a resultant of competitory response tendencies and the nature of stimuli in the social environment.

Conditions of Conflict

The main reason for analyzing the accompanying conditions of conflict separately is that particular sources which result in the analytic preconditions do not account for the origin, form, intensity, duration, reduction, or resolution of conflict. This can be demonstrated by Dahlke's . . . analysis of race riots, which, he argues, are highly probable when (*a*) the period is one of change and mobility; (*b*) the minority group has an outstanding trait or characteristic which can become a basis for negative assessments; (*c*) lawful authorities assign the minority group a subordinate status; (*d*) one or more associations or organizations direct the attack against the minority; (*e*) the press and other media have been minority-baiting; and (*f*) suitable personnel (students and marginal workers) are available for initiating action.

Clearly, the notion of conditions opens up a wide range of relevant factors. In calling attention to the analytic separation of these factors, we mean only to say that certain elements inherent in the nature of parties to conflict, in the interaction relationships between parties, and in the social context will often account for the origin, form, intensity, duration, limits, and resolution of conflict. Conditions are not, then, a special category of factors but a way of viewing the impact of the elements to be discussed in succceeding sections.

To illustrate in a preliminary fashion, we list sample propositions:

PROPOSITION 24: *Mediation increases the possibility of resolving conflict when parties are small. . . .*

PROPOSITION 25: *Realistic conflict need not be accompanied by hostility and aggressiveness. . . .*

PROPOSITION 26: *It is more difficult to mediate controversy where costs of aggressive conflict are high. . . .*

PROPOSITION 27: *Social conflict cannot be integrative and functional in the absence of community. . . .*

PROPOSITION 28: *Ideological conflict is more intense and the parties thereto are more intransigent because of objectification of issues and lack of inhibitions on personal attacks. . . .*

PROPOSITION 29: *A high degree of intimacy between the parties, as contrasted with a high degree of functional interdependence, will intensify conflict. . . .*

In addition, two other conditioning factors are of importance. Our specification of the essential properties of conflict relations stressed the power component. To the extent that conflict is over the nature of the respective roles of the parties in decision-making with respect to mutual interests, the form, intensity, and duration of the conflict will depend on the length of time it takes to test the power relationship conclusively and the means available to each party for exerting control. Intensity will also be affected by the cruciality of the decision-making functions at issue. A long war, a long strike, or a long bargaining period may indicate roughly an equal power equation or the failure to find adequate indexes of power. Another condition of great importance is the amount of information available to, and interpreted correctly by, the parties to conflict. . . .

The Social Context of Conflict

The conditions discussed above were those primarily confined to the parties and to their relationship. However, it is axiomatic that conflict occurs in, affects, and in turn is affected by, a surrounding environment. Conflict must be researched and analyzed against the background of the total social system in which it occurs. . . .

Social change affects conflict in a number of ways. Changes are constantly shifting the bases of potentially antagonistic interests and the relative power positions of individuals and groups. As the value potentiality of the social environment shifts, new demands, new frustrations, and new incompatibilities arise. Population growth, invention, urbanization, mobility—indeed, all the changes which result in and are resultants of greater social complexity—affect the sources of conflict, the nature and number of parties to conflict, the instrumentalities of conflict, the issues of conflict, modes of settlement, and so on. . . . The same general point applies to international conflict, which has its own social context:

PROPOSITION 30: *Important alternations in the balance of forces as between societies occur as a result of profound changes internal to one or more societies. . . .*

Social organization will determine the number and kinds of parties to conflict within any society. In a complex industrial urban society realistic conflict will tend to be carried on by highly organized groups having diverse memberships and specialized representatives and negotiators. In a less complex communal society, there will tend to be more direct, face-to-face interpersonal conflict. Social differentiation (status, occupational roles, power positions, etc.) will tend to define lines of consensus and cleavage. . . . In a recent book, *Race and Culture Contacts in the Modern World,* Frazier organizes his analysis around the ecological, economic, political, and social organization. The impact of the social context on racial conflict is clearly shown. For example, economic racial conflict does not arise where the division of labor is based on objective standards of competitive success. . . . Whyte's study, *Pattern for Industrial Peace,* is concerned with a more immediate context of conflict: the relation between company structure and labor-management relations. Changes in organization are correlated with three stages of development: from disorganized conflict to organized conflict to organized co-operation.

Interinstitutional strain, as in the case of religious and political institutions in the United States, may create intrapersonal conflict (religious versus secular values) and/or intergroup conflict over such issues as public aid to parochial schools. . . . Coser . . .and Williams . . . have argued that a "loosely organized society" with many crisscrossing pressures and influences on individuals and groups reduces the possibility of single, rigid, and intense conflicts which divide the whole society or a large segment of it and also provides stability despite extensive conflict. Thus a multiplicity of potential or actual conflict situations, combined with shared values which cut across lines of cleavage, prevents any one conflict situation or kind of conflict (e.g., religious) from dominating the relations of sizable groups and large numbers of individuals. Closely related to this is Simmel's notion of safety-valve institutions which channel hostility and drain off residual conflict responses. . . .

This suggests another significant aspect of the social context of conflict. Normally, no matter how serious a conflict exists between particular groups and individuals, there will always be *disinterested or neutral,* but nonetheless affected, outsiders (or, indirectly, "third" parties). If conflict completely divides a local, national, or international community, which means in effect that there are no outsiders, solutions become very difficult indeed. This is partly because there are no available neutral conciliators or mediators and partly because no one has a vested interest in the cessation of conflict. . . . Both labor and management in the United States have been compelled to recognize a "public interest," and one of the functions of the United Nations is to mobilize world-wide pressure on disputants.

The availability and permissibility of the instrumentalities of conflict are obviously dependent on the social environment. Firearms are strictly controlled in most societies as a means for settling interpersonal conflict. In many Latin-American countries military rebellion is a recognized mode of carrying on political conflict. It took many years for the strike to be sanctioned as a proper instrument in industrial conflict. There has been a long history of attempts to establish legitimate and illegitimate uses of war as an instrument of national policy.

One of the major problems of the social order at all levels of society is the control of violent conflict. Hence one of the tasks of public policy, social engineering, and scientific study of human behavior is to determine what kinds of social arrangements are conducive to non-violent conflict. . . .

PROPOSITION 31: *The more integrated into the society are the parties to conflict, the less likely will conflict be violent. . . .*

But, as important as violent conflict is as a basic form or type, the problem is, in fact, much broader. Order and conflict (all types) are persistent states of any social system. While to an extent they are, or appear to be, opposites, both can and must exist side by side. Furthermore, the relationship between them will determine the degree of social stability. Basically, the stability-instability balance will be a resultant of the success or failure of the normative order in regulating conflicts of interest. . . . Conflict induces a constant pressure of factual situations on the normative order. In turn, conflict is in some manner controlled by social norms. As already remarked, social change—its rate and direction—is an ultimate source of conflict because, as the factual social order undergoes transition, new incompatibilities and antagonistic interests arise. The relevant regulatory norms either will accommodate (permit) acceptable "solutions" or will be modified (or perhaps consistently violated) to take account of the actual power relations between the parties.

If we are interested in generalizing propositions about social conflict from one area of behavior to another, it is obviously necessary to compare relevant social contexts. . . . To the extent that the social environments of industrial and international conflict differ, *some* propositions will not hold for both. For example, it is unclear whether the international social environment has yet produced a reservoir of mediators and conciliators such as exist in most complex industrial societies. Perhaps one of the reasons that the propositions from racial and ethnic intergroup conflict do not apply to religious conflict is that the social context even in a single society is different. Thus far in the United States, for example, there has been clear separation between religious and political institutions (church and state), while racial and ethnic factors permeate family, educational, economic, and political institutions.

The Functions of Conflict

Since preoccupation with conflict often centers on its most violent, abhorrent, and socially costly forms, it is likely that the average reader will regard *all* conflict as universally bad. Proposition 13, listed above, boldly states the contrary view. There is no way of evaluating this proposition unless the function and consequences of conflict are systematically examined. It is noteworthy that most contemporary social scientists lay stress on the constructive consequences of conflict relations. . . . Coser has summarized sociological thinking on this point with particular reference to social groups. Dubin's five central propositions . . . constitute a broader thesis: intergroup conflict is a fundamental institutionalized social process which determines the direction of social change and, in effect, defines social welfare. . . .

. . .

PROPOSITION 32: *Conflict sets group boundaries by strengthening group cohesiveness and separateness. . . .*

PROPOSITION 33: *Conflict reduces tension and permits maintenance of social interaction under stress. . . .*

PROPOSITION 34: *Conflict clarifies objectives. . . .*

PROPOSITION 35: *Conflict results in the establishment of group norms. . . .*

PROPOSITION 36: *Without conflict, accommodative relations would result in subordination rather than agreement. . . .*

The foregoing is a brief reminder that there are important positive social functions served by conflict. Evidence discussed by writers in support of Propositions 32–36 would tend to support the more general Proposition 13 presented earlier. This perspective does not, of course, imply that conflict is not often dysfunctional and very costly. One of the most difficult problems in conflict analysis is to arrive at a method for determining the dividing line between constructive functions and dysfunctions. Clearly, the question of the cost of social conflict involves different relevant criteria. It may seem a macabre joke to emphasize the constructive consequences of conflict in an age of nuclear weapons. . . . On the other hand, no scholar, reformer, critic, or politician has ever denied that conflict is an all-pervasive fact of human life, nor does anyone deny that society persists in spite of violent and costly conflict. As a matter of fact, the functional and dysfunctional aspects of conflict are opposite sides of the same coin.

As a crude first approximation to a meaningful distinction, it might be suggested that conflict is, *on balance*, dysfunctional to the extent that its positive functions are impaired or neutralized under certain conditions. For example, the normal course of a realistic conflict may under some circumstances generate, instead of relieve, hostility or tension. Indeed, a realistic conflict may be transformed into a nonrealistic conflict, which may, in turn, undermine institutionalized modes of resolving realistic conflict and also raise costs far beyond what is proportionate to any advantages accruing to the parties or affected bystanders. A long strike which results in obscuring objectives, in an almost total breakdown of interaction and mutual dependence, in hostility which becomes unrelated to the goals of the parties, and in confusion of actual power relations is dysfunctional and wasteful. Functional conflict encourages collaboration and a more efficient division of labor between parties because of heightened consciousness of purpose and strengthening of positions taken. It is one of the characteristics of dysfunctional conflict that it is difficult to say, as time goes on, what the conflict is about.

Violence at the international level is often accompanied by a tragic lack of reliable knowledge about the objectives and power potentials of the respective contenders and by inadequacy of machinery through which the positive functions of conflict can be realized. In terms of the whole thesis being developed here, the most abhorrent and costly social conflicts should be viewed not as abrupt breaks in "order" and "co-operation" but as transitions or abrupt shifts from one kind of conflict relationship to another. However, it is quite likely that predominantly dysfunctional conflict will lead to a cessation of interaction at some point.

While socially useful and socially undesirable consequences of conflict can and should be kept separate, it is probably true that they go together. From some vantage points at least, it is difficult to imagine any conflict having only one kind of consequence. Therefore, part of the problem of differentiation of the functional and dysfunctional aspects of conflict is the identification of conditions under which dysfunctional consequences can be minimized. A fundamental research question is, then, How and why do the dysfunctional consequences come to predominate?

Summary

Though the framework for conflict analysis outlined so far has centered on the concept, types, sources, conditions, context, and functions of conflict, it is clear from the brief comment and propositions that such aspects cannot be discussed without mentioning the connection between relevant party characteristics and the conflict relationship, the nature of conflict interaction itself, and the problem of conflict resolution and control. We shall therefore develop the framework one step further in the next two sections by considering two major foci of conflict analysis—party characteristics and interaction. . . .

THE PARTIES TO CONFLICT: IMPLICATIONS OF NATURE, NUMBER, AND INTERNAL CHARACTERISTICS

The term "party" here will be taken to include individual actors, culture, coalition, social class, personality, nation, organization, organism, system, or group. Party refers to analytic units, regardless of level of generality, *between* which, or in some cases *within* which, conflict takes place. It is assumed that each of these unit types may be viewed operationally as an abstraction of certain observable tendencies and actions of persons and of certain relationships.

Identification and Establishment

This raises the question of identification, which often is not self-evident or given in the particular situation. At the same time, we have proposed that one of the preconditions of a conflict relationship is visibility of parties to each other. Logically, this implies that if the parties are *not subjectively* identifiable, conflict, as defined, cannot exist, though potentially it may be likely if and when identification does take place. It is one of the notable caprices of social conflict that parties may be misidentified, i.e., and individual or group may be *assumed* to be the opponent in a clash of mutually incompatible goals or values when objectively such is not the case at all. As a matter of fact, one of the major features of a sequence of preconflict-conflict-postconflict actions and reactions may be a process of establishing visibility and/or changing identifications of parties. Matters are further complicated by the social context, which may include, as noted, bystander or neutral elements which are affected but not technically involved. The line between party and non-party may be a fine one indeed. Sympathy strikes, for example, would seem to be instances of where unions not parties to a particular conflict become, in effect, by their correlated action parties to another (and new) conflict. And, if the sympathy strike occurs in a highly integrated industry, the sympathy strike may actually add a party to the original conflict.

The problem of the identity of parties to conflict is not just a methodological exercise. An observer's identification and the participants' identification may or may not coincide. What may appear to be a realistic conflict between labor and management may, in fact, be what has been called an "induced" conflict, i.e., one between officials on both sides. . . . For example, political party conflict is often the induced kind. Once the distinction is made, its base seems obvious, but the implications are perhaps not so obvious. Not only is diagnosis of the *sources* of such conflicts likely to be in error (or at least incomplete), but the conditions and effective modes of resolution may be quite different. One general hypothesis might be: *Induced conflict is likely to be more intense than realistic conflict because of the coincidence of group and personal values.* A second general hypothesis might be: *Induced conflicts arise more from imbalance or ambiguity of power relations, whereas realistic conflicts arise more from incompatibility of objectives.* A third general hypothesis might be: *Induced conflicts are not readily susceptible to normal mediation procedures.*

In the sphere of international affairs, an observer might argue that, in a given case, governments are the real parties, whereas, subjectively, whole nations may be perceived as parties. Apart from the fact that in the social world it is the latter which really counts, actors in conflict situations attempt to manipulate the nature and number of parties. Diplomats and foreign policy-makers may attempt to *delimit* severely the parties to international conflict by separating the government from the people of a foreign nation: "Our quarrel is not with you but with your leaders." Conversely, governmental leaders may attempt deliberately to *extend* either the number or size of opposing parties by saying to a whole population: "This conflict directly involves your welfare, and you had better restrain your leaders or else." The practice of equating group interests and general welfare represents (among other things) an attempt to enlarge the size or change the constituency of one party. It might be supposed that the enlargement-through-changed-identification tendency, where manifest in a monolithic or highly stratified social context, would cause conflict to spread. The establishment of visible and recognized parties is thus part of the conflict process. The following proposition will illustrate:

PROPOSITION 37: *The early stages of conflict are often carried on with the object of establishing the intergroup nature of conflict. . . .*

A proportionately large number of strikes at the beginning of the organized labor movement supports the conclusion that one of the primary objectives was recognition of the union as a party in industrial conflict. . . . On the other hand, a party to conflict may be created by the search for an "enemy" and by another party—provided, of course, that there is conflictful interaction, once the latter has been found.

Number of Parties

. . .

Actually, little seems to be known about the effect on social conflict of the sheer number of parties. On a common-sense basis it would seem that the larger the number of parties to a conflict, the more complex the power relations and the more ambiguous the incompatibility of values. Several tentative hypotheses may be suggested:

1. *The larger the number of parties, the more difficult it will be to discover a common solution, in which all parties can achieve at least some gain over previous power positions.*
2. *The larger the number of parties, the less intense will be the non-realistic components of the conflict relationship.*
3. *There is a persistent tendency to reduce multiple-party conflict to two-party conflict via coalitions and blocs.*

If one of the functions of conflict is the clarification of goals and the exploration of common aims, this will depend on the distribution of reliable information among parties and the potential existence of an area of value compatibility. An increase in the number of parties enhances the chance of communications failure and reduces the range of alternative solutions acceptable to all parties. On the other hand, a large number of parties will tend to diffuse hostility and antagonism because more outlets or objects are provided. The tendency to reduce the number of parties to conflict is obviously due to the need to make power more effective and to arrive at a clear-cut definition of power relations which is somewhat stable. Diffuse power relations are notoriously unstable. The general hypothesis would be: *Social conflict tends toward bipolarization of power relations and to centralize the bases of effective power. . . .*

Internal Characteristics of Parties

The problem here is a dual one: the determination of relevant characteristics and the linking of these to clearly differentiated units of analysis. If we keep in mind what has been said previously, it is possible to suggest a crude check list of characteristics. Naturally, since it is not at all clear a priori what range of internal characteristics is relevant to particular types of conflict situations, any list must be derived in part from the postulated properties of conflict, in part from hypothesized relationships between characteristics of parties and aspects of conflict, and in part from further empirical investigation. The following dimensions might serve as a point of departure: *motives, values, and attitudes; beliefs, perceptual frameworks, and information; degree of internal organization and intraparty relationships; size; strength; and extraparty factors having internal implications. . . .*

1. It has already been indicated that some observers (for example, Propositions 1, 2, and 10 above) attribute the source of conflict to motivational, value, and attitudinal factors and that other observers have linked these same party characteristics to the conditions of conflict (for example, Proposition 16 above). To take one arena, there are numerous psychoanalytic hypotheses bearing on international conflict and war, . . . of which the following are additional examples:

PROPOSITION 38: *Persons with character disorders have a predilection for public positions, and the public has a predilection for electing such persons. . . .*

PROPOSITION 39: *Intrapersonal conflict between aggressive impulses and socially sanctioned moral norms of behavior leads to projection of aggression on external groups. . . .*

In general, these hypotheses involve a causal connection between personality dynamics or psychological mechanisms operating at the individual actor level and some aspect of intergroup conflict. Individual attitudes or general personality characteristics are cited to account for, say, national policies leading to conflict or a war decision. More specifically, the implications of Brown's analysis of intrapersonal conflict for intergroup conflict are at issue.

We have noted earlier that the broad issue of the desirability of pushing intergroup conflict analysis to this depth of motivation is unsettled. There is agreement, implicitly or explicitly, that conflict should be viewed in the context of the needs, beliefs, perceptions, values, and attitudes of individuals and groups. However, there also seems to be agreement (*a*) that hostility, aggression, or particular personality disorders are not necessarily concomitants of conflict and (*b*) that realistic or objective conflict may itself induce prejudice, unfavorable stereotypes, and hostility. The latter point implies that the relationship between party characteristics and conflict interaction is reciprocal, not unilateral. More than this, not all individual responses are destructive; constructive responses can be conflict-inducing. Thus ethnocentricity may be functional in the sense of being a factor in group survival and cooperation, while at the same time it is a potential source or condition of conflict. Even were such not the case, counterhypotheses to the ones cited are present in the literature:

PROPOSITION 40: *The source of international tension resides between, rather than within, nations. . . .*

PROPOSITION 41: *Belligerents in recent wars have not enjoyed greater sexual, economic, or prestige frustrations, . . .*

nor have they been more viciously manipulated by their leaders than have non-belligerents. . . .

There are two important points to be considered in evaluating or verifying propositions of this kind. First, the nature of the analytic unit which is to be denoted as the party to conflict becomes crucial. Is a nation, as a group, to be thought of in terms of its whole population or only in terms of the officials who act in its behalf? Proposition 2 seems to include all members of a nation, including policy-makers, and hence flies in the face of much evidence that official decisions are the result of rational processes. Proposition 38, on the other hand, hypothesizes a link between personality factors affecting masses of individuals in society and the selection of officials who have "character disorders" which presumably influence national policies. Propositions 2 and 38 both typically assume complete identity or homogeneity of motives, values, attitudes, and perceptions among citizens and between citizens and policy-makers and also ignore the organizational setting in which governmental decisions are made. Now it is perfectly conceivable that rational policy-makers may feel bound to act on the basis of a public opinion, which, in turn, is formed by underlying non-rational or irrational personality factors. Thus the aggressive tendencies of the people as a whole *could* lead to a conflict policy formulated by policy-makers who were not themselves subject to these tendencies. However, this is quite a different proposition.

Similarly, is a labor union, as a party to conflict, to be designated as the entire membership or as the union leaders? Kerr's distinction between real and induced conflict implies that the latter is related to characteristics of union and management officials and not to characteristics of union membership and a company viewed as collectivities. Nor would we expect to apply a psychoanalytic hypothesis concerning individual behavior to a complex organization or a system in Boulding's terminology without the significant qualification that in each case we referred to certain individuals whose behavior was the focus of analysis. It is perfectly permissible to speak of organizational or system goals, ideology, information, and so on, as long as the properties of such entities are not confused with those of individual actors considered as total personalities.

Second, motivation, values, and attitudes as party characteristics must be related to a specific situation, to a particular conflict interaction context. . . . We must do more than specify a psychological mechanism which is unrelated to an objective state of affairs; rather, we must seek emotional predispositions which cause individuals to perceive and react to real conflict situations.

A somewhat different perspective on the relationships between individual characteristics and intergroup relations is offered by Guetzkow in his *Multiple Loyalties: Theoretical Approach to a Problem in International Organization*. . . . One of the basic propositions which emerges from this study is:

PROPOSITION 42: *Citizen loyalty to the nation and citizen loyalty to some kind of supranational organization are not incompatible, provided that the latter is perceived to meet new or independent needs*. . . .

Behind this proposition is a more general one to the effect that multiple loyalties may or may not produce conflict within the individual, thus leading him to withdraw one set of loyalties in favor of another or to be caught in indecisiveness. In a preliminary test of the proposition, Guetzkow used UNESCO survey data and compared multiplists (those citizens with both national and supranational loyalties), patriots (those citizens with exclusive loyalty to the nation), and the alienated (those whose loyalties were primarily supranational). Results were then correlated with such indexes as education, economic status, age, and attitude toward the future. The larger problem being explored here is, of course, the impact of loyalty to one group or set of values on the relations of groups or sets of values. Does loyalty to one preclude loyalty to others? Does loyalty to one group necessarily enhance the possibility of group conflict because multiple loyalties cannot be held by the individual? Guetzkow's thesis appears to represent the positive side to the cross-pressures thesis noted above: cross-pressures mitigate against exclusive loyalties and hence reduce conflict potential; but, to the extent that multiple loyalies can be accommodated, mutually exclusive loyalties to different groups or values need not induce conflict within the individual and may foster intergroup collaboration.

The role of values in conflict analysis can be highlighted by a reminder that value incompatibility is, by definition, an element in conflict. Hence the examination of the respective values (preferred state of affairs, standards of conduct, criteria of choice among goals and actions, etc.) of opposing parties is inescapable. More specifically, ideological and religious conflict should be mentioned in this connection. Very often opposed values can be compromised or partially accommodated, but often they cannot. Ideological conflict may be marked by the fact that a basic value of one party (e.g., freedom of speech in a free society) requires the absolute denial of a basic value of another party (e.g., an official ideology in a totalitarian society). Religious conflict may be marked not only by a clash of ultimate values but by a commitment to conversion of those of different faith. . . . In general, the more inclusive or broader the claim, the less susceptible is the conflict to some form of resolution. The conditions under which religious and other values tend to become inclusive or the conditions under which incompatible value commitments can be held without inducing conflictful behavior are thus extremely important.

2. Propositions 2, 4, 10, and 19 refer to traits shared by so many individual members of a group that the behavior of the group as a whole is alleged to reflect them. But none of them states anything about intraparty relations or the nature and degree of organization among individual members or components. Another dimension of party characteristics concerns these factors. These propositions, two of which have been cited previously, will illustrate:

PROPOSITION 43: *Conflict between the Soviet Union and the United States is to be understood partly in terms of institutional rivalry. . . .*

PROPOSITION 1: *Intragroup harmony and solidarity reduce intergroup friction. . . .*

PROPOSITION 9: *Conflict with outgroups increases internal cohesion. . . .*

PROPOSITION 44: *Conflict between loosely organized groups (i.e., members are only peripherally involved in group activities or loyalty) is less intense. . . .*

PROPOSITION 45: *As organizations become more bureaucratic, nonrealistic conflict decreases, induced conflict increases. . . .*

PROPOSITION 46: *Internal political structures which effectively channel and accommodate discontent are less likely to exhibit external aggressiveness. . . .*

The range of factors suggested is, of course, extensive, even in this small selected set of propositions. Perhaps the most critical point is obvious enough: there is a basic reciprocal functional relationship between the structure and internal dynamics of any group and intergroup conflict interaction. In analyzing these functional relationships, it is once again necessary to bear in mind that propositions will differ, depending on whether we are discussing unorganized individuals as comprising a group, leader-follower, or citizen–policy-maker relations; a heterogeneous political organization; a complex bureaucracy; a total political or social system; or a particular set of institutions. . . . It is difficult to tell whether there is a limited number of strategic aspects of intraparty organization which yield hypotheses of broad generality. At first glance, the existing literature seems to suggest at least three related aspects: (1) degree of internal cohesion and intimacy; (2) degree of centralization of internal control, including group representatives or a bureaucracy; and (3) degree and exclusiveness of commitment to group or organizational values.

Intraparty organization and relations may or may not contribute to either the inducement of conflict or its resolution and control. Familiar propositions fall roughly into two categories—positive and negative. Positive ones are associated with the general view of conflict as a fundamental interaction process which serves needed social functions. Negative ones stress the role of intraparty characteristics in the origin, intensification, and enlargement of conflict. Obviously, this reflects the fact that internal cohesion, centralization of control, and exclusiveness of commitment to group values may be empirically either functional or dysfunctional. On the one hand, for example, all three aspects are functional in the sense that clarification of opposed goals and mobilization of power are facilitated. On the other hand, dysfunctional consequences may follow—needless intensification, enhancement of non-realistic factors, and enlargement of conflict beyond the parties whose interests are really at stake.

What is more important, perhaps, is that the three aspects point to the "management of forces" which conflict requires. The quality of leadership and morale becomes significant in the instigation and maintenance of conflict relations. No analysis of social conflict would be adequate without due attention to leadership as a party characteristic. This is implied at several points in the foregoing scheme, particularly in connection with motivational elements and induced conflict. . . . It would be desirable to formulate a set of leadership roles and role functions and to relate these to types, sources, context, conditions, and consequences of conflict.

One kind of leadership role might be that of the intellectual. Among other things, the intellectual leader is one who uses and creates ideas, and one consequence is to objectify conflict. Earlier we hypothesized that depersonalization or objectification tended to intensify conflict, to neutralize certain limits on modes of resolution. Joining these propositions and assuming each to be true to some extent, we emerge with a general hypothesis: *Effective intellectual leadership tends to intensify social conflict.* Empirical investigation would be required to confirm or refute this statement and to ascertain the conditions under which it holds. . . . It would be interesting to compare conflict situations in which intellectual leadership was present with those in which it was either negligible or absent.

Another relevant internal characteristic of parties to conflict follows naturally from the discussion of management of conflict. . . . Clearly, a conspiratorial group (e.g., the

Communist party) or an organized interest group (e.g., the National Association of Manufacturers) is much more conflict-oriented than is a company like General Motors. One would expect that the former types would pay much more attention to the "management of forces" and to the relationship between internal organization and conflict interaction. In general, it might be expected that the more central conflict is to the operations of a group or organization, the more highly developed will be the techniques of conflict waging. For groups and organizations whose missions are not primarily conflict-directed, conflict avoidance or quicker resolution might be expected.

3. The size and strength of parties are two further dimensions. Implications of these gross variables may be in some sense obvious, but propositions embodying them are much less numerous. A well-known relationship between party size and conflict has been observed in the case of interethnic and interracial opposition. In general, it is said that, as a minority group increases in size, conflict is intensified or arises in the first instance. Where the Negro population is small relative to whites in southern communities, conflict over segregation is less intense. High intensity seems to be correlated with a 60–40 or near 50–50 ratio, though the exact numerical proportion has not been ascertained. Religious conflict appears less serious or nonexistent where, say, Protestants are almost completely surrounded by Catholics and vice versa. . . . Coser observes that small parties tend to make themselves rigid and inelastic, to withstand pressure toward dissolution, and also tend to absorb the whole individual person in group commitment. . . . Hence smaller groups may engage in more intense conflict relations and may be much more intransigent regarding resolution. The content or issues of conflict may be affected by group size: the larger the group, the lower the common denominator of group goals.

Party strength has several ramifications and is related to a fundamental property of conflict interaction already discussed, namely, the power relation. Paradoxically, the need for and accomplishment of a readjustment of power relations is both a source of conflict . . . and a function of conflict. . . . A further paradox is that in some cases the readjustment of power relations requires, or aims at, the complete destruction or crippling of an opposing party, and, in other cases, the weakening of one of the parties beyond a certain point is a distinct disadvantage to the other. Power is an object of conflict and a conditioner of conflict: relative weaknesses may lead to conflict, and the comparative strength of parties will partially determine the new power relation which emerges from conflict. Previous distinctions will be helpful here, among them the differentiation of institutionalized and non-institutionalized conflict.

In the case of institutionalized conflict where continuity of interaction and regularized rules or expectations are essential, the conflicting parties have a vested interest in each other's strength. . . . There is considerable evidence that industrial conflict has become much more stabilized as unions have grown stronger. Proposition 8 . . . above suggests that, as unions gain power, the duration of strikes is decreased. Furthermore, the enforcement of rules of conduct and mutual obligations which result from conflict interaction depends heavily on a minimum self-control (i.e., power to control internal decisions) by the two parties involved. In the case of non-institutionalized conflict, these considerations probably do not apply. Indeed, it may well be that it is precisely the lack of vested interest in continuity and stability which accounts for the instability and inconclusiveness of much non-institutionalized conflict.

Another facet of the party-strength factor relates to sources of conflict. This is epitomized in the following proposition already mentioned:

PROPOSITION 17: *Changes in the relative power positions of nations are the source of tension leading to international conflict. . . .*

Although applied to phenomena of international conflict, the proposition would appear to apply to most intergroup conflict, except perhaps where groups are unorganized individuals or where conflict is religious in nature. We should also draw a distinction between the recognized and the unrecognized power of groups, that is, a factual change in the power status of one party which is not accepted as a condition of interaction by an opposing party. As noted earlier, the establishment of recognized parties may be the key factor in the initial phase of conflict. Group weakness, on the other hand, may induce conflict where the capacity for enduring frustration of group wants or needs is low. . . .

Obviously, one of the primary conditions of conflict interaction is the respective influence that two parties can bring to bear on each other in the attempt to control outcomes or otherwise direct behavior along intended lines. Factors range from the capacity to endure threatened deprivation to the capacity to inflict damage, from bargaining skill to flexibility of requirements. The central underlying problem is the identification and measurement of the bases of effective reciprocal influence in conflict interaction. More scholarly effort has been expended on the analysis of potential power and on the calculation of gross power factors available to conflicting parties than on the determination of why under particular conditions a bargain is closer to the desired optimum result of one party than the other, or why one party yields more control over joint decision-making to the other. Conflict analysis clearly joins another strategic focus of analysis—social power. Conceivably, the overemphasis on the more dramatic forms of conflict resolution, such as force or financial superiority, has tended to obscure this broader connection. . . .

4. Finally, we come to extraparty factors which affect the links between intraparty characteristics and conflict interaction. The concept of context is once again relevant. Three propositions, drawn from different areas of social conflict, will indicate the general point:

PROPOSITION 18: *Religious intergroup conflict is most likely to develop and to be intense when there are no cross-pressures at work within the individual. . . .*

PROPOSITION 47: *To the extent that workers and unions are integrated into the general society, the propensity to strike is decreased. . . .*

PROPOSITION 48: *The higher the level of prosperity, the less intense the conflict between ethnic and racial majorities and minorities.*

Proposition 18 implies that when individuals are affected by shared values which offset or run counter to religious values which put them into opposition with others, religious conflict will be less likely to develop. For example, the Catholic and Protestant businessmen who share certain goals and prescribed behaviors are less susceptible to conflict on religious grounds than are Catholics and Protestants who do not share these goals and behaviors. Proposition 47 states, in effect, that when parties to industrial conflict are accorded roughly equal status, privileges, and opportunities, there is a tendency to avoid violent conflict. Proposition 48, a very familiar thesis, calls attention to the fact that psychological mechanisms and opposed interests are unlikely under conditions where the majority group does not regard improvement in the status of a minority group as a direct threat to its access to material goods which are becoming scarcer because of a decline in economic activity.

One basic question concerning conflict at the group, society, and international levels is: What social arrangements conduce to non-violent or non-aggressive conflict? On the basis of present evidence, the answer is not at all clear. Another basic question concerns the relations of major social conflicts to one another. Williams . . . has remarked on the canceling-out or non-cumulative incidence of conflict in American society. Coser . . . has alerted us to the significance of the degree of individual involvement in a single conflict group. A hypothesis worth examining might be formulated as follows: *The larger the number of conflicts in any particular context, the less likely that any one will become all-inclusive with respect to persons, groups, energies, and resources.* Wright suggests, on the other hand, that there is a tendency for all international conflict to become total and absolute. Under what conditions is either or both true?

. . .

CONFLICT AS AN INTERACTION SYSTEM

Conflict has been characterized as a basic social-interaction process, and the tendency toward some degree of institutionalization has been noted. The conflict relation has been postulated as existing in a social context and as embodying a power component. Hence it is not a long step to viewing conflict as a system in the general sense employed by Boulding. . . .

Modes of Resolution

There is a variety of methods for resolving or controlling conflict—many more than can be mentioned here. Arbitration, mediation (more often than not used synonymously with conciliation), negotiation, inquiry, legislation, judicial settlement, informal consensus (meeting of minds through discussion), the market, violence or force, authoritative command, and varieties of voting procedures are familiar ones. A range of techniques is implied in the phrase "intergroup therapy": interracial housing, co-operative living experiments, education for tolerance, interfaith movements, and so on. When "bargaining" and "negotiation" are not used in a specific technical sense, . . . these terms apply to many conflict situations. For each mode there are particular types—compulsory versus voluntary arbitration, concilation recommendations which are not binding versus those which are, majority vote versus unanimity, and so on. Essentially, modes may be regarded as a set of rules for handling the need for resolution or accommodation. Different rules produce different results in different situations, and the rules themselves are a frequent conflict issue. Furthermore, some modes are appropriate for some conflict systems and not others. Voting between an equal number of representatives of labor and management would nearly always be indecisive, while arbitration is hardly a suitable mode of settlement for conflict among political parties. . . . Modes of resolution are fundamentally related to the nature of conflict. Evidence indicates that proposed modes of resolution are often inappropriate. Thus no amount of "better understanding through better communication" by itself is going to resolve a genuine power conflict. Mediation cannot function effectively if conflict is between unorganized groups, because mediation requires representatives who can speak authoritatively enough for each group that agreements become binding. At any rate, conflict systems can and should be characterized according to their predominant mode (or combination of modes) of resolution. Basically, Dahl and Lindblom have analyzed the handling of political and economic conflict in terms of basic social processes in their *Politics, Economics, and Welfare.*

Given the growing significance of interorganizational conflict or conflict between highly organized groups, mediation deserves special attention. This mode probably now dominates or is coming to dominate the area of collective bargaining and is becoming more frequent in the area of international relations. . . . Jackson has analyzed eight propositions which, he argues, hold for both industrial and international relations; two are repeated here:

PROPOSITION 49: *Public debate is occasionally an aid in the mobilization of public interest, but extended public debate by the parties tends to harden their views.*

PROPOSITION 50: *Techniques for getting parties together on agreement, once mediation has started, are very similar in international and labor fields.*

Such propositions must be evaluated in the light of similarities and differences between the two areas of conflict. . . . Nonetheless, there is substantial agreement among experts on the conditions of successful mediation. It is agreed on all sides that the personal qualifications and professional skills of the mediator are essential to mediation success. Something might be gained from a comparison of the model qualities of an industrial mediator, which can be found in the literature, with the attributes and skills of Dr. Ralph Bunche and Secretary-General Hammarskjöld, who have functioned effectively as mediators for the United Nations. The progress of mediation at the international level would seem to be heavily dependent on an available group of knowledgeable and trusted mediators. Experience with this problem within societies might be revealing for future developments in international organization. Moreover, Kerr's . . . distinction between tactical and strategic mediation may be useful. Rather than being aimed at basic solutions to major issues, Kerr sees tactical mediation as resulting in reduced irrationality, removal of non-rational conflict elements, creation of possible new solutions, and assistance in the graceful retreat of parties from overly rigid positions. Various agencies and processes within the United Nations, many hidden from public view, should be examined as manifestations of tactical mediation. Observations based on industrial mediation . . . indicate definite phases to the conflict resolution process. The initial phase is likely to be one of strong language and positions of apparent inflexibility —a phase the layman is probably most familiar with and which he either mistakes for the general tenor of the whole process or assumes to be irrelevant. This spectacular phase, unless seen in the light of a sequential set of phases, may be very misleading. In more general terms, the ceremonial aspect of conflict resolution through mediation turns out to be functional, and its abolition, which many equate with the "solution" to conflict, would have serious consequences for the likelihood of eventual agreement. However, if conflict becomes entirely or predominantly ceremonial, complexity and rigidity of rules may be the reason. . . .

In considering conflict resolution, the distinction between violent (or aggressive) and non-violent modes provides another way of classifying systems. Wars, strikes, riots, armed rebellions, and physical assaults are all violent or aggressive modes. From many points of view the chief problem is to channel conflict resolution into non-violent, non-aggressive modes. Some writers blame the seriousness of human conflict on ultimate weapons available . . . , and violent modes have been in some respects overemphasized as the essence of conflict systems. The over-emphasis on violent modes has, of course, been a reflection of their cost, overtness, and dramatic impact, but it has had the effect of obscuring the relation between non-violent and violent modes, of inspiring superficial solutions, and of divorcing modes of resolution from the underlying nature of conflict interaction. A general hypothesis can be stated as follows: *The possibility of aggressive conflict or employment of violence tends to set a terminal point to controversy.* A related general hypothesis is: *The more destructive the means available to both parties to a conflict, the less likely is it that the ends for which conflict is waged can be served if such means are used.* At first glance, these tentative propositions may be an affront to the reader who is thinking of frequent wars and strikes and who reads and hears threats among superpowers possessing nuclear weapons. Obviously, these hypotheses imply important conditions and qualifications. The first implies a common interest in joint survival and some degree of functional interrelatedness between the parties. The second implies a rough equality of capacity to administer destruction and the absence of values which decree total elimination of one or both parties. . . .

Several familiar reminders are appropriate here. In the evolution from individual or group self-help to the monopoly of the instrumentalities of force in the hands of government, it is essential to note that violent modes of conflict settlement did not disappear but were *institutionalized,* i.e., their employment was subject to restrictive conditions and other modes of resolution were made available. The same thing can be said of strikes: as mediation and other modes of resolution of industrial conflict have grown in significance, the strike was *not* abolished but was related to the other modes in the collective-bargaining system in such a way as to curb its use without removing it as an incentive to agreement. It hardly seems likely that mediation could have developed if strikes had been abolished. Similarly, it may be seriously questioned whether international mediation would develop merely because nuclear weapons were abolished. Many disarmament solutions neglect the central function of violent modes: to make bargaining more conclusive and more effective. Attempts by conflicting parties to control violent modes can be interpreted as a recognition that the utility of aggressive conflict has become severely limited.

The necessity to relate the nature of conflict situations to modes of resolution can be seen in another connection. There is, of course, a substantial literature on bargaining generally and on effective strategies in "social games." For the most part, attention is focused on descriptions of bargaining and games of strategy and on prescriptions for rational behavior where opposing parties are making choices under conditions of uncertainty. We should say in passing that, although this type of analysis employs formal mathematical or economic models which, as yet, have had relatively little empirical application to a wide range of social conflicts, very useful insights into the nature of conflict have been forthcoming. . . . It is assumed that bargaining can and should lead to an intersection of demands by parties to conflict such that both "win" . . . and there are strategies in social games which will yield optimum results (this may involve minimizing losses) to the opponents under given conditions. Psychologists, on the other hand, have been concerned with situations in which there is ambivalence toward alternative states of affairs or outcomes and in which conflict is intensified precisely because plus and minus values either do not cancel out or cannot be "resolved" by the choice of a particular value or combination of values. This suggests that value conflict, in the sense of ideological conflicts mentioned above, requires a different type of mode of resolution from those prescribed in bargaining strategies or game theory. For the latter kind of conflict, some sort of value integration seems required, that is, conflicting goal values are converted into instrumental values serving a superordinate goal value. For example, two independent nations may not be able to reach a mutually satisfactory trade bargain because any alternative point of mutually beneficial agreement may have other negatively valued (including non-economic adverse consequences) aspects. But, by organizing themselves into a single trade unit (economic union), trade relations may subserve a higher value, such as a more advantageous all-round division of labor between them or closer political ties.

. . .

Power Relations

In a previous section we discussed party strength as a factor in the general relationship between party characteristics and conflict interaction. Clearly, however, power is a relational concept, and it is the nature and distribution of power among the parties *and* relative to the issues of conflict which are significant. Accommodation to preconflict changes in comparative party strength and clarification of mutual control over decisions have also been established as functions of the conflict relation. Thus the power-relations component of any conflict system consists of the respective bases of effective influence on which the parties can operate *and* the allocation of control over decision which occur during the interaction. There seems to be no inherent reason why, empirically, the bases of influence and distribution of control over behavioral choices cannot be identified and measured with some degree of precision whether the parties are unorganized groups or individuals or bureaucracies. . . .

If we can assume for a moment that power relations have been at least crudely defined, two characteristic patterns might serve to differentiate conflict systems: (1) *diffuseness* and *specificity* and (2) *stability* and *instability*. In most situations it is likely that these concepts represent a continuum rather than mutually exclusive polar opposites. Diffuseness-specificity implies a distinction between a system characterized by a broad range of effective bases of influence and ambiguity of control over decisions, as against a system embodying a narrow range of effective bases of influence and definite prescriptions for control over decisions. This dimension appears to be related to other variables—the number of parties and internal organization. Interracial or interethnic conflict would appear, in general, to manifest multiple parties and lack of centralized relations within parties. Face-to-face relations among parties are likely to cover a number of life-situations and hence to offer several possible influence relationships. In contrast, labor-management conflict is predominantly characterized by centralized interaction and formal allocation of decision-making power.

An unstable power relation is one in which no durable resolution of power conflicts or establishment of regular joint decision-making patterns is possible (or has been achieved) and/or in which there is no accepted means of measuring the power balance. The perishable nature of coalitions is probably related to the difficulty of stabilizing power relations under certain conditions. Instability accompanies shifting agenda of issues, i.e., the relationship must accommodate a large number of issues generally unpredictable in advance and rapid changes in internal characteristics of parties. When the bases of effective influence are primarily of a subtle psychological kind rather than force or economic bargaining, indexes of power are difficult to determine. This seems to be true of say, party conflict in the French Chamber of Deputies and of contemporary international politics.

What are the implications of the power factor for the problem of resolution and control of conflict? For one thing, to the extent that the function of conflict is the clarification and stabilization of power relations, modes of resolution which omit or cannot basically affect these relations are likely to be ineffective. . . . It is not only that opposed goals are at stake in conflict situations but that control over the choices governing alternative goals and means is also at stake. "Human-relations" approaches which attempt exclusively to create a sense of common goals while by-passing the joint decision-making phase may therefore be wide of the mark in many situations.

The difficulty of estimating power in advance of a concrete test is undoubtedly a major obstacle in preventing conflict or in reducing the likelihood of extreme conflict. . . . Hence the problem of social conflict resolution may be viewed in a dual aspect: the necessity to devise advance measurements of power outcomes and the substitution of small-scale (i.e., discussion or vote) methods for large-scale (i.e., a strike or war) methods in trials of power. In effect, the parties to conflict need to know beforehand whether a better decision can be reached via one mode of resolution than by another. A straw vote, an advisory court opinion, and a mediation process are all examples of ways of avoiding premature or mistaken trials whose possibly adverse consequences cannot be avoided, once they occur. Misinformation or guesses concerning conflict outcomes tend to result in situations in which all parties lose or in which interaction is completely disrupted and therefore must be painfully re-established. . . .

Despite the universal common-sense recognition of the need for face-saving and graceful retreats when ultimate tests of power are bound to be adverse or inconclusive, we know little about the effective detection and accommodation of this stage in a conflict interaction. In areas of disorganized social conflict typified by diffuse and unstable power relations, the possibility of dysfunctional interaction is much greater, especially in the case of unrealistic conflict.

Nature and Degree of Institutionalization

The foregoing comments lead to another dimension of conflict systems. Institutionalization of conflict generally means continuity of interaction; regularized procedures for handling changes in conditions, goals, and power; interdependence of parties; and the creation of new norms. . . . Out of institutionalized conflict come new social policies. As conflict is partially resolved at various stages through time, certain issues disappear, and a common law governing formerly disputed matters is built up. Ways of measuring power relations and correcting imbalances without aggressive conflict or violence are developed. Institutionalization requires the combination of conflict and co-operation, since rules and procedures cannot function in the absence of voluntary obedience or enforcement through sanctions. . . . Even war, the ultimate in conflict, is cooperative to the extent necessary to permit communication between enemies and administration of mutually advantageous rules. Thus the frequent rigid dichotomy between harmony and opposition, co-operation and conflict, is very misleading. . . . Co-operation can be antagonistic and can result from bribed interdependence. In any event, institutionalized conflict and co-operation go together. Co-operation does not imply an absence of conflict or vice versa.

Non-institutionalized conflict or conflict interaction having a low degree of institutionalization is marked by chronic recurrence of unsettled issues, by an absence of agreed procedures for review of relations, and by discontinuity of interaction or drastic shifts in the mode of resolution. This type of system is correlated, if not casually linked, with diffuse and unstable power relations. Hypothetically, a higher degree of institutionalization is similarly linked to more specific and stable power relations. A general hypothesis, which could be tested empirically, is: *The higher the degree of institutionalization, the greater the consistency and balance of strength of the parties to conflict.* The pressures of functional interdependence between parties and the need to preserve predictable conflict relations result in modes of resolution which stop short of the complete destruction or crippling of one of the parties. Indeed, it is no accident that wars, for example, seem to be terminated while there is still an entity for the victor to deal with, some minimal organization to make possible a new formulation of the now altered power relation.

There are noteworthy differences in the nature of institutionalization of conflict. The conflict relation may be autonomous in the sense that the parties voluntarily establish an informal social control of their interactions. Or a conflict relation may be regulated by legal norms enforced from outside the conflict system. Industrial collective bargaining in Great Britain is an expression of the former and collective bargaining in the United States is an expression of the latter. International conflict is for the most part a mixture, with predominant emphasis on autonomy. The growth and success of industrial bargaining suggest that the appropriate social context of conflict can permit autonomous conflict resolution as exemplified by experience in Great Britain.

Another pattern of institutionalization relates to centralization and decentralization of conflict systems. In general, political institutionalization is centralized with respect to some area of jurisdiction (or political unit), while the institutionalization of economic conflict, in free societies at least, is more decentralized. Centralized institutionalization of conflict is exemplified by national legislation, a local ordinance binding on all members of the community, or by an authoritative Supreme Court decision. Decentralized institutionalization is exemplified by the market. Hence social policies which accommodate conflicting goals, demands, and needs may evolve from a central decision-making agency which lays down rules and determines power relations or from the cumulative impact of a number of separate bargains whether between individuals or firms or between consumers and producers. . . .

There is good reason to assume, in the absence of strong evidence to the contrary, a persistent tendency toward institutionalization of social conflict. From the foregoing, three directions of this tendency can be inferred. First, particular institutionalization for particular kinds of conflict may evolve. Second, institutionalization may be based on the support of existing machinery in the social context outside a given conflict system. Third, these two patterns may be combined. Conflict which is essentially disorganized, unrealistic, characterized by diverse modes of resolution, diffuse and unstable power relations, and, on balance, more dysfunctional than functional, tends to lead to institutionalization through mechanisms operating in the social context—usually a centralized institution. Conflict which manifests the opposite properties tends to lead to autonomous, decentralized, and more particularistic institutionalization. Racial conflict would probably fall into the first category and industrial conflict clearly into the second. The conditions leading to a combination are not immediately clear. Presumably, the general character of the culture and social organization would be controlling. . . .

It is difficult to escape the conviction that the resolution and control of social conflict are intimately related to the nature and degree of institutionalization. Superficially, it would appear that conflict relations are functional and stable (i.e., predictable and subject to semiautomatic adjustment to new conditions) to the extent that *appropriate* institutionalizaion exists, The fact that wars and strikes are institutionalized in an important sense in no way undercuts the argument that it is the institutionalization of other modes and the relationship of various modes within an institutional framework which are crucial.

Direct, Unmediated Systems versus Mediated Representational Systems

Another aspect of conflict systems which can be analytically differentiated is closely bound up with the previous dimension. Again, intuitive observation suggests a sizable difference between much interpersonal and unorganized group conflict, on the one hand, and organized intergroup or interorganizational conflict, on the other. The model for the latter, which would cover a large sector of social conflict, can be indicated briefly:

1. The relationships among two sets of representatives or bargainers and the relationships among each set of bargainers or representatives
   a) The values and perception of the representatives or bargainers
2. The nature of the membership or constituency represented
   a) The values and preceptions of the memberships
   b) Degree of unity and kinds of relations among members
3. The relationship between representatives or bargainers and the membership or constituency
   a) Nature and consequences of authority relationship
   b) Nature and function of leadership
4. The role of the mediator or mediating agencies (if present)
   a) Qualities and effectiveness of mediation
   b) Relationship of mediating function to the social context
5. Interrelation of bargaining or representational system to social context
   a) Institutional links (e.g., sanctions)
   b) Non-institutional links (e.g., interested publics)

This model, though highly general and though it includes no basis for deriving links among the five sets of variables, does offer a possibly fruitful method of organizing and classifying propositions which then could be connected in the description and explanation of a conflict system which conformed to the underlying assumptions. Furthermore, direct unmediated systems could be analyzed in terms of the presence or absence of the five components. Nor is there any reason why the other characteristics of conflict systems discussed above could not be incorporated in the model as well as the party characteristics, also discussed above. It should be noted that the model is not restricted to formal mediation as a mode of resolution. If non-institutionalization and institutionalization imply a continuum, then the closer to the non-institutionalization end a particular system is, the less likely is the system to conform to the specifications of the model.

System Limitations and Boundaries

Finally, we come to the limitations on conflict, a subject best left to this point because so much of what has been said bears on it. Since conflict has been so often associated with social instability, waste, destruction, random outbursts of violence, and long-drawn-out struggles, it is easy to equate conflict with a breakdown of control or to underestimate its limits. But social conflict behavior is rarely, if ever, random and without limitations.

One of the properties of any system is that it is boundary-maintaining. That is, for the purposes at hand, an observer can usually discover empirical distinctions between the related parts which comprise the system and other phenomena which are either unrelated or, from the observer's standpoint, unimportant. Thus the parties to conflict and the conflict interaction (including its components) can be empirically separated from what was earlier called the "social context." The social context consists of non-system factors which the observer *does* think are important. Apart from system boundaries (or limits) in this sense, the other meaning of limitation on conflict concerns those factors (inside or outside the system) which tend to affect the intensity, duration, enlargement, and mode of resolution of the conflict interaction process. As presented by Boulding, the proper way to connect system and non-system boundaries and limitations is by a concept of an "open system," i.e., one which is characterized by internal changes in relationships among constituent parts *and* one which is susceptible to influences from outside its boundaries. Implicitly, at least, many propositions on conflict are based on a closed system or on an ever expanding system or on a system which manifests only disequilibrium as its essential property. There is ground for distrusting all three as approaches to the study of conflict.

Major limitations on conflict can be listed briefly. Intra-system limits are (1) functional interdependence between parties, (2) regulation through institutionalized norms and procedures, (3) the need for continued communication between parties, (4) conflict cost, (5) availability and feasibility of certain modes of resolution, (6) inertia and organizational inefficiency of parties, (7) ignorance or misunderstanding, and (8) avoidance taboos. Most of these are self-evident on the basis of the preceding discussion. Thus the implications of conflict cost as a limitation on conflict are rather obvious. It may be that some conflict systems have as their outstanding feature the desire of one or both parties to inflict maximum disorder on the conflict relationship—subversion or a rebellion would be examples. Nonetheless, in conflict systems having predominantly highly institutionalized non-violent modes of resolution, there is a limit on tolerable disorder. The restoration of order following a disruption of normal interaction places a burden on each party. The contractual spacing of conflict resolution, e.g., a one-year or more union-management agreement, confirms this natural limitation. Even during a steel strike, a union will assign some of its members to keeping open-hearth furnaces banked.

The last three limitations have not been mentioned before. Party weakness has been mentioned as a source of conflict under some conditions, but inertia and organizational inefficiency may also limit conflict. Many social conflicts become less intense or die out altogether because one or both parties simply run out of sustained drive. Conflict relations may be emotionally satisfying and substantively rewarding, but they are also burdensome. Sustained conflict, if vigorously waged, puts a great premium on energy and resources, neither of which is unlimited in supply. Ignorance and misunderstanding are normally cited as sources and conditioners of conflict. However, it is not always recognized that these same factors may also prevent or minimize conflict. How much more conflict would there be if individuals and groups really thoroughly and correctly understood each other's motives, words, and deeds? . . . Diplomatic language, often dismissed as double talk, makes possible "planned misunderstandings" which keep tensions down and provide opportunity for clarification prior to ultimate or aggressive measures. Avoidance taboos, a term mostly employed by social anthropologists, denote behavioral restraints which have not been broadly examined as a limiting factor in conflict. Everyone is aware of "things which are just not said or done," regardless of provocation. Such restraints, if operative at enough key junctures of interpersonal and intergroup relations, may be a much more powerful limitation on conflict than is realized. Religious conflict in the contemporary United States is undoubtedly restrained by avoidance taboos.

Limitations arising outside any conflict system can be classified as follows: (1) shared cultural and social values which neutralize or dominate conflicting values; (2) institutional sanctions against certain kinds of power relations and modes of resolution; (3) third parties interested in control or resolution; (4) crisscrossing of other conflict systems which prevents enlargement or bipolarization around any single system; and (5) "cross-pressures" which create ambivalences within parties.

To the extent that there are "natural limits" to conflict, the lesson for the problem of resolution and control would seem to be this: *Social strategies designed to keep conflict functional and to prevent violent or aggressive conflict ought to be based in part on deliberate attempts to capitalize on natural limits*. This may involve giving up notions of "abolishing" conflict, of "final" resolutions, and may direct attention to less obvious control devices. Avoidance taboos, for example, may be easier to inculcate and enforce than centralized political controls. Clarification and invigoration of existing common values may be more feasible than finding formulae for reconciling some conflicting values. . . .

THE KENNEDY EXPERIMENT

Amitai Etzioni

THE PATTERN of events between June 10 and November 22, 1963, provided a partial test of a theory of international relations. The essence of the theory is that psychological gestures initiated by one nation will be reciprocated by others with the effect of reducing international tensions. This tension reduction, in turn, will lessen the probability of international conflicts and wars.

Examining this theory in light of the 1963 experiment, I ask: (a) What are the main propositions of the theory? (b) What initiatives were actually taken by the United States in the experiment period, and how did the Union of

Reprinted from *The Western Political Quarterly,* Vol. 20, No. 2, Part I (June, 1967), pp. 361–380.
Note: This article grew out of my work at the Institute of War and Peace Studies at Columbia University. I am grateful for the research assistance of Sarajane Heidt and Robert McGheean. Since this article was written two books have appeared which provide additional documentation for the points made but seem not to affect the conclusions reached: See Theodore C. Sorensen, *Kennedy* (New York: Harper & Row, 1965), esp. chap. XXV, and Arthur M. Schlesinger, Jr., *A Thousand Days* (Boston: Houghton Mifflin, 1965), esp. pp. 888–923. Additional treatment of this subject is included in my *The Active Society: A Theory and Political Process* (New York: Free Press of Glencoe, 1968).

Soviet Socialist Republics react? (c) What were the effects of these initiatives and responses on inter-bloc relations, and to what degree did these effects conform to the expectations of the theory? (d) What other factors, not accounted for by the theory, could have produced all or part of these effects? (e) What factors limited both the scope and the extent of the experiment, and under what conditions could it be replicated or extended?

A PSYCHOLOGICAL THEORY OF INTERNATIONAL RELATIONS

The theory views the behavior of nations basically as that of persons who have strong drives that motivate their pursuit of goals, influence their choice of means, and distort the communications they send and receive. It suggests that nations, when in conflict, tend to be caught in a spiral. The hostility of one as perceived by the other evokes his hostility, which in turn is perceived by the first side, further increasing *his* hostility. Arms races, in which the participant countries increase the level of their armaments because the other countries are doing so, are viewed as an expression of such upward spiraling of hostile reactions.

Psychological analysis of international behavior has been so discredited[1] that most political scientists and members of sister-disciplines might find their patience tried when asked to examine such a theory. It should therefore be stressed from the outset that the evidence provided below, although partial, provides some new support for some elements of the psychological approach. While the more extreme version of the theory remains unsupported, a moderate version is strengthened enough to stand among the major hypotheses on international behavior that are to be explored further. After a brief recapitulation of the theory and its two versions the evidence speaks for itself.

According to both versions of the theory, a high level of hostility generates psychological blocks that prevent the sides from facing international reality. Various defense mechanisms are activated: for one, a high level of tension tends to produce a *rigid* adherence to a policy chosen under earlier conditions, e.g., the sides increase armaments and hold to a hostile posture ("cold war"), though armaments have been procured beyond military needs and hostile feelings are no longer justified in view of changes in the character and intentions of the opponent.[2] These changes are *denied,* another mode of defensive behavior, to make the continuation of the earlier policy psychologically possible.

Further, fears of nuclear war, *repressed* since they are too threatening to be faced, express themselves in stereotyping and paranoia, indications of which advocates of the theory find in the conduct of nations locked in a state of international tensions. *Stereotyping* is represented by the divisions of the world into black and white, good and bad, nations,[3] and the manipulation of information by selecting among and distorting the content of communications, so that positive information about one's adversary is ignored and negative information about one's own side disregarded. Blocked or distorted communication between the sides thus prevents "reality-testing" and correction of false images.

Stereotyping is often accompanied by *paranoia.* Whatever the adversary offers is interpreted as seeking to advance his own goals and as a trap for us. If the Soviets favor complete and general disarmament, this in itself brings Americans to point to disarmament as a Communist ruse.[4] A possibility of a genuine give-and-take is ignored. The same repressed fear, the psychological analysis continues, causes even reasonable concessions to the other side, made as part of a give-and-take, to be seen as submission or, to use the political term, appeasement. The labeling of bargaining behavior as disloyal or treacherous impedes negotiations that require open-mindedness, flexibility, and willingness to make concessions even though not sacrificing basic positions and values.

What could a therapy be? How, the psychologists ask, can the vicious circle of hostile moves and counter-moves be broken? The answer is similar to psychoanalytic technique—increased and improved communication. Communication can be increased by visits of Americans to Russia and Russians to

America, exchange of newspapers, publication of American columns in Soviet newspapers and vice versa, by summit conferences, and the like.[5] Communication will become less distorted and tensions will be reduced if one of the sides begins to indicate a friendly state of mind. While such indications will be initially mistrusted, if continued they will be reciprocated, reducing hostility which in turn will reduce the counter-hostility, thus reversing the cold war spiral. Once the level of tension is reduced, and more communication is received from the other side, there will be an increased ability to perceive the international reality as it is, which will further reduce tensions. Joint undertakings are also favored because psychological experiments with children have shown that the introduction of shared tasks helps to reduce hostility.[6] International cooperative research, joint exploration of the stars, oceans, and poles, joint rather than competitive development aid, are hence favored.[7]

There are significant differences in the extent to which this theory claims to explain international behavior. Strongly put, it suggests that "war starts in the minds of man" and "the situation is what we define it to be." In this interpretation, the causes of war are psychological and can be fully explained in psychological terms. Arms are merely an expression of these attitudes of mind.[8] If attitudes are modified, arms will either not be produced or have no threatening impact. The people of New Jersey, it is pointed out, do not fear nuclear arms held by New Yorkers.

More moderate versions of the theory view psychological factors as one aspect of a situation that contains economic, political, and military dimensions as well. Just as triggers without hostilities do not make a war, so hostilities without arms cannot trigger battles. Moreover, even if armaments were initially ordered to serve a psychological motive, once available they generate motives of their own to propel hostile postures and wars. Thus one can hold the psychological theory with varying degrees of strength.[9] Osgood, in most of his writings on this subject, has advanced the stronger version,[10] while this author subscribes to the more moderate one.[11]

A second line of variation centers on where the blame for triggering the spiral is placed. Some writers tend to view the sides as equally at fault with no "real" reason for a cold war other than misunderstanding. For example, Stalin only wished to establish weak friendly governments on his Western borders, a desire which the West misperceived as expansionistic. Others tend to put more of the blame on the West or on the East. All of these interpretations can be coupled with the psychological analysis on the grounds that regardless of the initiator and whether the initial cause was real or imagined, the same process of psychological escalation is at work. The therapy, hence, remains the same. To insist that the side that triggered the process be the one to take the initiative to reverse it, is viewed as immature behavior.

Next, there are important differences in the steps suggested to break the cycle. It is generally agreed that measures which require multilateral negotiations are not appropriate for the initiation of tension reduction. The high level of hostility and mutual suspicions invariably disrupts the negotiations, and the mutual recriminations that follow increase rather than reduce the level of international tensions. Unilateral steps are therefore needed. The important differences between the two versions of the theory concern the nature of these steps. Jerome Frank, for instance, stresses that the initiatives must be clear, simple, and dramatic to overcome the psychological barriers,[12] for any minor concessions will be seen as a trap to encourage the opponent to lower his guard. Actually, in Frank's judgment, unilateral renunciation of nuclear weapons might well be the only sufficiently large step to break the vicious cycle.[13] More moderate interpretations call for significant reductions of arms as initiatives; still more moderate interpretations seek to restrict the unilateral steps to purely symbolic gestures not involving any weakening of the military strength of the initiator even though some arms reduction, such as the cutting of arms surpluses, might be recommended.[14]

Finally, there are those who believe that the transition from a "cold war" to a "stable peace" would be achieved by a chain of unilateral initiatives followed by reciprocations by the other side, while others believe that such exchanges would open the way to effective multilateral negotiations. The unilateral-reciprocal approach, it is suggested, is needed to create the atmosphere in which important international accommodations such as broad-based arms reduction schemes can be introduced, but those in themselves cannot be introduced in this way because the unilateral-reciprocation approach can carry only comparatively simple communications, and the sides are unlikely to make major arms reductions unless those of the other side are made simultaneously.[15]

AMERICAN INITIATIVES

The Kennedy experiment can be viewed as a test of a moderate version of the psychological theory that seeks to use symbolic gestures as unilateral initiatives to reduce tension to get at other factors, leading toward multilateral negotiations.

The first step was a speech by President John F. Kennedy at the American University on June 10, 1963, in which he outlined "A Strategy of Peace." While it is not known to what degree the President or his advisors were moved by a psychological theory, the speech clearly met a condition of this theory—it set the *context* for the unilateral initiatives to follow. As any concrete measure can be interpreted in a variety of ways, it is necessary to spell out the general state of mind these steps attempt to communicate.[16]

The President called attention to the dangers of nuclear war and took a reconciliatory tone toward the Soviet Union in his address. He said that "constructive changes" in the Soviet Union "might bring within reach solutions which now seem beyond us." He stated that "our problems are man-made . . . and can be solved by man." Coming eight months after the 1962 Cuban crisis, when the United States and Russia stood "eyeball to eyeball," such statements marked a decisive change in American attitudes. United States policies, the President added, must be so constructed "that it becomes in the Communist interest to agree to a genuine peace," which was a long way from the prevailing sentiment that there was little the United States could do, so long as the Soviet Union did not change. Further, there was doubt that the Soviet Union was capable of a genuine interest in peace. Nor did the President imply that all the blame for the cold war rested with the other side; he called on Americans to "re-examine" their attitudes toward the cold war.

Beyond merely delivering a speech, the President announced the first unilateral initiative—the United States was stopping all nuclear tests in the atmosphere and would not resume them unless another country did. This, it should be noted, was basically a psychological gesture and not a unilateral arms limitation step. The United States at that time was believed to command about five times the means of delivery of the Soviet Union and to have them much better protected, and had conducted about twice as many nuclear tests including a recent large round of testing. American experts believed that it would take about one to two years before the information from these tests was finally digested, that in all likelihood little was to be gained from additional testing even after that date,[17] and that if testing proved to be necessary it could be conducted in other environments, particularly underground. Thus, in effect, the President used the termination of testing as a psychological gesture.

The steps that followed had much the same quality. Kennedy's speech, delivered on June 10, was published in full during the next few days in the Soviet government newspaper, *Izvestia,* as well as in *Pravda* with a combined circulation of 10,000,000, a degree of attention rarely accorded a Western leader. Radio jammers in Moscow were turned off to allow the Russian people to listen without interruption to the Voice of America's recording of the speech, a fact that was reported in the United States and, therefore, had some tension reduction effect on both sides. Premier Khrushchev followed on June 15 with a speech welcoming the Kennedy initiative. He stated that a world war was not inevitable and that the main danger of conflict stemmed from the arms race and the stockpiling of nuclear weapons. Khrushchev reciprocated on the psychological-military side by announcing he had ordered that the production of strategic bombers be halted. The psychological nature of this step is to be seen in that the bombers were probably about to be phased out anyway and that no verification was offered for cessation of production.

In the United Nations, the Soviet Union on June 11 removed its objection to a Western-backed proposal to send observers to war-torn Yemen. The United States reciprocated by removing, for the first time since 1956, its objection to the restoration of full status of the Hungarian delegation to the United Nations.

Although the United States had proposed a direct America-Russia communications link at Geneva in late 1962,[18] the Soviets finally agreed to this measure on June 20, 1963. Next, attention focused on the test ban. Following the United States' example, Russia reciprocated by not testing in the atmosphere, so that until the treaty was signed, both sides refrained from such testing under an understanding achieved without negotiation but rather through unilateral-reciprocal moves. This development, in line with the moderate version of the theory, led in July to multilateral negotiations and a treaty, signed on August 5, 1963. The signing of the treaty was followed by a number of new proposals for East-West agreements. Foreign Minister Gromyko, on September 19, 1963, called for a "non-aggression pact between the members of the Warsaw Treaty [*sic*] and the members of the North Atlantic bloc" and asked for a peace treaty with Germany. President Kennedy came before the United Nations and dramatically suggested, on September 20, 1963, that the United States and the Soviet Union explore the stars together. Also mentioned repeatedly in the front-page news in those weeks were the possible exchange of observer posts at key points to reduce the danger of surprise attack; expansion of the test treaty to include underground testing; direct flights between Moscow and New York; and the opening of an American consulate in Leningrad and a Soviet one in Chicago.

The next step actually taken came in a different area—a

symbolic reduction of the trade barriers between East and West. As part of the cold war, the United States and, following its guidance, other Western nations had sharply limited the trade between East and West. Not only was trading of a long list of strategic material forbidden, but trade in other materials required an export license that was difficult to obtain. Restrictions were also imposed on the credits Russia could obtain. There were occasional violations of these bans, especially by traders in Western countries other than the United States, but the total East-West trade remained very small.

On October 9, 1963, President Kennedy approved the sale of $250 million's worth of wheat to the Soviet Union. The almost purely psychological nature of that step is not always understood. As the test ban treaty had, for reasons mentioned above, a limited military significance, so the wheat deal had little commercial importance. The barriers to East-West trade were *not* removed; credit and license barriers were maintained. The President himself said that this decision did not initiate "a new Soviet-American trade policy,"[19] and such trade remained a small fraction of the total Soviet foreign trade. The total value of the wheat the United States actually sold was $65 million. The main values of the deal were, hence, as a gesture and in the educational effect of the public debate which preceded the Administration's approval of the deal.

October brought another transformation of a unilateral-reciprocal understanding into a binding, multilateral formal agreement. This time it concerned the orbiting of weapons of mass destruction and, once more, though it appeared to be a military measure, it was largely a psychological one. The United States had formerly decided, after considerable debate, that it was not interested in orbiting nuclear bombs.[20] The Soviet Union, as far as could be determined, had reached a similar conclusion. Neither side orbited such weapons while it was watching the other side. On September 19 Gromyko suggested such a pact, and Kennedy indicated that the United States was willing. An agreement in principle was announced on October 3, and the final resolution was passed in the General Assembly on October 19, with the approval of both powers. Its immediate effect was to publicize and formalize an area of agreement that had in effect existed in the preceding years. Another measure, psychological in nature, was an exchange of released spies. While spies had been exchanged under a variety of circumstances in the past, the October 1963 exchange served the new policy.

In late October and in the first three weeks of November, there was a marked slow-down of American initiatives, and reciprocation to Soviet initiatives almost completely stopped. The reasons were many: the Administration felt that the psychological mood in the West was getting out of hand, with hopes and expectations for more Soviet-American measures running too high;[21] allies, especially West Germany, objected more and more bitterly;[22] and the pre-election year began, in which the Administration seemed not to desire additional accommodations. The present *posture* seemed best for domestic purposes. There had been some promising signs for those who favored disarmament, and no matters of grave enough importance were involved so that even if all went sour—if the Soviets resumed testing, orbited bombs, etc.—no credible "appeasement" charge could be made by Republicans. There was an expectation that moves would be renewed after the elections. For the election year, however, even such measures as air and consular treaties were delayed.[23] (The experiment was actually resumed after the election; the factors that prevented its success merit a study in their own right.[24])

SOVIET RESPONSES

One of the prevalent criticisms against the unilateral initiatives theory is that the Soviets might not respond to such initiatives.[25] The Soviets, it is said, are Marxists and quite aware of the difference between real and symbolic moves. A policy of symbolic gestures would appeal only to people who think in Madison Avenue terms and not in political, military, and economic ones. The evidence on this point is fairly clear. For each move that was made, the

Soviets reciprocated. Kennedy's "Strategy for Peace" speech was matched by a conciliatory speech by Khrushchev; Kennedy's unilateral declaration of cessation of tests was followed by a cessation of the production of strategic bombers; spies were traded for spies, etc. The Russians showed no difficulties in understanding the gestures and in responding to psychological initiatives; and they participated in a "you move–I move" sequence rather than waiting for simultaneous, negotiated, agreed-upon moves. Further, they shifted to multilateral-simultaneous arrangements once the appropriate mood was generated, as reflected in the test-ban treaty and outer space resolution.

Another "danger" critics of unilateral initiatives warned of was that the Soviets might reciprocate "below par" and thus accumulate an advantage. While these matters are not readily measurable, it seems that the Russian reciprocations were "proportional" to the American ones. Khrushchev's speech might have been somewhat less elegant than Kennedy's, but it would be difficult to defend the proposition that announcing a halt to the production of bombers is lower in value than the declaration of cessation of tests, both basically psychological gestures. Spies were exchanged for spies; the test treaty and the space ban involved substantively identical, strategically similar, commitments. In short, neither side seemed to have made a disproportionate gain.

While the warnings of the critics were not realized, a danger that seems not to have been anticipated by the United States Government did materialize: the Russians responded not just by reciprocating American initiatives but by offering some initiatives of their own, in the spirit of the *détente*.[26] Washington was put on the spot: it had to reciprocate if it were not to weaken the new spirit, but it could lose control of the experiment. The first test came at the very outset, when Russia took the initiative and suddenly removed its objection to the sending of United Nations observers to Yemen. The United States reciprocated, as previously mentioned, allowing the restoration of full status to the Hungarian delegation to the United Nations. The United States also responded handsomely to Russia's initiative on a space ban. It found it more difficult, however, to respond to the other Russian initatives. The United States agreed to the wheat deal, but only after hesitation that was sufficient to reduce the gesture's value. It never quite succeeded in making a good case for its objection to a non-aggression pact between the North Atlantic Treaty Organization and the Warsaw Treaty Organization. (The argument that this would involve a recognition of East Germany was a thin one, for several wordings were suggested that would circumvent this difficulty.) It was felt that a non-aggression pact between these two was already covered within the United Nations charter, which would be weakened if the message were rearticulated in another document. In other cases the United States was unconcerned about such duplication, for instance, between the Organization of American States and the United Nations.[27] The United States hesitated in responding to the Soviet initiative on an air treaty, as well as on more encompassing moves regarding Germany and disarmament. Despite this reluctance, however, there were enough initiatives and reciprocations as well as multilateral measures within the three months to allow a partial testing of the theory. What was the effect of the gestures and counter-gestures?

THE PSYCHOLOGICAL IMPACT

The first steps in June 1963 did not produce what later became known as the Soviet-American *détente,* or the 1963–64 thaw in the cold war. In accord with the preceding psychological analysis, they were rather received with much ambivalence and suspicion. The *New York Times* seems to have reflected accurately the mood the author observed in Washington at the time, when it stated on June 16, 1963, that

> . . . there was a new threat of international peace in the air this week, the kind of threat that leaves sophisticates smirking and the rest of us just dumbfounded. The "accommodators," as outraged Republicans call them, were simply delighted. The "cold

warriors," as the accommodators call them, regarded conciliation as a shrewd new tactic.[28]

Thus, even the initiating side was not convinced that there really was a new line, and, if we may assume that Russian authorities read the *New York Times,* they too could hardly have been immediately persuaded.

In line with the theory, Kennedy's initiation speech included recognition of Russia's achievements ("We can still hail the Russian people for their many achievements—in science and space, in economic and industrial growth, in culture and in acts of courage") and suffering ("And no nation in the history of battle ever suffered more than the Soviet Union suffered in the course of the Second World War"). These statements seemed to have weakened the rigid image that was typical of the cold war period.

The impact of the speech was felt outside the seats of government. In the United States, "from around the country came a generous flow of messages echoing all these responses, but more approving than not. And from around the globe came new bursts of hope kept alive by quick signs of interest in Moscow."[29] A *New York Times* correspondent in Moscow reported that "the ready approval of its contents by ordinary Russians was evident in the reactions of Muscovites who lined up at kiosks to buy newspapers."[30] But the main turning point came when the test treaty—considered an important "breakthrough"—was successfully negotiated. That at first hopes for a treaty ran low, and that it took great effort to obtain it only increased the significance of its ratification.

The treaty to partially ban thermonuclear tests was the central gesture of the Kennedy experiment. Until it was reached, gestures and counter-gestures were met with caution, if not skepticism. When in early July Khrushchev offered a ban on tests in sea, air, and space (as was ultimately agreed), but coupled this offer with a suggestion of a non-aggression pact between the North Atlantic Treaty Organization and the Warsaw Treaty Organization, the *New York Times* referred to the offer as "Another Booby Trap?"[31] A week later, discussing the test treaty negotiations, the same source reflected the mood in the capital: "If these talks are successful, it is generally believed that a new chapter in East-West relations will open. But there are grave doubts on all sides that such a new chapter is indeed at hand."[32] Thus, a test ban was viewed as having major tension-reduction potential, but there was much doubt whether it would be achieved. A Washington reporter still refers to the *détente* at this point with a question mark and explores at length the possibility "that the Soviet Union did not really want an agreement"[33] (i.e., was negotiating in bad faith). An American report from Moscow indicated that "Mr. Khrushchev would also hope that conclusion of a partial test-ban treaty would create an atmosphere in which he could negotiate other advantageous agreements, especially on Germany."[34]

The treaty was negotiated in July, signed in August, and ratified in September. Thus, for more than two months, it served as the focus for discussions about Soviet intentions, the possibility of peaceful co-existence, and the dangers of nuclear war; and the Senate hearing helped to keep the debate alive. Its ratification was therefore not merely one more gesture in an international sequence of pseudo-events,[35] but a major educational act. The American public that entered the period with ambivalent attitudes toward a test-ban treaty, remembering the arbitrary resumption of testing by the Soviet Union in 1961, after three years of voluntary moratorium, as well as the 1962 Cuban crisis, was now strongly in favor of the agreement. Louis Harris reports that a national poll taken in July, before the negotiations on the treaty had begun, found that 52 per cent of the population strongly supported a treaty. This percentage had risen to 81 by September when the treaty was ratified.[36] The tone of the press also changed; there was now an "official amity" between the United States and the Soviet Union.[37] While some newspapermen, accustomed to sudden shifts in international winds, continued to be cautious, a report from Moscow stated:

> As Secretary of State Rusk left the Soviet Union today, after six days of discussions with Soviet leaders, it appeared almost

certain to Western observers here that a surface of calm would descend on East-West relations. . . . The prospect, it is believed, is for a long period of manifold negotiations at all levels and in many cities and countries on all sorts of issues. . . . The feeling is that the Russians are generally interested in maintaining the current state of improved relations with the West. They are believed to be hoping for a minimum of friction.[38]

The correspondent who had reported smirking and dumbfoundedness over any possible thaw in June now stated that "we have cleared the air and cleared the atmospheres and warmed the climate and calmed the winds."[39] The test-ban treaty had allayed many of the doubts about Russian intentions.

Following the signing of the treaty came a number of new proposals to improve East-West relations and further extend the *détente*. While none of these materialized in this period, the repeated and frequent offering of various tension-reduction measures had some effect in itself. Actually, hopes rose so quickly that late in August, Secretary of Defense McNamara warned that it was perilous to relax in a "euphoria," and Kennedy cautioned in September that the test ban was "not the millennium."

By late October, almost no new American initiatives were taken, and those of the Soviet Union were not reciprocated. The press referred to a "pause in the thaw"; there was a marked slow-down in tension reduction though efforts continued, as we shall see, to preserve the measure of *détente* that had been achieved. The assassination of President Kennedy and the beginning of the election year ushered in a year of more or less stable semi-*détente*.

What are the conclusions from this brief and incomplete test of the theory? Certain of the central hypotheses were supported: (a) unilateral gestures were reciprocated; (b) reciprocations were proportional; (c) unilaterally reciprocated gestures reduced tensions; (d) unilaterally reciprocated gestures were followed by multilateral-simultaneous measures, which further reduced tensions; (e) initiatives were "suspected," but, when continued, they "got across"; (f) the gestures and responses created a psychological momentum that pressured for more measures, a reversal of the cold war or hostility spiral; (g) when measures were stopped, tension reduction ceased (we shall see the significance of this point below); (h) the relatively more consequential acts were initiated multilaterally or were transformed from an initially informal, unilaterally reciprocated basis to a formal, multilateral one.[40]

Not all the assumptions and derivations of the theory were as clearly supported. Most important, it is impossible to tell, without re-running history for "control" purposes, whether multilateral negotiations could have been successfully undertaken without the "atmosphere" first having been improved by unilateral steps. The fact, however, that both the test treaty and the space ban were first introduced on a unilateral-reciprocal basis and that even in the reduced tension condition these measures were hard to defend before Congress, suggests that, if not preceded by tension reduction, they either might have failed, or the risks of failure would have been sufficiently high for the Administration to refrain from introducing them. (Attempts to advance a test ban in earlier periods failed.)[41]

Also, the Kennedy experiment was only a partial application of the theory: the gestures were not the clear signals a full test theory would require. Thus, for instance, to gain the Senate's consent for a test-ban treaty, its value for American security was stressed.[42] It would allow, it was said, stopping of testing while we were ahead both in number of tests and weapons technology. Further, President Kennedy made it clear that the United States would "vigorously and diligently" pursue its underground nuclear test program.[43] The wheat deal was interpreted in a similar fashion,[44] e.g., as a show of Russia's weakness. Further, during the whole period, American observers provided various interpretations of the gestures as other than efforts to communicate a desire for peaceful co-existence (e.g., the *détente* exacerbates the Soviet-Sino rift). While a policy is often supported by a large variety of arguments, and the self-serving ones are usually emphasized when facing Congress, their preponderance could not but have had negative side-effects on Soviet-American relations. Also, the same gestures would have been more effective had they been introduced with less hesitation, and if Soviet initiatives had been met with less ambivalence.

Above all, since the process was halted, one cannot tell whether psychological measures open the door to "real" give-and-take or are essentially meaningless in the absence of basic and lasting settlements of differences and conflicts. The fact remains, however, that gestures that were almost purely psychological in nature led to an American-Soviet semi-*détente* lasting from June 1963 until now. Whether more of the same could have brought about more fundamental changes cannot be learned from this case.

ALTERNATIVE EXPLANATIONS

Even though the adoption of the measures advocated by the theory yielded the expected psychological results, there still remains the possibility of spuriousness; i.e., that the result was produced by factors other than those specified by the theory. We need, then, to ask what other factors could account for the *détente*? Two alternative sources of tension reduction most often cited are examined below; we shall see that they do not invalidate the claim that the unilateral-initiatives approach deserves credit for the *détente*. It is, however, always possible to claim that still another factor was at work; there is no final test against spuriousness. But until it is actually shown that there was another factor that caused the specified effects, we are justified in holding that the theory has been strengthened by the Kennedy experiment. This is especially so, as we can trace directly the contribution of the unilateral initiatives to the *détente*.

The first explanation is that of catharsis. According to this theory, the door was opened for a *détente* after the Cuban blockade discharged a large amount of frustration that Americans had accumulated over the cold war years. Traditionally, Americans have expected that wars will be short, end with an American victory, followed by the restoration of peace. In contrast, the cold war required a continual state of mobilization and prolonged tensions without the prospect of victory. The resulting frustration was deepened by the widely held belief that the Communists were more successful than the West in Asia, Latin America, and Africa. Under the pressure of these frustrations, it is often suggested, efforts to reach accommodation with Russia became viewed as showing weakness, and a "tough" *verbal* posture was popular. The establishment of a Communist government in Cuba, Soviet successes in space, the fiasco of the 1961 Bay of Pigs invasion, and the positioning of Soviet missiles in Cuba in 1962 all further deepened American frustration. While initially the 1962 blockade raised many fears, once it proved not to lead to war and to yield a Soviet retreat, it became the first American victory in a long time. While the blockade's successes were widely viewed as supporting the "tough" line, suggesting that power politics could be used in the nuclear age, the psychological effect was in the opposite direction, one of cathartic release. One of the values of the psychological line of analysis is to highlight such differences between verbal postures and underlying emotional commitments. Fierce posture on one level need not be accompanied with the same on the other. "Tough" words may cover a moderate feeling. In this case, it is said, the Cuban showdown increased the American public's emotional willingness to accept arms control negotiations with the Soviet Union.

The other interpretation associates the initiation of the *détente* with the unfolding of a different psychological process —the effects of the increased visibility of the disintegration of the blocs. In 1962 Communist China attacked the Soviet Union publicly, criticizing Soviet involvement in Cuba as "adventurism" and its retreat as "defeatism." Russia, like America, continued its economic and military support to India when it came under Chinese attack in 1962. About the same time, the American-French dispute forced itself on the public's attention.

Initially, the popular American press, apparently reflecting the opinion of the public at large, tended to ignore or regard as a "put-up job" the split in the East and to underplay the rift in the West. But the rifts finally gained recognition with the hostile rejection of Mao and of De Gaulle partially replacing that earlier focused on the Soviet Union. The Soviets now seemed "reasonable" and "responsible" compared to Communist China, for Russia appeared willing to share with us the concern over nuclear proliferation and dangers of war provoked by over-eager allies.

Some evidence to support the effect of this bifurcation of the bloc images in generating the *détente* can be seen in the press. A typical *New York Times* Sunday review-of-the-news section ran the following captions: "Conflict in East," "Russia vs. China," and "U.S. vs. France"; and last—"East vs. West."[45] Direct reporting of the relationship between changes in the intra-bloc situation and those which were inter-bloc was also common. For example:

> The answer seems to hinge on whether Premier Khrushchev really wants a test ban. One school of thought is that he does. The argument runs that Moscow's relations with Peking have reached the point virtually of open rupture. Consequently, Premier Khrushchev is thought to be willing to deal with the West, especially if one result of such dealing might be increased difficulty for Peking in acquiring nuclear capability.[46]

It is not implied that the only effect of the decline in the solidarity of the blocs was to bring the two superpowers closer to each other. In reality, the Soviet Union was occasionally reluctant to agree to American proposals so as not to lose points in its fight with China over control of the Communist movement in third countries. Similarly, the United States was not always eager to agree to Soviet initiatives for fear of displeasing West Germany and thus playing into the hands of France. But the consciousness of deep differences of interest within the blocs, even when they agitated against agreement between the bloc leaders, had the psychological effect of reducing inter-bloc tensions. The recognition of the splits in the alliances undermined the prevailing simplistic image of the forces of light fighting the forces of darkness. As a result, it is suggested, the ideological fervor of the international atmosphere declined, tension was reduced, and *détente* was enhanced.

Such a weakening of ideological fervor is important for the initiation of negotiations which give and take, because otherwise politicians find it hard to face their voters with the outcomes of the negotiations. As long as any give and take, even when completely symmetrical, tends to be viewed as a concession, if not outright appeasement, ideological disarmament is needed to allow the public to see that some genuine bargaining is possible, and that certain kinds of accommodation serve both sides to the disadvantage of neither.

At the same time, bifurcation of the bloc images shifted the focus of the xenophobia. Regarding the Communist camp, China became, with considerable disregard of its actual foreign policy, the villain; in the West, the focus of American self-righteousness was now De Gaulle. These two replaced the previous preoccupation with Soviet Russia. Xenophobia, it is suggested, was rechanneled rather than reduced. (Or, more technically, a new object was substituted rather than the drive extinguished or significantly weakened.)

All these psychological processes might have been feeding into each other. Catharsis, bifurcation of images, and unilateral initiatives might all have contributed to the *détente* as well as to each other. For instance, catharsis might have eased the initiation of a policy of unilateral initiatives, and in turn the resultant reduction of inter-bloc tensions accelerated bifurcation of the bloc images, which made easier the further reduction of tensions through additional unilateral initiatives.

We still remain with the difficult question of the relative weight of the three processes in bringing about the *détente*. While it is impossible to answer this question with precision, it seems that while catharsis and bifurcation might have helped, they were not necessary prerequisites to the resultant situation; unilateral initiatives alone could have produced the effect. The best evidence for this is found in the examination of two other occasions in which a thaw was achieved—the 1959 Camp David spirit, and the 1955 Geneva spirit. These cannot be analyzed within the limits of this paper, but they seem to show the validity of the assertion that unilateral initiatives can bring about a *détente* without the support of the other two psychological processes.

It also should be noted that the 1963–64 thaw did not immediately follow the termination of the Cuban crisis, in the sense that no *détente* existed between November 1962 and June 1963 (though this still would not rule out the role of catharsis as a preparatory condition). Similarly, while the bifurcation of the bloc images was deepened in 1962, it existed before, and was as much caused by the *détente* as it effected the *détente*. Above all, the effect can be most directly traced to the unilateral initiatives; it started with them, grew as they grew, and slowed down only as they decreased.

THE EFFECTS OF SABOTAGE

Sabotage is a traditional tool of foreign policy, going back at least to the ancient Greek states. In the age of mass democracies, one of its forms is that of creating international pseudo-events to affect the psychological atmosphere in a direction counter to that of the prevailing policy. In some formulations of the psychological theory, this problem is disregarded, for nations are conceived as analogous to individuals, thus being able to shift policies in the manner of one man changing his mind.[47] In formulations which take into account the existence of vested interests in the continuation of inter-bloc tensions, both overt opposition to tension reduction and sabotage are expected.[48] The lesson of the U-2 flight which triggered the termination of the 1959 thaw was analyzed before the 1963–64 *détente* took place. It showed the need of policymakers to realize that many governmental activities have a communicative value, and that if a government seeks to communicate that it has shifted to a new posture, measures are to be taken to ensure that no activities are undertaken or continued that conflict with the new posture. This point is to be emphasized, as some inconsistency is often deliberately introduced in the policy of most countries. For example, the U.S. position on M.L.F. for a while attempted to assure the Russians that there would be no proliferation of arms while at the same time encouraging the West Germans to hope for some control of nuclear weapons. But when one engages in psychological campaigns, consistency has a high value because "out-of-character" steps largely undermine the effect of the campaign on recipients who, the psychological theory suggests, are suspicious to begin with.

The foregoing discussion assumes that the U-2 flights were continued due to an oversight (neglecting to cancel this "hostile" activity as the change in posture took place), or were a planned attempt to reap the benefits of continued violations of Soviet territories on one level, while trying to reduce tensions on another. If, on the other hand, the flights were an act of sabotage by a service or group within it not concurring with the change in policy, then it would seem that if the American government is to follow a tension-reduction policy, a tightening of internal controls is necessary[49]

The lesson of the U-2 incident is that it is necessary to anticipate both unwitting and deliberate sabotages and prepare a proper response. Several observers suggested that Premier Khrushchev was, for domestic reasons, looking for a way out of the 1959 *détente* and that the U-2 just provided an excuse. But the possibility that the Russian premier was really embarrassed before his fellow members of the powerful Presidium, some of whom objected to the *détente,* cannot be ruled out. That would suggest that he had not foreseen an act of sabotage and was not prepared to act in a way that would diffuse its chilling effect on the thaw. Further, Eisenhower's insistence that he personally ordered the flight and his refusal to make apologetic comments, behavior which is common in such circumstances, made Khrushchev's accommodation in favor of continuation of the *détente* more difficult—if he desired to continue. It also gave him a ready excuse if he were looking for one, although in this case he might sooner or later have found one anyway. The fact that Khrushchev was unwilling to terminate the Camp David atmosphere without such an excuse, suggests that he was not particularly anxious to terminate it at all. Moreover, had time been gained by not providing such an excuse, the pro-*détente* motives and forces might have prevailed. Drawing on all this, I suggested in 1962 that unilateral initiatives be guarded against sabotage, and, if it occurred anyway, the sabotage should be rapidly defused rather than allowed to damage the *détente*.[50]

We have already seen that domestic forces and politics as well as allies prevented the United States from giving a clear signal of a shift to a Strategy for Peace. Several leading Democratic senators and important representatives of the military objected to the test-ban treaty; the wheat deal was made with much hesitation and debate; and various tension-provoking interpretations were given to the *détente* policy. Direct acts of sabotage also occurred, but their effect on the *détente* was much more limited than the U-2 flight; they were treated more in accord with the theory.

An example of an "out-of-character" event is found in a note struck by President Kennedy himself, when, during a speech at West Berlin's City Hall on the twenty-sixth of June, he not only described himself as a Berliner and repeated the usual statements regarding America's commitment to Germany's defense but added, in tones familiar to the pre-*détente* period:

> There are many people in the world who really don't understand—or say they don't—what is the great issue between the free world and the Communist world. Let them come to Berlin.
>
> There are some who say that Communism is the wave of the future. Let them come to Berlin.
>
> And there are some who say in Europe and elsewhere—"We can work with the communists." Let them come to Berlin.
>
> And there are even a few who say it's true that Communism is an evil system but it permits us to make economic progress. Let them come to Berlin.

Khrushchev, giving a counter speech a few days later in East Berlin on the occasion of Ulbricht's birthday, chose not to reciprocate in kind, and thus the incident was soon forgotten.

The "tailgate" clash on the route to West Berlin on October 10–12 came closer to undermining the Kennedy experiment. Briefly, what happened was that the Americans riding in a convoy to West Berlin refused to dismount for a head count, and the Russians would not allow them to pass. The Russians claimed they usually were granted the right to count the passengers, but the West claimed this was the case only if more than thirty soldiers were involved, and there were fewer this time. (When fewer, the Russians looked over the tail-gate, hence the name of the incident.) When the Russians countered that there were more than thirty, the United States answered that the balance were civilian drivers who did not "count"; the Russians claimed that they did. The Americans tried to break through; the Russians blocked the route with armed carriers. Headlines around the world projected for two days an image of two sides standing "eyeball to eyeball," finger on the trigger, in a typical cold war test of will, lacking any *détente*-like spirit. Finally, the crisis was resolved, and the convoy was allowed to pass.

Although who was to blame for the incident is by no means clear, this is of little importance to the analysis of its effect on America-Russia relations: tensions mounted rather than declined, and to most American newspaper readers the fault was completely Russian, and the senselessness of the act amidst a *détente* heightened anew their suspicions of Russia's good faith. The *New York Times* declared that "the provocative Soviet behavior on this matter has set back the cause of the *détente*, reinforced Western suspicion of Moscow."[51] The *Herald Tribune*'s editorial on October 12 was entitled, "The Soviet Mask Slips." It claimed that "the wholly unjustifiable display of Soviet pettifogging at the entrance of Berlin, then, will be taken by the American government and people as an indication that the protestations of Mr. Khrushchev and of Mr. Gromyko concerning Russia's desire for more friendly relations with the U.S. are just a mask."

But once the incident was settled, the explanation encouraged by Washington was that there was a "misunderstanding" about the rules and not a new Soviet pressure on the West or a shift in Russian policy away from *détente*.[52] Others attributed the incident to abuse of authority by low-ranking Soviet officers. One reliable American journal published an account that provided evidence suggesting the issue was largely caused by American army officers.[53] A second interpretation, seeking to defuse the effects of the incident, was that Berlin was an "abnormal" situation, excluded from the general *détente* the Russians otherwise did favor.[54] While the incident left the *détente* marred, especially as it was about to be slowed down anyway, these interpretations, encouraged by Washington and London, succeeded in restricting its damage. This was in sharp contrast to the impact of the U-2 flight.

A second incident, which occurred on October 31, 1963, had almost exactly the same pattern. An American scholar, Professor Frederick C. Barghoorn, was arrested in Moscow on espionage charges. President Kennedy stated that the charges were "unwarranted and unjustified" and that they "badly demaged" Soviet-American relations. Western newspapers again asked if Russia were shifting away from the conciliatory "Spirit of Moscow," and the conservative press sounded its "I told you so" horns. The professor was released, and it was almost immediately suggested that "the arrest might have been carried out by security officers . . . anxious to throw a monkey wrench into Premier Khrushchev's policy of 'co-existence' with the West."[55] Khrushchev chose not to identify with the arrest but let the Professor go because of the "personal concern" of President Kennedy.[56] Later, although the incident had left its mark, its impact was, once again, defused. American sources further helped to dissipate the resultant tensions by suggesting that "they still found it conceivable that something had occurred to arouse their [the Russians'] suspicions about the professor."[57] In each case, then, when a dissonant note was sounded during the Kennedy experiment, it was soon softened and modified to protect the main theme. Thus, both the fragility of the *détente* and the mechanisms to safeguard it were demonstrated.

PSYCHOLOGICAL VS. "REAL" FACTORS

By far the most difficult question to answer is what gains can be achieved from a *détente* in other than psychological terms. The 1959 *détente* was the shortest and yielded nothing; the 1955 *détente* was longer and brought about the neutralization of Austria, the main instance since World War II in which territory held by the Red Army was released to a society with Western institutions. There is a widely held belief that the 1955 *détente* could have yielded much more, possibly an arrangement regarding Germany and Berlin, but this must remain speculation. The 1963 *détente* led to a partial test ban and a ban on the orbiting of weapons of mass destruction, both steps of largely psychological value. Whether or not it did prepare the ground for additional steps is yet unknown.

There remains a more general question which is of a different order from the analysis of any one period and its psychology: how important are psychological factors in affecting international behavior? Answers range from theories which imply these factors are all-important to those which view the determinants of international relations to be exclusively "real" factors. The correct view is probably somewhere between the extreme positions. Certainly factors other than psychology are relevant, and it can easily be demonstrated that psychological factors have "real" consequences. The question then is one of the *relative* importance of these factors.

While we are unable to provide a definite answer to this question, several comments can be made. First, the advent of nationalism and mass media has increased the importance of psychological forces. Second, the consequences of these forces seem to have increased with the introduction of nuclear deterrence forces, because deterrence is itself a psychological concept and is therefore affected by such factors as credibility, fear, and misperception.

In addition, the present study suggests that psychological forces are most important when the sides wish to *initiate* a change in policy but seem not to be strong enough to *sustain* the change when it is not supported by other factors. When other processes agitate for change (e.g., a new congruence in Soviet-American interests with regard to the spread of nuclear arms), a modification of psychological variables in the same direction makes the new policy easier to introduce. Moreover, the psychological forces might get somewhat "out-of-hand" and bring about changes in policy above and beyond what other considerations seem to suggest. (For example, in 1958 the United States sought to *negotiate* a moratorium on nuclear testing but not to bring about its initiation. When Russia suddenly declared a moratorium unilaterally, the United States felt it had no choice but to reciprocate. This did not, however, lead to additional arms control measures.) On the other hand, it seems that the psychological factors are basically well in hand; they cannot be used to bring about a policy that is a major departure from the policy other forces favor. Thus, in general, psychological factors have *significant auxiliary* and *limited independent* effects.

A study of the "actors" who are affected by psychological factors might in large part illuminate the reasons for the preceding statement. Most statements about "international tensions" are actually referring to states of mind of citizens rather than relations among nations or among the governing elites of the nations.[58] The kind and degree of influence of the citizenry on foreign policy is a complicated question that cannot be explored here. But it might be suggested that to a great extent *the effect of psychological factors on international behavior of a state is that of the citizens on foreign policy-making elites*. In the pre-nationalist stage, the mass of the citizens had little effect on foreign policy, and psychological factors were, therefore, relatively unimportant. In totalitarian societies, citizens have less influence on foreign policy than in democratic ones; hence psychological factors are relatively less consequential there.

In democratic societies, public opinion is determined through a complicated process in which the public, its local leaders, the mass media, the national elites, and various social and economic processes are working on each other. In the short run, one of the most outstanding features is that the national leadership is confronted with the public opinion it helped to crystallize at earlier points in time. Once a context (or *gestalt*) is established, there is a demand for consistency. Seeming inconsistency activates various psychological processes, such as the feeling of betrayal. Thus, at various points American Administrations have felt they could ill-afford politically to support the admission of Communist China to the United Nations, because the American public was educated against it, and the Administration believed that no amount of short-run explanation could change public opinion to make the political costs low enough. The Kennedy experiment, it seems, was much more oriented toward the American people than toward the Russians or any international "tensions." Its primary purpose, it seems, was not to affect international relations directly but to increase the range of options the Kennedy Administration could take up without running high political risks from a public steeped in cold war psychology. Thus the policy of unilateral initiatives can be said to have worked, and the experiment to have been successful. A wider range of foreign policy options was made politically feasible.

Part V

The Problem of the Public

BEHAVIORAL STUDY OF OBEDIENCE

Stanley Milgram

This article describes a procedure for the study of destructive obedience in the laboratory. It consists of ordering a naive S to administer increasingly more severe punishment to a victim in the context of a learning experiment. Punishment is administered by means of a shock generator with 30 graded switches ranging from Slight Shock to Danger: Severe Shock. The victim is a confederate of the E. The primary dependent variable is the maximum shock the S is willing to administer before he refuses to continue further. 26 Ss obeyed the experimental commands fully, and administered the highest shock on the generator. 14 Ss broke off the experiment at some point after the victim protested and refused to provide further answers. The procedure created extreme levels of nervous tension in some Ss. Profuse sweating, trembling, and stuttering were typical expressions of this emotional disturbance. One unexpected sign of tension—yet to be explained—was the regular occurrence of nervous laughter, which in some Ss developed into uncontrollable seizures. . . .

OBEDIENCE is as basic an element in the structure of social life as one can point to. Some system of authority is a requirement of all communal living, and it is only the man dwelling in isolation who is not forced to respond, through defiance or submission, to the commands of others. Obedience, as a determinant of behavior, is of particular relevance to our time. . . . From 1933 to 1945 . . . millions of

Reprinted from *Journal of Abnormal and Social Psychology*, Vol. 67, No. 4 (1963), pp. 371–378. (All footnotes, references, and tables have been deleted.)

innocent persons were systematically slaughtered on command. Gas chambers were built, death camps were guarded, daily quotas of corpses were produced. . . . These inhumane policies may have originated in the mind of a single person, but they could only be carried out on a massive scale if a very large number of persons obeyed orders.

Obedience is the psychological mechanism that links individual action to political purpose. It is the dispositional cement that binds men to systems of authority. Facts of recent history and observation in daily life suggest that for many persons obedience may be a deeply ingrained behavior tendency, indeed, a prepotent impulse overriding training in ethics, sympathy, and moral conduct. . . .

. . .

. . . It must not be thought all obedience entails acts of aggression against others. Obedience serves numerous productive functions. Indeed, the very life of society is predicated on its existence. Obedience may be ennobling and educative and refer to acts of charity and kindness, as well as to destruction.

GENERAL PROCEDURE

A procedure was devised which seems useful as a tool for studying obedience. It consists of ordering a naive subject to administer electric shock to a victim. A simulated shock generator is used, with 30 clearly marked voltage levels that range from 15 to 450 volts. The instrument bears verbal designations that range from Slight Shock to Danger: Severe Shock. The responses of the victim, who is a trained confederate of the experimenter, are standardized. The orders to administer shocks are given to the naive subject in the context of a "learning experiment" ostensibly set up to study the effects of punishment on memory. As the experiment proceeds the naive subject is commanded to administer increasingly more intense shocks to the victim, even to the point of reaching the level marked Danger: Severe Shock. Internal resistances become stronger, and at a certain point the subject refuses to go on with the experiment. Behavior prior to this rupture is considered "obedience," in that the subject complies with the commands of the experimenter. The point of rupture is the act of disobedience. A quantitative value is assigned to the subject's performance based on the maximum intensity shock he is willing to administer before he refuses to participate further. Thus for any particular subject and for any particular experimental condition the degree of obedience may be specified with a numerical value. The crux of the study is to systematically vary the factors believed to alter the degree of obedience to the experimental commands.

The technique allows important variables to be manipulated at several points in the experiment. One may vary aspects of the source of command, content and form of command, instrumentalities for its execution, target object, general setting, etc. The problem, therefore, is not one of designing increasingly more numerous experimental conditions, but of selecting those that best illuminate the *process* of obedience from the sociopsychological standpoint.

. . .

METHOD

Subjects

The subjects were 40 males between the ages 20 and 50, drawn from New Haven and the surrounding communities. Subjects were obtained by a newspaper advertisement and direct mail solicitation. Those who responded to the appeal believed they were to participate in a study of memory and learning at Yale University. A wide range of occupations is represented in the sample. Typical subjects were postal clerks, high school teachers, salesmen, engineers, and laborers. Subjects ranged in educational level from one who had not finished elementary school, to those who had doctorate and other professional degrees. They were paid subjects were told that payment was simply for coming to $4.50 for their participation in the experiment. However, the laboratory, and that the money was theirs no matter what happened after they arrived. . . .

Personnel and Locale

The expirement was conducted on the grounds of Yale University in the elegant interaction laboratory. (This detail is relevant to the perceived legitimacy of the experiment. In further variations, the experiment was dissociated from the university, with consequences for performance.) The role of experimenter was played by a 31-year-old high school teacher of biology. His manner was impassive, and his appearance somewhat stern throughout the experiment. He was dressed in a gray technician's coat. The victim was played by a 47-year-old accountant, trained for the role; he was of Irish-American stock, whom most observers found mild-mannered and likable.

. . .

Procedure

One naive subject and one victim (an accomplice) performed in each experiment. A pretext had to be devised that would justify the administration of electric shock by the naive subject. This was effectively accomplished by the cover story. After a general introduction on the presumed relation between punishment and learning, subjects were told:

> But actually, we know *very little* about the effect of punishment on learning, because almost no truly scientific studies have been made of it in human beings.
>
> For instance, we don't know how *much* punishment is best for learning—and we don't know how much difference it makes as to who is giving the punishment, whether an adult learns best from a younger or an older person than himself—or many things of that sort.
>
> So in this study we are bringing together a number of adults of different occupations and ages. And we're asking some of them to be teachers and some of them to be learners.
>
> We want to find out just what effect different people have on each other as teachers and learners, and also what effect *punishment* will have on learning in this situation.

Therefore, I'm going to ask one of you to be the teacher here tonight and the other one to be the learner.
Does either of you have a preference?

Subjects then drew slips of paper from a hat to determine who would be the teacher and who would be the learner in the experiment. The drawing was rigged so that the naive subject was always the teacher and the accomplice always the learner. (Both slips contained the word "Teacher.") Immediately after the drawing, the teacher and learner were taken to an adjacent room and the learner was strapped into an "electric chair" apparatus.

The experimenter explained that the straps were to prevent excessive movement while the learner was being shocked. The effect was to make it impossible for him to escape from the situation. An electrode was attached to the learner's wrist, and electrode paste was applied "to avoid blisters and burns." Subjects were told that the electrode was attached to the shock generator in the adjoining room.

In order to improve credibility the experimenter declared, in response to a question by the learner: "Although the shocks can be extremely painful, they cause no permanent tissue damage."

Learning task. The lesson administered by the subject was a paired-associate learning task. The subject read a series of word pairs to the learner, and then read the first word of the pair along with four terms. The learner was to indicate which of the four terms had originally been paired with the first word. He communicated his answer by pressing one of four switches in front of him, which in turn lit up one of the four numbered quadrants in an answer-box located atop the shock generator.

Shock generator. The instrument panel consists of 30 lever switches set in a horizontal line. Each switch is clearly labeled with a voltage designation that ranges from 15 to 450 volts. There is a 15-volt increment from one switch to the next going from left to right. In addition, the following verbal designations are clearly indicated for groups of four switches going from left to right: Slight Shock, Moderate

Shock, Strong Shock, Very Strong Shock, Intense Shock, Extreme Intensity Shock, Danger: Severe Shock. (Two switches after this last designation are simply marked XXX.)

Upon depressing a switch: a pilot light corresponding to each switch is illuminated in bright red; an electric buzzing is heard; an electric blue light, labeled "voltage energizer," flashes; the dial on the voltage meter swings to the right; various relay clicks are sounded.

The upper left-hand corner of the generator is labeled Shock Generator, Type ZLB, Dyson Instrument Company, Waltham, Mass. Output 15 Volts–450 Volts.

Details of the instrument were carefully handled to insure an appearance of authenticity. The panel was engraved by precision industrial engravers, and all components were of high quality. No subject in the experiment suspected that the instrument was merely a simulated shock generator.

Sample shock. Each naive subject is given a sample shock on the shock generator, prior to beginning his run as teacher. This shock is always 45 volts, and is applied by pressing the third switch of the generator. The shock is applied to the wrist of the naive subject, and has its source in a 45-volt battery wired into the generator. This further convinces the subject of the authenticity of the generator.

Shock instructions. The subject is told to administer a shock to the learner each time he gives a wrong response. Moreover—and this is the key command—the subject is instructed to "move one level higher on the shock generator each time the learner flashes a wrong answer." He is also instructed to announce the voltage level before administering a shock. This serves to continually remind subjects of the increasing intensity of shocks administered to the learner.

Preliminary and regular run. Pretests revealed that the procedure of reading words and administering shocks requires some practice before it can be handled smoothly. Therefore, immediately preceding the regular run, the teacher is given a preliminary series of 10 words to read to the learner. There are 3 neutral words in the practice series (i.e., words that the learner answers correctly), so that shocks are administered for 7 of the words, with the maximum shock at 105 volts (moderate shock). Almost all subjects master the procedure by the time the preliminary run is over.

Subjects are then presented with a second list, and are told that the procedure is the same as for the first list; the experimenter adds, however:

> When you get to the bottom of the list, repeat it over again, and continue giving shocks, until the learner has learned all the pairs correctly.

The experimenter instructs the subject to:

> start from 15 volts and increase the shock level one step each time the learner gives a wrong answer.

Feedback from the victim. In all conditions the learner gives a predetermined set of responses to the word pair test, based on a schedule of approximately three wrong answers to one correct answer. In the present experimental condition no vocal response or other sign of protest is heard from the learner until Shock Level 300 is reached. When the 300-volt shock is administered, the learner pounds on the wall of the room in which he is bound to the electric chair. The pounding can be heard by the subject. From this point on, the learner's answers no longer appear on the four-way panel.

At this juncture, subjects ordinarily turn to the experimenter for guidance. The experimenter instructs the subject to treat the absence of a response as a wrong answer, and to shock the subject according to the usual schedule. He advises the subjects to allow 5–10 seconds before considering no response as a wrong answer, and to increase the shock level one step each time the learner fails to respond correctly. The learner's pounding is repeated after the 315-volt shock is administered; afterwards he is not heard from, nor do his answers reappear on the four-way signal box.

Experimenter feedback. At various points in the experiment the subject may turn to the experimenter for advice on whether he should continue to administer shocks. Or he may indicate that he does not wish to go on. It was important to standardize the experimenter's responses to these inquiries and reactions.

If the subject indicated his unwillingness to go on, the experimenter responded with a sequence of "prods," using as many as necessary to bring the subject into line.

Prod 1: Please continue, *or* Please go on.
Prod 2: The experiment requires that you continue.
Prod 3: It is absolutely essential that you continue.
Prod 4: You have no other choice, you *must* go on.

The prods were always made in sequence: Only if Prod 1 had been unsuccessful, could Prod 2 be used. If the subject refused to obey the experimenter after Prod 4, the experiment was terminated. The experimenter's tone of voice was at all times firm, but not impolite. The sequence was begun anew on each occasion that the subject balked or showed reluctance to follow orders.

Special prods. If the subject asked if the learner was liable to suffer permanent physical injury, the experimenter said:

> Although the shocks may be painful, there is no permanent tissue damage, so please go on. [Followed by Prods 2, 3, and 4 if necessary.]

If the subject said that the learner did not want to go on, the experimenter replied:

> Whether the learner likes it or not, you must go on until he has learned all the word pairs correctly. So please go on. [Followed by Prods 2, 3, and 4 if necessary.]

Dependent Measures

The primary dependent measure for any subject is the maximum shock he administers before he refuses to go any further. In principle this may vary from 0 (for a subject who refuses to administer even the first shock) to 30 (for a subject who administers the highest shock on the generator). A subject who breaks off the experiment at any point prior to administering the thirtieth shock level is termed a *defiant* subject. One who complies with experimental commands fully, and proceeds to administer all shock levels commanded, is termed an *obedient* subject.

Further records. With few exceptions, experimental sessions were recorded on magnetic tape. Occasional photographs were taken through one-way mirrors. Notes were kept on any unusual behavior occurring during the course of the experiments. On occasion, additional observers were directed to write objective descriptions of the subjects' behavior. The latency and duration of shocks were measured by accurate timing devices.

Interview and dehoax. Following the experiment, subjects were interviewed; open-ended questions, projective measures, and attitude scales were employed. After the interview, procedures were undertaken to assure that the subject would leave the laboratory in a state of well being. A friendly reconciliation was arranged between the subject and the victim, and an effort was made to reduce any tensions that arose as a result of the experiment.

RESULTS

Preliminary Notions

Before giving an account of the experimental results, it is instructive to consider how persons predict others will perform when commanded to administer powerful shocks to another person. Fourteen Yale seniors, all psychology majors, were provided with a detailed description of the experimental situation. They were asked to reflect carefully on it, and to predict the behavior of 100 hypothetical subjects. More specifically, they were instructed to plot the distribution of obedience of "100 Americans of diverse occupations, and ranging in age from 20 to 50 years," who were placed in the experimental situation.

There was considerable agreement among the respondents on the expected behavior of hypothetical subjects. All respondents predicted that only an insignificant minority would go through to the end of the shock series. (The estimates ranged from 0 to 3%; i.e., the most "pessimistic" member of the class predicted that of 100 persons, 3 would continue through to the most potent shock available on the shock generator—450 volts.) The class mean was 1.2%. The question was also posed informally to colleagues of the author, and the most general feeling was that few if any subjects would go beyond the designation Very Strong Shock.

Result of Experiment I

Subjects accept situation. With few exceptions subjects were convinced of the reality of the experimental situation, that they were administering shocks to another person, and the most potent shocks were extremely painful. In the post-experimental interview subjects were asked: "How painful to the learner were the last few shocks that you administered to him?" Subjects were instructed to indicate their answers on a printed 14-point scale ranging from "Not at all painful" to "Extremely painful." The modal response was 14 (Extremely painful) with the mean at 13.42.

Signs of extreme tension. Many subjects showed signs of nervousness in the experimental situation, and especially upon administering the more powerful shocks. In a large number of cases the degree of tension reached extremes that are rarely seen in sociopsychological laboratory studies. Subjects were observed to sweat, tremble, stutter, bite their lips, groan, and dig their fingernails into their flesh. These were characteristic rather than exceptional responses to the experiment.

One sign of tension was the regular occurrence of nervous laughing fits. Fourteen of the 40 subjects showed definite signs of nervous laughter and smiling. The laughter seemed entirely out of place, even bizarre, Full-blown, uncontrollable seizures were observed for 3 subjects. On one occasion we observed a seizure so violently convulsive that it was necessary to call a halt to the experiment. The subject, a 46-year-old encyclopedia salesman, was seriously embarrassed by his untoward and uncontrollable behavior. In the post-experimental interviews subjects took pains to point out that they were not sadistic types, and that the laughter did not mean they enjoyed shocking the victim.

Distribution of scores. It had been conjectured that persons would not, in general, agree to administer shocks beyond the level designated as Very Strong Shock. . . . The obtained distribution of scores deviates radically from the prediction.

. . .

Upon command of the experimenter, each of the 40 subjects went beyond the expected breakoff point. No subject stopped prior to administering Shock Level 20. (At this level—300 volts—the victim kicks on the wall and no longer provides answers to the teacher's multiple-choice questions.)

Of the 40 subjects, 5 refused to obey the experimental commands beyond the 300-volt level. Four more subjects administered one further shock, and then refused to go on. Two broke off at the 330-volt level, and 1 each at 345, 360, and 375 volts. Thus a total of 14 subjects defied the experimenter. It is instructive to reprint their remarks at the point of defiance, as transcribed from the tape recordings:

[0124] I think he's trying to communicate, he's knocking. . . . Well it's not fair to shock the guy . . . these are terrific volts. I don't think this is very humane. . . . Oh, I can't go on with this; no, this isn't right. It's a hell of an experiment. The guy is suffering in there. No, I don't want to go on. This is crazy. [Subject refused to administer more shocks.]

[0123] He's banging in there. I'm gonna chicken out. I'd like to continue, but I can't do that to a man. . . . I'm sorry I can't do that to a man. I'll hurt his heart. You take your check. . . . No really, I couldn't do it.

These subjects were frequently in a highly agitated and even angered state. Sometimes, verbal protest was at a minimum, and the subject simply got up from his chair in front of the shock generator, and indicated that he wished to leave the laboratory.

Of the 40 subjects, 26 obeyed the orders of the experimenter to the end, proceeding to punish the victim until they reached the most potent shock available on the shock generator. At that point, the experimenter called a halt to the session. (The maximum shock is labeled 450 volts, and is two steps beyond the designation: Danger: Severe Shock.) Although obedient subjects continued to administer shocks, they often did so under extreme stress. Some expressed reluctance to administer shocks beyond the 300-volt level, and displayed fears similar to those who defied the experimenter; yet they obeyed.

After the maximum shocks had been delivered, and the experimenter called a halt to the proceedings, many obedient subjects heaved sighs of relief, mopped their brows, rubbed their fingers over their eyes, or nervously fumbled cigarettes. Some shook their heads, apparently in regret. Some subjects had remained calm throughout the experiment, and displayed only minimal signs of tension from beginning to end.

DISCUSSION

The experiment yielded two things that were surprising. The first finding concerns the sheer strength of obedient tendencies manifested in this situation. Subjects have learned from childhood that it is a fundamental breach of moral conduct to hurt another person against his will. Yet, 26 subjects abandon this tenet in following the instructions of an authority who has no special powers to enforce his commands. To disobey would bring no material loss to the subject; no punishment would ensue. It is clear from the remarks and outward behavior of many participants that in punishing the victim they are often acting against their own values. Subjects often expressed deep disapproval of shocking a man in the face of his objections, and others denounced it as stupid and senseless. Yet the majority complied with the experimental commands. This outcome was surprising from two perspectives: first, from the standpoint of predictions made in the questionnaire described earlier. (Here, however, it is possible that the remoteness of the respondents from the actual situation, and the difficulty of conveying to them the concrete details of the experiment, could account for the serious underestimation of obedience.)

But the results were also unexpected to persons who observed the experiment in progress, through one-way mirrors.

Observers often uttered expressions of disbelief upon seeing a subject administer more powerful shocks to the victim. These persons had a full acquaintance with the details of the situation, and yet systematically underestimated the amount of obedience that subjects would display.

The second unanticipated effect was the extraordinary tension generated by the procedures. One might suppose that a subject would simply break off or continue as his conscience dictated. Yet, this is very far from what happened. There were striking reactions of tension and emotional strain. One observer related:

> I observed a mature and initially poised businessman enter the laboratory smiling and confident. Within 20 minutes he was reduced to a twitching, stuttering wreck, who was rapidly approaching a point of nervous collapse. He constantly pulled on his earlobe, and twisted his hands. At one point he pushed his fist into his forehead and muttered: "Oh God, let's stop it." And yet he continued to respond to every word of the experimenter, and obeyed to the end.

Any understanding of the phenomenon of obedience must rest on an analysis of the particular conditions in which it occurs. The following features of the experiment go some distance in explaining the high amount of obedience observed in the situation.

1. The experiment is sponsored by and takes place on the grounds of an institution of unimpeachable reputation, Yale University. It may be reasonably presumed that the personnel are competent and reputable. The importance of this background authority is now being studied by conducting a series of experiments outside of New Haven, and without any visible ties to the university.

2. The experiment is, on the face of it, designed to attain a worthy purpose—advancement of knowledge about learning and memory. Obedience occurs not as an end in itself, but as an instrumental element in a situation that the subject construes as significant, and meaningful. He may not be able to see its full significance, but he may properly assume that the experimenter does.

3. The subject perceives that the victim has voluntarily submitted to the authority system of the experimenter. He is not (at first) an unwilling captive impressed for involuntary service. He has taken the trouble to come to the laboratory presumably to aid the experimental research. That he later becomes an involuntary subject does not alter the fact that, initially, he consented to participate without qualification. Thus he has in some degree incurred an obligation toward the experimenter.

4. The subject, too, has entered the experiment voluntarily, and perceives himself under obligation to aid the experimenter. He has made a commitment, and to disrupt the experiment is a repudiation of this initial promise of aid.

5. Certain features of the procedure strengthen the subject's sense of obligation to the experimenter. For one, he has been paid for coming to the laboratory. In part this is canceled out by the experimenter's statement that:

> Of course, as in all experiments, the money is yours simply for coming to the laboratory. From this point on, no matter what happens, the money is yours.[1]

6. From the subject's standpoint, the fact that he is the teacher and the other man the learner is purely a chance consequence (it is determined by drawing lots) and he, the subject, ran the same risk as the other man in being assigned the role of learner. Since the assignment of positions in the experiment was achieved by fair means, the learner is deprived of any basis of complaint on this count. (A similar situation obtains in Army units, in which—in the absence of volunteers—a particularly dangerous mission may be assigned by drawing lots, and the unlucky soldier is expected to bear his misfortune with sportsmanship.)

7. There is, at best, ambiguity with regard to the prerogatives of a psychologist and the corresponding rights of his subject. There is a vagueness of expectation concerning what a psychologist may require of his subject, and when he is overstepping acceptable limits. Moreover, the experiment occurs in a closed setting, and thus provides no opportunity for the subject to remove these ambiguities by dis-

cussion with others. There are few standards that seem directly applicable to the situation, which is a novel one for most subjects.

8. The subjects are assured that the shocks administered to the subject are "painful but not dangerous." Thus they assume that the discomfort caused the victim is momentary, while the scientific gains resulting from the experiment are enduring.

9. Through Shock Level 20 the victim continues to provide answers on the signal box. The subject may constitute this as a sign that the victim is still willing to "play the game." It is only after Shock Level 20 that the victim repudiates the rules completely, refusing to answer further.

These features help to explain the high amount of obedience obtained in this experiment. Many of the arguments raised need not remain matters of speculation, but can be reduced to testable propositions to be confirmed or disproved by further experiments.

The following features of the experiment concern the nature of the conflict which the subject faces.

10. The subject is placed in a position in which he must respond to the competing demands of two persons: the experimenter and the victim. The conflict must be resolved by meeting the demands of one or the other; satisfaction of the victim and the experimenter are mutually exclusive. Moreover, the resolution must take the form of a highly visible action, that of continuing to shock the victim or breaking off the experiment. Thus the subject is forced into a public conflict that does not permit any completely satisfactory solution.

11. While the demands of the experimenter carry the weight of scientific authority, the demands of the victim spring from his personal experience of pain and suffering. The two claims need not be regarded as equally pressing and legitimate. The experimenter seeks an abstract scientific datum; the victim cries out for relief from physical suffering caused by the subject's actions.

12. The experiment gives the subject little time for reflection. The conflict comes on rapidly. It is only minutes after

the subject has been seated before the shock generator that the victim begins his protests. Moreover, the subject perceives that he has gone through but two-thirds of the shock levels at the time the subject's first protests are heard. Thus he understands that the conflict will have a persistent aspect to it, and may well become more intense as increasingly more powerful shocks are required. The rapidity with which the conflict descends on the subject, and his realization that it is predictably recurrent may well be sources of tension to him.

13. At a more general level, the conflict stems from the opposition of two deeply ingrained behavior dispositions: first, the disposition not to harm other people, and second, the tendency to obey those whom we perceive to be legitimate authorities.

CHILDREN AND FOREIGNERS

Henri Tajfel

NATIONALISM is an attitude, a way of feeling and a mode of thinking about certain issues, which is shared by millions of people in a large variety of cultural contexts. It seems unlikely that this compound of beliefs, value judgments and emotions springs fully into existence in adolescence or adulthood without some background process of growth. This is certainly so in the case of awareness of racial differences: there is good evidence that such awareness exists at a very early age. It is also true that—at least in multi-racial societies—this awareness is supported by a series of easy props for recognition of outgroups. We can actually see and

Reprinted from *New Society*, Vol. 7, No. 196 (June 30, 1966), pp. 9–11.

hear the differences in some of the strangers in our midst.

There are no such simple perceptual supports for the concepts of "own" and "alien" in the case of nations. The proper use of terms such as "English" or "French" represents an achievement at a fairly high level of abstraction. A good deal of work has been done in the last 30 years or so on the development in children of the capacity to manipulate abstract concepts; but very little of this work was concerned with concepts which are rooted in strongly entrenched value judgments. National stereotypes, as has often been shown, are shot through with affective or emotional evaluations; they are early learned, widely used and subject to very slow change.

If, then, children do assimilate early these evaluations of large categories of people by national labels, it is likely that they do so in a conceptual vacuum. The value judgments apply to people; but the underlying classification of people into groups has no real existence to the child.

The second problem highlights the first. Most of the experimental work on intergroup relations in social psychology is concerned with face-to-face groups. National attitudes and behavior related to them present a rather different problem. One's own "group" consists in the main of people one doesn't know; this applies even more clearly to other groups. But this lack of background of personal relations does not mean that attitudes do not translate themselves into behaviour towards individuals classified as "one's own" or "other." To take an extreme case, a Nazi did not have to know personally an individual Jew in order to behave towards him in a highly determined and predictable fashion. Millions of tourists abroad display every year less dramatic forms of the same phenomenon. Their frequent isolation is probably partly due to their readiness to act on the basis of crude general notions, coupled with a refusal or unwillingness to seek new information. The same applies to the actions of hosts towards their visitors, temporary or permanent. Attitudes towards large-scale human groups affect behaviour even when they are not rooted in personal knowledge of individuals representing these groups.

PATTERN OF PREFERENCES

About two and a half years ago we started an exploratory research project with the aim of gathering some facts about the development of these attitudes in children. We wanted to elucidate through these facts the underlying emotional and cognitive processes and their relation to one another. The work has been done in several European countries. In the remainder of this article I shall briefly summarise a few of the findings.

I said earlier that it is likely that children develop early some form of attitude towards foreign countries. One way in which the existence of such attitudes can be established is through the degree of consensus displayed by children in the pattern of their preferences concerning foreign countries. In one of the first studies we have done in Britain (which was later repeated in Austria, Belgium and Greece) a test was included in which children aged from six to eleven were asked to express their preferences relating to America, France, Germany and Russia. The four countries were presented in all the six possible pairings, and for each of the pairs the child was asked to state which of the two he "liked better." From these judgments, a rank order of preference for the countries was obtained for each child. The table shows the percentage of children assigning each country to the top (or bottom) two positions, and is thus a measure of the preference consensus of the group. As will be seen, at the age of nine to eleven the degree of consensus is very high indeed. Thus 85 per cent are agreed in placing America in the two ranks which expressed higher preference, and the same proportion placed Russia in the two lower preference ranks. As one goes back to age six to seven, consensus is also marked.

We also sought to compare the degree of children's consensus concerning preferences with their consensus concerning matters of fact. As an item of information which would be fairly basic and unambiguous, we finally chose the size of the countries concerned. The children were presented with 17 black plastic squares of varying sizes. The square of median size was designated as representing the size of the child's own country. The children were asked to point to the squares which would then relatively represent the size of the four foreign countries.

In the scoring of the responses, only those in which *either* Germany *or* France were seen as larger than *either* America *or* Russia were considered as incorrect. In other words, in the correct set of responses America and Russia had to be ranked either 1 or 2 in size, France and Germany either 3 or 4. This method allowed for a direct comparison with the preference judgments: in both cases the four rank positions have been reduced to two categories (1 and 2 against 3 and 4) for presentation in the table. Ranks 1 and 2 represent higher preference or greater size: ranks 3 and 4 lower preference or smaller size.

The important feature to notice in the table is that, for the younger children of six to seven, *all* the preference judgments are more strongly polarised than the size judgments. Thus, for example, these children are more likely to "know" that France is one of the nicer two countries than that it is

Polarisation of Preference and Size Judgments in Britain

	% of Subjects out of Total Samples			
	Age 6-7		*Age 9-11*	
	%	*Ranks*	*%*	*Ranks*
America				
Preference	63	1,2	85	1,2
Size	58	1,2	90	1,2
Russia				
Preference	70	3,4	85	3,4
Size	52	1,2	70	1,2
France				
Preference	68	1,2	88	1,2
Size	59	3,4	82	3,4
Germany				
Preference	58	3,4	83	3,4
Size	48	3,4	78	3,4

one of the smaller two; and similar statements can be made for each of the other three countries used. It should be added that the data from a comparable sample of children in Belgium indicate that this precedence of learning of preferences over factual information relating to the same four foreign countries does not hold there.

The development of the emotional significance to the child of his own national membership was studied with the help of a different method. Children of the same age range as in the previous study were presented individually with a set of 20 especially prepared and standardised photographs of young men, all English. For each of the photographs the child was asked to decide whether he liked the person or not. The child did this by placing each photograph in turn in one of four boxes respectively labelled "I like him very much," "I like him a little," "I dislike him a little," "I dislike him very much." During a second session about a fortnight later the child was told that some of the people he had previously seen were English and some were not, and he was asked to guess for each photograph whether the person was English or not. Two boxes were used for this purpose, one for each of the two categories. One half of the children had the two sessions in the order just described. For the other half, nationality assignment came first and the preference rating second.

THEIR OWN NATIONALITY

The analysis of data was conducted in several ways which all show that there is a highly significant tendency for children to "like better" those people whom they assign to the category "English." We conducted the same study (with the same set of photographs of English people) in Austria, Belgium and Holland, asking the children to assign them to their own nationality and express their preference on this basis. It may be worth noting that in all these countries the photographs were divided about equally (and approximately in the same proportions as in England) into own nationals and others. In addition, in Italy two sets of photographs were used (the English one and a specially prepared Italian set), and in Israel the variable of ethnic affiliation (European and Oriental) of the children and of the persons photographed was introduced. All the data apart from the Italian ones have been analysed and they all show the same preference for photographs assigned to their own national category. Apart from this general result, several aspects of the findings throw additional light on some interesting features of this phenomenon.

Of the three samples (English, Belgian and Dutch) for which age trends are already available, the first two show a *decrease* of the correlation between national assignment and preference as the children grow older. This trend is particularly clear in the English data. It would be unwise, however, to infer from this that children start out by being highly chauvinistic at the age of six to seven (the correlation between the two sets of responses is enormous at that age in the English sample; it is of the order of 0.92) and then come to a more balanced view of things. It is more likely that at the younger ages the emotional cue is the only one available to the children for making their nationality assignments.

DEVELOPING STEREOTYPES

It is also possible that with increasing age a physical stereotype of one's own nation group begins to develop, and that the components of this sterotype in different photographs are not necessarily the same as the features in individual faces, which lead children to prefer them. From a comparison between the English, Dutch and Belgian data we have some evidence supporting this assumption. If some form of a physical stereotype of "own" national group exists, it would not be surprising to find that this stereotype is rather similar in the countries of northwest Europe. We found quite substantial correlations in the data from the three countries in the assignment of photographs to "own" category. Perhaps even more suggestive is the fact that without exception the correlations increase with age. These data, therefore, seem to fit in with the assumption that a physical stereotype of one's own national group does exist and that it becomes more articulate with increasing age. It may well be that this is a "negative" stereotype in the sense of a general consensus in northwestern European countries about who does not look like a native.

The findings described so far provide factual information which is needed before one can proceed further with empirical studies of the growth of national attitudes in children. This evidence allows the conclusion that such attitudes do exist to an appreciable extent, that children assimilate very early the generally accepted value judgments about salient foreign countries, that this happens in almost complete absence of any factual information about these countries, and that their own national membership acquires just as early (if not earlier) an emotional significance which can trigger off a whole set of responses.

With this sort of information in the background, it is possible to ask more complex questions concerning the relation between this early crystallisation of emotional attitudes and the development of modes of thinking about foreign countries and their nationals. Two studies of this nature can be briefly summarized. One conducted in Leiden was concerned, among other things, with children's ideas about similarity or dissimilarity between various countries as related to their likes or dislikes of these countries. The results were, on the whole, quite clear: the greater the difference between two countries in a child's preference system, the more dissimilar they are seen to be.

When children who earned high scores on preference for their own nationals in the photograph study just described were compared with those who earned low scores, a fairly complex judgmental phenomenon revealed itself. Those who most preferred their own nationals tended to see foreign countries either as very different from each other or as very similar to each other; those whose responses in the photograph study tended to be less ethnocentric avoided these two extremes in their conception of differences between foreign countries. Both these extremes reflect in their different ways the degree of salience to the child of his ideas about "foreign" or "alien."

DESERT ISLAND CHOICE

Another study, conducted in Oxford, explored the child's capacity to understand that members of disliked national groups would act on the basis of the same principles as members of own or liked national groups. The study consisted of several situations, including one in which the child had to take decisions for captains of boats as to who should be saved among many people stranded on a desert island. Both the captains and the people they were to save belonged to various nationalities for which the child's relative preferences had previously been established. The number of people that each captain was allowed to take off the island was limited to four. (The boats, the captains, the people on the island and the island itself were all concretely represented.) The results show fairly clearly that as one moves from liked to disliked countries there is an increasing difficulty in visualising the situation from the point of view of the "other." The same conclusion applies to the child's capacity to divorce his attributions of likes and dislikes *by* nationals of other countries from his own system of preferences.

We undertook several other studies concerned with these and related problems. The most important implication which emerges from them can perhaps be summarised as follows: thinking about large human groups in a rational and adequate manner is a complex conceptual achievement made even more difficult by the early intervention of emotional biases of various kinds. Many of these biases are introduced in the school curricula themselves. We do not expect a child to be able to learn without help the intellectual skills involved in most subjects taught at school. And yet, somehow or other, we assume that he is able to learn to deal rationally with a complex human problem by some kind of autonomous magic which he is supposed to evolve without any systematic educational support. Both on the basis of common sense and of the sort of evidence that we were able to gather this is obviously an untenable assumption. The policy of educational laissez faire in this field is consequently just as untenable—particularly in primary schools.

BOUNDARIES OF PUBLIC TOLERANCE: THE PUBLIC OPINION POLLS

A. T. Steele

. . . AMERICAN opinions on China are not only extremely diverse but also subject to much shifting and adjustment to conform to changing situations. They are tied, however, to certain underlying attitudes—for example, anticommunism—which change much more slowly, or not at all.

The volatility of public opinion on some issues is illustrated by the fluctuating views on Viet-Nam. Many people who formerly regarded the Viet-Nam war as little more than a civil conflict between Vietnamese factions later came to view it in a more serious light as the testing ground for United States ability to halt the spread of Chinese Communist influence into Southeast Asia. The effect was to strengthen public support for American policy in this area.

This illustration raises the question of the approximate limits of public consent in the matter of American policy toward China. In other words, how far could the United States government go toward easing or stiffening its policy

Reprinted from *The American People and China* (New York: McGraw-Hill Book Company, 1966), pp. 94–105.

without provoking strong opposition from the American public? The immobility of many of our national leaders and legislators on the China question is based on the assumption that public opinion is solidly behind our policy as it stands and that any attempt to modify or even reexamine it would provoke devastating political reactions from the voting public. Is this true?

. . . It is possible, through public opinion polls, to determine how strongly opinions on China are held, which way the winds of change are blowing and the approximate limits of elasticity in public thinking at a given time. In exploring these matters in this study, reliance has been placed mainly, but not exclusively, on two public opinion polls undertaken on our behalf. One was the nationwide sampling conducted by the Survey Research Center (SRC) of the University of Michigan. . . . Carried out in May and June 1964, it involved interviews with a representative sample of 1,501 persons across the country. The other survey, made in 1963 by Samuel Lubell Associates, based its findings on 169 "man-in-the-street" interviews in Eastern, Midwestern and Southern towns. The Lubell report, though not published for general circulation, produced some revealing information on the contrasting images of China and Russia in American eyes and on major trends in American thinking on the China question. It was supplemented, in 1965, by a few additional findings.

The Survey Research Center's poll revealed a disturbing lack of knowledge among the general public on even the most elementary facts of the China situation: more than one-fourth (28 per cent) of the public was not aware that China is now ruled by a Communist government; and 39 per cent of those who did know of the Communist government could not think of any other Chinese government. In evaluating the SRC's findings it needs to be borne in mind that on some questions of policy the polling organization excluded from its questioning those who were apparently unaware of either of the two regimes. It was felt that to invite opinions about a foreign regime from people who did not know of its existence might lead to serious distortions in the findings. Nevertheless, one cannot ignore the probability that in a crisis situation many of these people would be stimulated into having an opinion and taking sides and, therefore, would have to be counted.

For the purposes of this study it was decided that perhaps the best way to get a rough measure of the flexibility of public opinion on China policy would be to determine public reactions to various hypothetical initiatives by the President of the United States. This approach was based on the fact that it is usually the President who initiates legislation relating to China and that it is his influence that is most persuasive for or against any measure. Thus, public response for or against his recommendations would tend to indicate the amount of "give," if any, in public attitudes. Therefore, when interviewers of the Survey Research Center went to the people with a series of questions on China, they led into the difficult area of China policy with this statement:

> Now the President of the United States might decide that it was in our best interests to take certain new actions with regard to Communist China. For each thing I mention, would you tell me how you would feel about it if the President suggested that action?

This statement was followed by a series of five questions, each relating to a particular phase of U.S. policy. In the returns on these questions, the respondents were divided into those who *definitely* favored and *probably* favored each proposition and those who definitely *opposed* and *probably* opposed each one. This subdivision of categories is worth noting, since it provides a clue to the intensity, or lack of it, with which opinions are held. We can assume that those with strongly held opinions are more likely to persist in them and to fight for them than those whose views are lightly held. By the same token, we can assume that those whose views are not strongly held are more likely to alter them with changing circumstances. Translated into political terms, this means that a view held by an intensely and actively committed minority can often prevail over the view of an indifferent majority.

The Survey Research Center's findings are discussed below. The commentaries on these findings are based on material from various sources, including the Lubell survey.

On the Question of Communication

QUESTION: Suppose the President suggested visits between Americans and people from Communist China—like newspapermen from each country visiting each other?

ANSWERS:

Definitely favor following his suggestions on this	41%	73%
Probably favor following his suggestion on this	32%	
Probably be against following his suggestion on this	6%	16%
Definitely be against following his suggestion on this	10%	
No idea whether I'd favor or be against it	10%	
Not ascertained	1%	
Total	100%	

There are no surprises here. As has been pointed out, if there is any question of China policy on which there is overwhelming agreement in all of our public opinion samplings, it is on the desirability of increased communication between the American and Chinese peoples. As far back as 1957, when the Chinese Communists seemed receptive to the idea of an exchange of newspaper correspondents and our State Department was being negative about it, the National Opinion Research Center (NORC) asked the American public the following question: "Do you think our government should allow American reporters to visit Communist China or not?" The replies even then were emphatically favorable: Should, 65 per cent; Should not, 23 per cent; Don't know, 12 per cent.

On Willingness to Exchange Ambassadors with Communist China

QUESTION: Suppose the President suggested that we exchange ambassadors with Communist China the way we do with other countries?

ANSWERS:

Definitely favor **following his suggestion on this**	**24%**	**51%**
Probably favor **following his suggestion on this**	**27%**	
Probably be against **following his suggestion on this**	**11%**	**34%**
Definitely be against **following his suggestion on this**	**23%**	
No idea **whether I'd favor or be against it**	**14%**	
Not ascertained	1%	
Total	**100%**	

The response to this question is consistent with the generally favorable attitude of the public toward increased communication with Communist China and the negotiation of high-level differences. However, we must avoid reading too much meaning into the answers. An exchange of ambassadors involves diplomatic recognition, but it is doubtful whether all persons responding to the question understood its full meaning. From the establishment of the Peking regime, in October 1949, public opinion polls have shown a generally consistent but variable opposition to diplomatic recognition of the Communist government. A Gallup poll in October 1949 showed only 25 per cent of the public in favor of recognition; an NORC poll in January 1950, only 11 per cent. In November 1954, just after the Korean War, an NORC poll found 55 per cent of the public favorable to recognizing the Communist regime (with 30 per cent opposed and 15 undecided). But a Gallup poll in October 1964 indicated that there had been a stiffening of attitude on this question in the intervening decade. In 1964, Gallup asked this question: "Do you think it would be in the interests of the United States to establish diplomatic relations with Communist China within the next five years or not?" The returns were as follows: Would be, 36 per cent; Would not be, 39 per cent; Don't know, 25 per cent.

On Negotiation with China on Asian Problems

QUESTION: Suppose the President suggested that we talk over problems of Asia with Communist China and try to come to some agreement with them?

ANSWERS:

Definitely favor following his suggestion on this	37%	71%
Probably favor following his suggestion on this	34%	
Probably be against following his suggestion on this	7%	19%
Definitely be against following his suggestion on this	12%	
No idea whether I'd favor or be against it	9%	
Not ascertained	1%	
Total	100%	

It is interesting that the consistently antagonistic attitude of the American public toward the Chinese Communists has been accompanied by an equally consistent desire for peace and harmony through negotiation of our differences. The overwhelmingly favorable response to the suggestion of negotiation with Communist China, above, follows a pattern of opinion that has remained virtually unchanged for a decade. In April 1955, NORC asked a nationwide sampling: "Do you think it would be a good idea or a bad idea for U.S. representatives to meet with Chinese Communist leaders to try to reach an agreement on some of the problems of Asia?" The replies were: Approve, 70 per cent; Disapprove, 21 per cent; Qualified, 3 per cent; Don't know, 4 per cent. Substantially the same question has been put to the American public on three or four occasions since then, always with substantially the same results. Leadership opinion, I found in interviews around the country, does not share the optimism of the general public on this subject. It tends to take a more serious view of obstacles standing in the way of agreement—notably the presently irreconcilable position of the two sides on Taiwan.

On the Question of Trade with Communist China

QUESTION: Suppose the President suggested selling things like wheat to Communist China?

ANSWERS:

Definitely favor following his suggestion on this	19%	43%
Probably favor following his suggestion on this	24%	
Probably be against following his suggestion on this	14%	47%
Definitely be against following his suggestion on this	33%	
No idea whether I'd favor or be against it	9%	
Not ascertained	1%	
Total	100%	

The public mood has been tested repeatedly on the nettlesome question of trade since the Communist takeover of the mainland, with generally inconclusive results. A Gallup poll in October 1949 showed a majority of those with opinions as being opposed to trade. Yet a sounding in January 1950 showed a slightly favorable sentiment. Views on trade were hostile, of course, during the Korean War and remained so for some months afterward. But a favorable trend developed in 1955, and an NORC poll in September of that year showed 55 per cent of those interviewed as favorable to trade in nonstrategic goods. Polling records indicate a predominantly disapproving attitude in 1956–57, but a poll in February 1961 showed the weight of opinion as favorable to the idea of the United States and Communist

China buying and selling goods to each other. The SRC poll, tabulated above, shows that there was slightly more sentiment against selling "things like wheat" to Communist China than in favor of it. Throughout these pollings, the margin of difference between the pros and cons on trade has generally been too narrow to show a clear pattern of preference. And the mixed reaction is consistent with the divided views of opinion leaders quoted in the previous chapter. A point to be noted in the SRC poll, however, is that while only 19 per cent of those questioned were *definitely* favorable to selling things like wheat to Communist China, no less than 33 per cent were *definitely* opposed. Here is a rather clear indication that those opposed to such trade told their views more strongly than those who favor it and would probably put up a strong fight against any serious attempt to modify the existing embargo.

On Admitting Communist China to the United Nations

QUESTION: Suppose the President suggested that we let Communist China join the United Nations?

ANSWERS:

Definitely favor following his suggestion on this	13%	31%
Probably favor following his suggestion on this	18%	
Probably be against following his suggestion on this	13%	53%
Definitely be against following his suggestion on this	40%	
No idea whether I'd favor or be against it	15%	
Not ascertained	1%	
Total	100%	

This is the one Presidential initiative of the five suggested that met with opposition from a clear majority of those questioned. The negative response fits into a pattern of opinion which has prevailed consistently since the question of Communist China's entry into the United Nations was first raised and no doubt is influenced by our government's firm, continued and well-publicized opposition to such entry. There has been a slow decline, however, in the percentage of the public opposing admission. The opposition was once overwhelming. In November 1953, for example, an NORC poll showed 74 per cent opposed to admission and only 12 per cent favorable.

There are those on the far right, in this country, who advocate U.S. withdrawal from the United Nations if Communist China is voted in over American objections. Is this view shared by the general public? Emphatically not. When SRC sought public reactions to this question, 75 per cent of those questioned said the United States should remain in the UN even if Communist China is admitted. Only 5 per cent favored withdrawal.

Lubell, in his 1963 sampling, also found public opinion strongly opposed to admission of Communist China to the United Nations. In later soundings (1965), following the nuclear explosions in China and the worsening of the situation in Viet-Nam, opposition remained strong, but there were some signs of uncertainty linked mainly to the deterioration in Viet-Nam. "Up to this point," Lubell informed this writer, "Viet-Nam had not been on people's minds. It was only after the Viet-Nam blow-up that the public realized the gravity of the situation and began to give more thought to China policy. Some people became less rigid in their outlook. There was a growing feeling that we should 'do something.' People who wanted to pull out of Viet-Nam tended to think we should admit Communist China to the UN. Those who wanted to fight on in Viet-Nam were against it. Public opinion on admission and recognition could be influenced either way by developments in Viet-Nam."

Lubell said that the most frequently mentioned reasons for opposing UN admission were that it would increase Communist power in the United Nations and that China, as an aggressor, had no place in an organization devoted to peace. Our commitment to Nationalist China was also cited fairly often as a reason for opposing UN admittance. Other typical quotes: "We should stick by our friends"; "They (the Communists) would have one more platform from which to disrupt things"; "They have nothing to offer—they are anti-everything"; "It would be like giving them a stamp of approval."

Arguments most used by the minority favoring Communist China's entry were (1) that mainland China is a world power, here to stay, and that we can no longer ignore her and (2) that bringing her into the UN may restrain or soften her. "How can you expect to develop friendship in isolation?" a New Jersey lawyer asked.

The Lubell interviews indicated that some of the opposition to admission would melt away if China showed herself less belligerent and more cooperative. A retail salesman in New Jersey said we should hold back UN admission "until they're more flexible and more peaceful." Other comments in the same vein: "They've got to calm down"; They won't listen to anyone"; "Their minds are made up"; "You can't deal with them." Several suggested resolving this dilemma by recognizing Communist China but not admitting her into the UN, on the theory that admission implies approval but recognition does not.

. . .

ATTITUDES TOWARD WAR AND PEACE IN ASIA

Among the broad conclusions that can be drawn from these samplings of American opinion is that a majority of the American people would favor a peaceful solution of outstanding differences with Communist China if it could be had on just and honorable terms. This is indicated by the overwhelming endorsement of the suggestion of negotiation with Peking on Asian problems. It shows up again in the response to SRC questions about Viet-Nam in which 46 per cent (61 per cent of those with opinions) said they would like to see a compromise settlement in that embattled land, even at the price of neutralization. And the strong sentiment against supporting the Nationalist Chinese in any attack against the Chinese mainland reflects a desire to avoid precipitating a war with China.

While the American people clearly are against aggressive action which would invite war with China, they have also demonstrated that they are willing to accept heavy risks in support of. U.S. commitments for the mutual defense of Taiwan and Viet-Nam. On the question of risking outright war, opinion has tended to vacillate with the changing situation and with our government's attitude of the moment. In 1955, to be sure, the public approved overwhelmingly when Congress authorized President Eisenhower to use U.S. armed forces, if necessary, to defend Taiwan. But in 1958, Gallup put this question to the public: "There's been much discussion whether this country should get into an all-out war with Red China over the Quemoy and Matsu Islands and over Formosa itself. How do you feel? Should the U.S. go to war for Quemoy and Matsu . . . should the U.S. go to war for Formosa?" Only 28 per cent said we should go to war for Taiwan, 32 per cent said we should not, and 40 per cent were undecided. Incidentally, only 18 per cent were willing at that time to get into an all-out war for Quemoy and Matsu, althought a 1955 question about "defending" Quemoy and Matsu had won approval from a majority of those with opinions.

The American public time and again has shown a reluctance to endorse war-risking action. But once the die is cast and the country embroiled, the people are sometimes prepared to take even bigger risks than their leaders are willing to approve. Such was the case during the Korean conflict when an NORC poll (June 1952) showed 61 per cent of the public in favor of bombing Communist supply bases inside China.

. . .

OVERLAPPING AND CONFLICT OF TERRITORIAL SELF-IMAGES

Ralph K. White

STUDENTS of animal behavior have often remarked on how quickly an animal will spring to the defense of a piece of territory with which he has identified himself and which he perceives as invaded by outsiders (McNeil, 1965, p. 17; Ardrey, 1963, pp. 33–58; Collias, 1944; Carpenter, 1934; Lorenz, 1952). "Territoriality" is a major basis of animal fighting. Similarly, history is full of examples of human fighting originating from the fact that more than one human group had identified itself with the same patch of land. Bosnia and other Yugoslav territory under Austrian rule, plus Serbia herself when Austria claimed a right to "punish" her, constituted the initial focus of World War I; the Polish Corridor, claimed by both Poland and Germany, and Danzig, an internationalized German city, were the initial focus of World War II; the Sudetenland was identified with by both Germans and Czechs; Alsace-Lorraine long poisoned the relationship between France and Germany; Israelis and Arabs claim Israel; Pakistanis and Indians claim Kashmir; French and Algerians identified with Algeria (there are some striking quotations from Frenchmen suggesting that for them Algeria was almost a part of their own body); French and Indochinese claimed Indochina; Communist China and "the Free World" identify with Taiwan (with both Communist and Nationalist Chinese treating it as self-evident that Taiwan is an integral part of China,

Reprinted from "Misperception and the Vietnam War," *The Journal of Social Issues*, Vol. 22, No. 3 (July, 1966), pp. 103–106. (Beginning of article has been omitted.)

though most of the Taiwanese feel differently); certain areas along the Sino-Indian border have caused fighting and great bitterness on both sides, with each side feeling that its own land had been infringed upon. With the growth of nationalism during the past century, irredentism in scores of places has become a potent source of conflict.

It is somewhat surprising that psychologists have paid so little attention to the territorial self-images of human groups, when they bulk so large in both animal behavior and human history, though there have been studies of the factors determining national identification (Karl Deutsch, 1953; Katz, 1965; Doob, 1966). A study is needed of two distinct psychological processes: the process by which a human group comes to identify firmly with a given piece of disputed land and to assume implicitly that it is "our" land, and the process by which strong emotions, some of which are probably unconscious, become mobilized when the territorial self-image is impinged upon by "outsiders." The way in which feelings about manhood and virility became an integral part of the territorial self-image would be of particular interest.

Presumably such feelings enter into both phases. In the first phase, the strength or potency of the national self-image is felt to be enhanced by expanding it into all territories that are actually subject to dispute and ambiguity. India, for instance, feels that its manhood would be diminished if it "weakly" gave up its claim to all of Kashmir; there is pain at the thought of accepting a diminished image of one's own nation on the map, and map-makers push their own nation's claims to the limit of what is plausible. In the second phase, once a given territorial image has become thoroughly identified with the national self, it is almost as if the territorial image were an image of the nation's physical body, and infringements upon it are reacted to as an individual might react to violations of his own body. The nation's territorial self-image becomes its body-image. The presence on one's "own" land of the "outsiders" who have conflicting claims to it is then perceived as obvious aggression, a challenge to one's own manhood, requiring even the risks and costs of war in order to drive them out.

Although this emphasizes the importance of land, it should be noted that it is not an "economic" interpretation of war. According to this hypothesis, it is not the economic or even the military significance of the land, rationally considered, that matters. What matters is the symbolic importance of the land as part of the national body-image. What counts emotionally in this context is not prosperity or even national power—there may be very little desire for power beyond the nation's own border, as the nation itself conceives that border—national integrity and self-respect, as symbolized by driving all invaders out of "our" territory.

The way in which all this applies to the North Vietnamese is similar to the various other examples cited above; the hypothesis is that they see South Vietnam as part of their national body, and see our pressure there as self-evidently a violation of their national body, and a challenge to their manhood. We have stepped over the boundary of their land, with guns in our hands.

The way in which it applies to American militants is a variation on the usual pattern, since Americans do not regard South Vietnam as America's own land at all. We mean it when we say we have no territorial ambitions there. We see ourselves rather as defending the right of a small and weak nation, South Vietnam, to its own land and its own integrity. But it can be argued that we have nevertheless identified with the soil of South Vietnam. Since 1945, we have seen ourselves as the champion of the whole of the Free World in its attempt to defend itself against Communist aggression; in a sense, therefore, our national body-image has expanded until it has become coextensive with the "Free World" itself, visualized as having a quite definite outer boundary that we feel we must defend at all costs, in much the same way that a nation feels it must defend its own boundary. In the eyes of American militants, that boundary, as far as Vietnam is concerned, is obviously the 17th Parallel.

Those who regard this boundary as part of the natural

order of things may forget (or perhaps have never learned) certain historical facts which are psychologically important enough to call for review at this point: that the great majority of the Vietnamese were elated by what they thought was independence under Ho Chi Minh's leadership immediately after World War II; that, with much trickery and bloodshed, the French tried to reimpose Western white rule upon Vietnam; that our own form of Western white influence (which we have never regarded as "rule" but which a great many Vietnamese naturally assimilated to their perception of French trickery, French warmaking, and French rule) began to be exerted in 1950, when we began giving major financial help to the French, and became predominant when we were largely instrumental in setting up Diem's regime; that during its later years, while we still supported Diem, his regime became quite generally hated; that the Catholics, of whom he was one and who were as a rule the most militant anti-Communists, were widely regarded by non-Catholics as semi-foreign and the stooges of foreigners; that most of the present military leaders are tainted by association with the French during the period of the long war for independence from France, while Ho Chi Minh is the chief symbol of that struggle and of its final victory; that the Communists' victory in 1954 gave them (and almost everyone else) the expectation that the whole country would in 1956 revert to the Communist government it had had in 1945; that the North Vietnamese made peace—giving up at the conference table what they could then have won rather easily on the battlefield—on the basis of what they took to be a general agreement, to be enforced by the French, that all-Vietnamese elections would be held in 1956 (Devillers, 1962, 211–12); that chiefly because of actions by Diem and his American backers, this expectation was never fulfilled; that this must have appeared to the Communists as a confession by Diem that the "people" would not support him.

All of this makes psychologically interesting the apparent assumption of a great many American militants that South Vietnam is self-evidently "our" (the Free World's) territory, that North Vietnamese Communists who cross the line as we have defined it are self-evidently invading "another country" rather than, as they claim, trying to "liberate" their countrymen from foreign rule, and that to regard our presence in Vietnam (from 1950 to now) as an infringement on Vietnamese soil is fantastic.

Among the militants who care greatly about peace—and there are many such—an additional factor probably has psychological importance: many have hoped that peace between East and West might be preserved by an increasing tacit acceptance, on both sides, of the existing boundary line between the two worlds. Irrational as it may be at certain points (especially where it cuts a nation in two) it is the only clear line we have had. We respected it when the Hungarian uprising gave us a moral right to intervene on behalf of a people most of whom seemed to be greatly distressed and clearly hostile to Soviet rule. We cared more about peace, then, than about extending "our" territory (the Free World) or liberating a people that wanted to be liberated. In Korea we defended the line, and since then many of us have thought of "holding the line" as one of the two essential ingredients in keeping the equilibrium between East and West, the other essential ingredient being that our military power should at least equal that of the Communists. In 1954 we said to ourselves, in effect: now the boundary line between the two worlds, as far as Vietnam is concerned, is the 17th Parallel; it has been divided as Korea was, and our job as keepers of the peace is to hold that line as we held the line in Korea.

In other words, we identified "ourselves" (the Free World) with South Vietnam, defined as a separate, non-Communist country. Very few of us were clearly aware, at that time, of the historical facts and of the psychological situation in Vietnam that made this a highly questionable identification. Partly because of the seeming analogy with Korea it became very firm in our minds before we were given any strong reason to challenge it. Many of us have used it ever since then as a fixed image and frame of reference for deciding who is "the aggressor," without challenging it at all.

At the same time, we kept another standard for judging what is the legitimate government of a given country: the principle of national self-determination. That principle is still very much alive, as is shown by our present commitment to let the people of South Vietnam determine their own destiny. If this means that a country on our side of the East-West boundary-line can freely "go Communist" if it wants to, then we have two criteria, one geographical and one psychological, that are capable of clashing. If and when they clash we may be forced to choose between them, instead of continuing to assume implicitly that it is always possible to retain both.

. . .

Notes

WAR, AFTERMATH, AND RECOVERY

Robert A. Dentler and Phillips Cutright

1 Robert W. O'Brien, *Readings in General Sociology,* 2d ed. (Boston: Houghton Mifflin Company, 1957), p. 44.
2 Robert Hagan, "The Myth of Civilian Defense," *Cambridge* 38 (November, 1961), pp. 12–13.

THE TERRITORIAL STATE IN INTERNATIONAL RELATIONS

John H. Herz

1 François Laurent, as quoted by Walter Schiffer, *The Legal Community of Mankind,* New York, 1954, p. 157.
2 See my *Political Realism and Political Idealism,* Chicago, 1951, pp. 206–221.
3 J. von Elbe, 'Die Wiederherstellung der Gleichgewichtsordnung in Europa durch den Wiener Kongress," *Zeitschrift für ausländisches öffentliches Recht und Völkerrecht,* IV (1934), pp. 226ff.
4 See Carl Schmitt, *Der Nomos der Erde,* Cologne, 1950, pp. 60ff.; also W. Schoenborn, "Über Entdeckung als Rechtstitel völkerrechtlichen Gebietserwerbs," in D. S. Constantinopoulos and H. Wehberg, eds., *Gegenwartsprobleme des internationalen Rechts und der Rechtsphilosophie,* Hamburg, 1953, pp. 239ff.
5 See M. M. McMahon, *Conquest and Modern International Law,* Washington, D.C., 1940; M. F. Lindlay, *The Acquisition and Government of Backward Territory in International Law,* London, 1926; and Robert Langer, *Seizure of Territory,* Princeton, N.J., 1947.
6 As witness the impression made on contemporaries by the destruction of the first ancient European unit to fall victim to these policies—Venice.
7 See Erich Eyck, *Bismarck,* II, Zurich, 1943, pp. 305ff.
8 Except for these cases, we find only marginal instances of complete obliteration. The annexation of the Free City of Krakow by Russia eliminated a synthetic creation of the Vienna settlement. British conquest of the Boer Republics, if considered as an instance of annihilation of European polities in view of the European origin of the inhabitants, happened at the very rim of the world, as it were, remote from the continent where the practice of non-annihilation prevailed.
9 Cf. also the remarkable stability of state units in the Western Hemisphere *qua* independent units; unstable as some of them are

domestically, their sovereign identity as units appears almost sacrosanct.

10 In League practice, therefore, membership applications of countries without this minimum were rejected (for instance, that of Liechtenstein; cf. Walther Schücking and Hans Wehberg, *Die Satzung des Völkerbundes,* 2d ed., Berlin, 1924, pp. 252ff.). The decline of genuine collective security in our time is apparent from the fact that, in contrast to this practice, the United Nations pays hardly any attention to the question of defensibility, particularly in connection with membership applications.

11 See my article, "Idealist Internationalism and the Security Dilemma," *World Politics,* II, No. 2 (January, 1950), pp. 157ff.; in particular, pp. 165ff.

12 B. H. Liddell Hart, *The Revolution in Warfare,* New Haven, Conn., 1947, p. 36. Suspicion of what would be in the offing, once man gained the capacity to fly, was abroad as early as the eighteenth century. Thus Samuel Johnson remarked: "If men were all virtuous, I should with great alacrity teach them all to fly. But what would be the security of the good, if the bad could at pleasure invade them from the sky? Against an army sailing through the clouds, neither walls, nor mountains, nor seas, could afford security" (quoted in J. U. Nef, *War and Human Progress,* Cambridge, Mass., 1952, p. 198). And Benjamin Franklin, witnessing the first balloon ascension at Paris in 1783, foresaw invasion from the air and wrote: "Convincing Sovereigns of folly of wars may perhaps be one effect of it, since it will be impracticable for the most potent of them to guard his dominions. . . . Where is the Prince who can afford so to cover his country with troops for its defense, as that ten thousand men descending from the clouds, might not in many places do an infinite deal of mischief before a force could be brought together to repel them?" (from a letter to Jan Ingelhouss, reproduced in *Life* magazine, January 9, 1956).

13 See Julius Stone, *Legal Controls of International Conflicts,* New York, 1954, pp. 611ff.

14 Some of the pertinent questions are discussed in a more comprehensive manuscript, "Reflections on International Politics in the Atomic Age," from whose initial chapters the preceding pages were adapted.

15 *The Open Mind,* New York, 1955, p. 141.

16 Roger Hilsman, "Strategic Doctrines for Nuclear War," in William W. Kaufmann, ed., *Military Policy and National Security,* Princeton, N.J., 1956, p. 42.

17 Thomas K. Finletter, *Power and Politics: US Foreign Policy and Military Power in the Hydrogen Age,* New York, 1954, p. 256.

18 The expectations connected with the situation of nuclear deterrence may serve as an illustration. Each side, so we may assume, wants to act "rationally"—that is, avoid resort to a war which

it knows would be suicidal; in this, in fact, is grounded the widespread present belief in the obsoleteness of major—i.e., nuclear—war. However, not knowing for sure that the other side can be trusted to behave rationally, each feels that the possibility of irrational behavior by the opponent must be included in its own calculations. For instance, assuming that rationally the United States would not permit itself to be provoked into nuclear action, can it rely on Soviet abstention from nuclear attack for similarly rational reasons? Or can the Soviets, who may actually believe that the "imperialist" powers are ready to inflict the worst on them, rely on Western rationality? And if, knowing that the other side may be swayed by considerations like these, one side takes these amended calculations as yardsticks for its own, what rational considerations remain? Policies then become so dependent on considerations of what you believe the other side believes, etc., ad infinitum, that no sane calculations are any longer feasible. One is caught here in the vicious circle inherent in the problem of the effects of assumptions (in behaviorist parlance, the problem of "anticipated reactions"), of what David Easton has called the possibility of an "infinite regress of effects" (*The Political System*, New York, 1953, p. 27). It may be doubted that even the theory of games as applied to international relations can cope with this one. And suppose that, sometime in the future, more than two major units "play"? In the face of this prospect, as Herbert Butterfield says, "The mind winces and turns to look elsewhere" (*History and Human Relations*, New York, 1952, p. 23).

19 J. Robert Oppenheimer, in "Atomic Weapons," *Proceedings of the American Philosophical Society*, XC (January 29, 1946), pp. 9f.

20 Hegel.

THE GROWTH OF TRANSNATIONAL PARTICIPATION

Robert C. Angell

1 The Western camp has the following members: United States, Canada, United Kingdom, Ireland, Iceland, Norway, Sweden, Finland, Denmark, West Germany, Netherlands, Belgium, Luxembourg, Switzerland, France, Spain, Portugal, Italy, Austria, Greece, Turkey, Israel, Australia, New Zealand, Japan, Republic of China, South Korea, South Vietnam and Hong Kong. The Communist bloc embraces: Soviet Union, Poland, East Germany, Czechoslovakia, Hungary, Rumania, Bulgaria, Albania, Mongolia, Peoples Republic of China, North Vietnam, North Korea and Cuba. All the rest of the nations are classified as uncommitted.

2 The 20 countries are Morocco, Uganda, Canada, Colombia, Uruguay, Venezuela, Hong Kong, India, Israel, Lebanon, Turkey,

Bulgaria, Czechoslovakia, Greece, Netherlands, Poland, Rumania, Spain, Yugoslavia and New Zealand.

3 The 13 countries are S. Africa, Cuba, Argentina, Brazil, Peru, Peoples Republic of China, Iran, Philippines, Singapore, West Berlin, East Germany, Sweden and Union of Soviet Socialist Republics.

REFERENCES

Harbison, Frederick H., and Charles A. Myers, *Education, Manpower, and Economic Growth* (New York: McGraw-Hill Book Company, 1964).

NONECONOMIC FACTORS IN THE INSTITUTIONALIZATION OF THE COLD WAR

Irving Louis Horowitz

1 See, for example, Emile Benoit, "Alternatives to Defense Production," *Disarmament and the Economy,* ed. Emile Benoit and Kenneth E. Boulding (New York: Harper & Row, 1963), pp. 203–220; Emile Benoit, "Economic Adjustments to Disarmament," *Economic Factors Bearing Upon the Maintenance of Peace* (New York: The Institute For International Order, 1960); and William S. Royce, "Economics of Disarmament," *The Nation,* Vol. 195, No. 6 (September 1962), pp. 105–109.

2 Irving Louis Horowitz, *The War Game: Studies of the New Civilian Militarists* (New York: Ballantine Books, 1963); and *Games, Strategies and Peace* (Philadelphia: American Friends Service Committee, 1963).

3 Irving Louis Horowitz, "Political Morality and Immoral Politics," *Council for Correspondence Newsletter,* No. 25 (April 1963); and Irving Louis Horowitz, 'On the Morality of Detente," *The Correspondent,* No. 28 (July-August 1963).

4 Murray L. Weidenbaum, "Problems of Adjustment for Defense Industries," *Disarmament and the Economy, op. cit.,* p. 67.

5 Philip Shabecoff and Joseph Lelyveld, "Defense Industry Shuns Plans for Possible Arms Ban," *The New York Times* (August 16, 1963), pp. 31, 37.

6 William Vickrey, "Fiscal Strategies for Shifting $22 Billions to the Civilian Economy," *A Strategy for American Security,* ed. Seymour Melman (New York: Lee Offset—Distributors, 1963), pp. 21–25.

7 Thomas C. Schelling and Morton H. Halperin, "Arms Control Will Not Cut Defense Cost," *Arms and Arms Control,* ed. E. W. Lefever (New York: Frederick A. Praeger, 1962), pp. 287–297.

8 John Kenneth Galbraith, *The Affluent Society* (Boston: Houghton Mifflin Co., 1958), pp. 349–356.

9 Richard C. Raymond, "Problems of Industrial Conversion," *Dis-*

armament: Its Politics and Economics, ed. Seymour Melman (Boston: The American Academy of Arts and Sciences, 1962), pp. 158–159.

10 Jules Henry, *Culture Against Man* (New York: Random House, 1963), p. 110.

11 David Riesman, "The Concept of National Purpose," *Council for Correspondence Newsletter,* No. 27 (June 1963), p. 11.

12 Irving L. Horowitz, "Consensus, Conflict, and Cooperation," *Social Forces,* Vol. 41, No. 2 (December 1962), pp. 177–188.

13 Abram Bergson, *The Real National Income of Soviet Russia Since 1928* (Cambridge: Harvard University Press, 1961), p. 362.

14 Marquis Childs, *St. Louis Post-Dispatch* (September 18, 1963).

15 Charles E. Osgood, "Questioning Some Unquestioned Assumptions about National Defense," *Journal of Arms Control,* Vol. 1, No. 1 (January 1963), p. 11. On this, see also Pitirim A. Sorokin, "Mutual Convergence of the United States and the U.S.S.R. to the Mixed Sociocultural Type," *International Journal of Comparative Sociology,* Vol. I, No. 2 (September 1960), pp. 143–176.

16 Henry A. Kissinger, "The Unsolved Problems of European Defense," *Foreign Affairs,* Vol. 40, No. 4 (July 1962), pp. 515–541; and also his essay "NATO's Nuclear Dilemma," *The Reporter* (March 1963).

17 Thomas C. Schelling, "American Aid and Economic Development: Some Critical Issues," *International Stability and Progress* (New York: Columbia University Press, 1957), pp. 127ff.

18 Roger Hagan, "Reciprocal Hardening," *Council for Correspondence Newsletter,* No. 26 (May 1963), p. 7.

19 Cf. *Economic and Social Consequences of Disarmament: Report of the Secretary General Transmitting the Study of His Consultative Group* (New York: United Nations Department of Economic and Social Affairs, 1962), pp. 45–46.

20 U.S. Arms Control and Disarmament Agency, *The Economic and Social Consequences of Disarmament* (Washington, D.C.: United States Arms Control and Disarmament Agency, March 1962), p. 35.

THE ANALYSIS OF SOCIAL CONFLICT—TOWARD AN OVERVIEW AND SYNTHESIS

Raymond W. Mack and Richard C. Snyder

REFERENCES

Andrzejewski, S., *Military Organization and Society.* London: Routledge, 1954.

Bernard, Jessie, *Conflict Resolution,* p. 111.

Bernard, Jessie, "Where Is the Modern Sociology of Conflict?" *American Journal of Sociology,* LVI (1950), 11–16.

Boasson, C., "The Relevance of Research to the Problems of Peace."

In *Research for Peace*, pp. 215–16. Oslo: Institute for Social Research, 1954.

Boulding, K., "Economic Issues in International Conflict," *Kyklos*, VI (1953), 99–115.

Center for Research on World Political Institutions, Publication No. 4. Guetzkow Princeton: Princeton University, 1955.

Chase, S., *Roads to Agreement*. New York: Harper & Row, 1951.

Chein, I., "Research Needs," *Journal of Social Issues*, XII (1956), 57–66 (for an appraisal of the lack of knowledge concerning religious conflict).

Chertok, E., "Sources of International Tension," *Bulletin of the Research Exchange on the Prevention of War*, III (1955), No. 17.

Coleman, J., "Social Cleavage and Religious Conflict," *Journal of Social Issues*, XII (1956), 45.

Cooper, J. B., "Psychological Literature on the Prevention of War," *Bulletin of the Research Exchange on the Prevention of War*, III (1955), 2–15.

Coser, L., *The Functions of Social Conflict*. Glencoe, Ill.: Free Press, 1956.

Cottrell, W. F., "Research to Establish Conditions for Peace," *Journal of Social Issues*, XI (1955), 13–20.

Dahlke, O., "Race and Minority Riots: A Study in the Typology of Violence," *Social Forces*, XXX (1952), 420.

Davis, A. K., "Conflict between Major Social Systems," *Social Forces*, XXX (1951), 31.

Douglas, A., "The Peaceful Settlement of Industrial and Intergroup Conflict," *Journal of Conflict Resolution*, I (1957), 72ff.

Dubin, R., *Conflict Resolution*, p. 179.

Farber, M., "Psychoanalytic Hypotheses in the Study of War," *Journal of Social Issues*, XI (1955), 33.

Frazier, E. F., *Race and Culture Contacts in the Modern World*. New York: Alfred A. Knopf, 1957.

Freeman, F. D., "Theory and Strategy of Action in Race Relations," *Social Forces*, XXX (1951), 86.

Glock, C. Y., "Issues That Divide: A Postscript," *Journal of Social Issues*, XII (1956), 40.

Hager, D. J., "Introduction: Religious Conflict," *Journal of Social Issues*, XII (1956), 3–11.

Jackson, E., *Meeting of Minds*. New York: McGraw-Hill Book Co., 1952.

Kahn-Freund, D., "Intergroup Conflicts and Their Settlement," *British Journal of Sociology*, V (1954), 201.

Kecskemeti, P., *Meaning, Communication, and Value*. Chicago: University of Chicago Press, 1952.

Kerr, C., "Industrial Conflict and Its Mediation," *American Journal of Sociology*, LX (1954), 230.

Klineberg, O., *Tensions Affecting International Understanding*. New York: Social Science Research Council, 1950.

Kluckhohn, C., "Values and Value-Orientations in the Theory of Action: An Exploration in Definition and Classification." In Talcott Parsons and E. A. Shils (eds.), *Toward a General Theory of Action.* 1951.

Kornhauser, A., R. Dubin, and A. M. Ross, *Industrial Conflict.* New York: McGraw-Hill Book Co., 1954.

Lockwood, D., "Some Remarks on 'the Social System,'" *British Journal of Sociology,* VII (1956), 134–45.

Parsons, T., "Certain Primary Sources and Patterns of Aggression in the Social Structure of the Western World." In L. Bryson *et al., Conflicts of Power in Modern Culture.* 1947.

Rickman, J., "Psychodynamic Notes," In H. Cantril (ed.), *Tensions That Cause Wars.* 1950.

Rose, A., "Needed Research on the Mediation of Labor Disputes," *Personal Psychology,* V (1952), 196–99.

Rose, A. M., and C. B. Rose, "Integroup Conflict and Its Mediation," *International Social Science Bulletin,* VI (1954), 25.

Sheppard, H. "Approaches to Conflict in American Sociology, *British Journal of Sociology,* V (1954), 324–42.

Simpson, G., *Conflict and Community: A Study in Social Theory.* New York: T. S. Simpson, 1937.

Singer, K., "Resolution of Conflict," *Social Research,* VI (1949), 230.

Sorensen, R. C., "The Concept of Conflict in Industrial Sociology," *Social Forces,* XXIX (1951), 263–67.

Williams, R. M., Jr., *The Reduction of Intergroup Tensions.* New York: Social Science Research Council, 1947.

Williams, R. M., Jr., "Religion, Value-Orientations, and Intergroup Conflict," *Journal of Social Issues,* XII (1956), 15.

Williams, R. M., Jr., *American Society.* New York: Alfred A. Knopf, 1950.

Wright, Q., *A Study of War.* 2 vols. Chicago: University of Chicago Press, 1942.

Wright, Q., "Criteria for Judging the Relevance of Researches on the Problems of Peace." In *Research for Peace,* pp. 68–82. Oslo: Institute for Social Research, 1954.

Wright, Q., "The Nature of Conflict," *Western Political Quarterly,* IV (1951), 198.

THE KENNEDY EXPERIMENT

Amitai Etzioni

1 See, for example, Kenneth Waltz, *Man, the State, and War* (New York: Columbia U. Press, 1959), chap. 3.

2 Gabriel A. Almond, *The American People and Foreign Policy* (New York: Praeger, 1960), p. xvi.

3 Urie Bronfenbrenner, a psychologist, found that when American

school children were asked why the Russians planted trees alongside a road, they responded that the trees blocked vision and "made work for the prisoners," whereas *American* trees were planted "for shade." *Saturday Review, January* 5, 1963, p. 96.

4 On disarmament as political gamesmanship, see John W. Spanier and Joseph L. Nogee, *The Politics of Disarmament* (New York: Praeger, 1962), chap. 2.

5 These ideas are also held by non-psychologically oriented writers. For example, see C. Wright Mills, *The Causes of World War III* (New York: Simon & Schuster, 1958), pp. 103ff.

6 A study often cited in this context is Muzafer and Carolyn Sheriff, *Groups in Harmony and Tension: An Integration of Studies on Intergroup Relations* (New York: Harper, 1953).

7 See discussions of the International Cooperation Year—for instance, the *Washington Post,* March 7, 1965.

8 In a statement typical of this line of argument, Erich Fromm points out: "This time the choice between violent-irrational, or anticipatory-rational behavior is a choice which will affect the human race and its cultural, if not its physical survival.

"Yet so far the chances that such rational-anticipatory action will occur are bleak. Not because there is no possibility for such an outcome in the realistic circumstances, but because on both sides there is a thought barrier built of clichés, ritualistic ideologies, and even a good deal of common craziness that prevents people—leaders and led—from seeing sanely and realistically what the facts are, from recognizing alternative solutions to violence. Such rational-anticipatory policy requires . . . a serious examination of our own biases, and of certain semipathological forms of thinking which govern our behavior." Erich Fromm, *May Man Prevail?* (Garden City: Anchor Books, 1961), p. 8.

9 For a discussion of various versions of this approach, see Arthur I. Waskow, *The Worried Man's Guide to World Peace* (New York: Anchor Books, 1963), pp. 74–82.

10 Charles E. Osgood, *An Alternative to War or Surrender* (Urbana: U. of Illinois Press, 1962), esp. chap. 3. See also John H. Kautsky, "Myth, Self-fulfilling Prophecy, and Symbolic Reassurance in the East-West Conflict," *Journal of Conflict Resolution,* 9 (March 1965), pp. 1–17; Raymond A. Bauer, "Problems of Perception and the Relations Between the United States and the Soviet Union," *Journal of Conflict Resolution,* 5 (September 1961), pp. 223–30.

11 Amitai Etzioni, *The Hard Way to Peace* (New York: Collier Books, 1962), esp. chap. 4, and *Winning Without War* (Garden City: Anchor Books, 1964), esp. pp. 21–26, 62–68, 209–12.

12 Jerome Frank, "Breaking the Thought Barrier: Psychological Challenges of the Nuclear Age," *Psychiatry,* 23 (1960), pp. 245–66.

13 *Ibid.,* pp. 263–65.

14 *The Hard Way to Peace, op. cit.*, esp. chap. 7.

15 *Ibid.*, pp. 95–98. Others view unilateral reciprocation as a much more encompassing measure. Schelling points out another difference in the policy's use—as a communication method (which can convey hostility as well as good will) and as a treatment of international conflicts. His approach is that of a communication method. Thomas Schelling, "Signals and Feedback in the Arms Dialogue," *Bulletin of the Atomic Scientists*, January 1965, pp. 5–10.

Another major difference is among those who favor continuing unilateral concessions if the other side does not reciprocate and those who would stop after awhile. Sibley favors continuing, even if this would involve unilateral disarmament. See Mulford Sibley, *Unilateral Initiatives and Disarmament* (Philadelphia: American Friends Service Committee, 1962), pp. 19–28. Osgood (*op. cit.*) is not completely clear on this point.

See also Arthur Herzog, *The War and Peace Establishment* (New York: Harper & Row, 1965), pp. 144, 159. Etzioni favors stopping after several steps (the number depends on the scope of each step); see *The Hard Way to Peace, op. cit.*, pp. 99ff. It is surprising to learn that Levine finds Etzioni unclear on this point on p. 56—Robert E. Levine, *The Armed Debate* (Cambridge: Harvard U. Press, 1963)—only to report the Etzioni position correctly on p. 228.

16 Such a speech had been advocated, in 1961. *The Hard Way to Peace, op. cit.*, p. 96. The importance of the context is overlooked by Levine, *op. cit.*, p. 327. Levine, belittling the role of gestures, argues that they have taken place "for years." He refers, of course, to such isolated acts as the closing of a military base or reducing travel restrictions, which took place in a cold war context without the context provided by a "strategy for peace."

17 Jerome B. Wiesner and Herbert F. York, "The Test Ban," *Scientific American*, 211 (1964), p. 27.

18 Richard D. Stebbins, *The United States in World Affairs 1963* (New York and Evanston: Harper & Row for The Council on Foreign Relations, 1964), p. 84.

19 *Documents on American Foreign Relations* (New York and Evanston: Harper & Row for The Council on Foreign Relations, 1962), pp. 182–93.

20 Mainly because these bombs are more difficult to deliver on target than when carried by air or missile. See Donald G. Brennan, "Arms and Arms Control in Outer Space," in Lincoln P. Bloomfield (ed.), *Outer Space* (New York: The American Assembly, 1962), p. 129. See also Amitai Etzioni, *The Moon-Doggle* (Garden City: Doubleday, 1964), pp. 118ff.

21 Max Frankel wrote on October 25, 1963, that "there is real concern here [in Washington] about the decay of the vigilance so

carefully developed in the non-Communist world and about the erosion of barricades erected against the spread of Soviet influence." *New York Times,* October 25, 1963, p. 6.

22 Adenauer, then still West German Chancellor, said of the *détente* that "only the stupidest calves choose their own butcher." *New York Times,* October 6, 1963, p. 6. For German objections to the treaty, see *Documents . . . , op. cit.,* 1963, pp. 26, 27; *Department of State Bulletin* (Washington, D.C.: G.P.O., September 2, 1963), pp. 353–55; United States Senate, *Executive Report* 3 (on Executive M), 88th Cong., 1st Sess., September 3, 1963.

23 *New York Times,* December 18, 1964, p. 1.

24 On December 17, 1964, air and consular convention negotiations were reopened. Further, on January 3, 1965, the United States and the Soviet Union expanded their cultural exchange agreement. On February 2, 1965, the United States unilaterally announced a new cutback in production of enriched uranium for atomic weapons. On February 5, 1965, as a "symbolic step toward curbing the spread of atomic weapons," the United States placed one of its reactors under international inspection. Also on February 5, the liquidation of 129 missile sites was announced, following an earlier announcement of the closing of other bases. This sequence, however, was simultaneous with the American escalation of the war in Vietnam in early 1965.

25 Robert A. Levine, "Unilateral Initiatives: A Cynic's View," *Bulletin of the Atomic Scientists,* 19 (January 1963), p. 22.

26 This could have been anticipated on the basis of previous Soviet conduct. *The Hard Way to Peace, op. cit.,* p. 107. For Russian moves that were not reciprocated by the United States, see Stebbins, *op. cit.,* pp. 76–77

27 Monzales M. Minerva, *Aspectos Politicos Del Sistema Inter-americano* (Mexico City: National University, 1961).

28 *New York Times,* June 16, 1963.

29 *Ibid.*

30 *Ibid.*

31 *Ibid.*, July 7, 1963, p. 1E.

32 *Ibid.*, July 14, 1963, p. 1E.

33 *Ibid.*, p. 5E.

34 *Ibid.*

35 This concept was introduced by Daniel J. Boorstein in *The Image* (New York: Atheneum, 1962), esp. pp. 9–12. A pseudo-event has the following characteristics: it is not spontaneously initiated; it is manufactured largely for publicity purposes; and it is intended to be a self-fulfilling prophecy, to create its own consequences.

36 *Washington Post,* September 16, 1963.

37 *New York Times,* August 4, 1963, p. 1E.

38 *Ibid.*, August 11, 1963, p. 3E.

39 *Ibid.*, September 22, 1963, p. 8E.

40 *The Hard Way to Peace, op. cit.*, pp. 99ff. That this was necessary was a point of some debate. See Waskow, *op. cit.*, pp. 75ff.
41 Spanier and Nogee, *op. cit.*, chap. 6
42 United States Senate, Committee on Foreign Relations, *Nuclear Test Ban Treaty: Hearings on Executive M*, 88th Congress, 1st Sess., August 12–17 (Washington, D.C.: G.P.O., 1963), pp. 97–109.
43 *Documents . . .* , op. cit., 1963, p. 27.
44 *New York Times,* October 14, 1963, p. 1E.
45 *Ibid.*, July 7, 1963, p. 1E.
46 *Ibid.* See also August 14, 1963, p. 1E, and August 25, 1963, p. 4.
47 Asked by a journalist if he believed that "nations act like people," Osgood is quoted as having answered, "I do." Herzog, *op. cit.*, p. 158.
48 *The Hard Way to Peace, op. cit.*, p. 104.
49 Sabotage has been suggested as an explanation for the out-of-character "tailgate" incident outside Berlin in October 1963. See Jean E. Smith, "Berlin, the Erosion of a Principle," *Reporter*, November 21, 1963, pp. 32–37.
50 *The Hard Way to Peace, op. cit.*, pp. 104–5.
51 *New York Times,* October 13, 1963, p. 8E.
52 *Ibid.*, October 20, 1963, p. 6E.
53 *Reporter,* November 21, 1963, p. 36.
54 *New York Times,* October 20, 1963, p. 6E.
55 *Ibid.*, November 17, 1963, p. 1E.
56 *Ibid.*
57 *Ibid.*, November 16, 1963, p. 3.
58 For a study of psychological factors affecting international relations by affecting the interaction of national representatives, see Bryant Wedge and Cyril Muromcew, "Psychological Factors in Soviet Disarmament Negotiation," *Journal of Conflict Resolution,* 9 (March 1965), pp. 18–37.

BEHAVIORAL STUDY OF OBEDIENCE

Stanley Milgram

1 Forty-three subjects, undergraduates at Yale University, were run in the experiment without payment. The results are very similar to those obtained with paid subjects.

Index

70 71 72 7 6 5 4 3 2 1